HISPANICS AND THE NONPROFIT SECTOR

D0916554

HISPANICS AND THE NONPROFIT SECTOR

HERMAN E. GALLEGOS AND
MICHAEL O'NEILL, Eds.

The Foundation Center
New York • 1991

Library of Congress Cataloging-in-Publication Data

Hispanics and the nonprofit sector / edited by Herman E. Gallegos and
  Michael O'Neill.
    p. cm.
  Includes bibliographical references (p.) and index.
  ISBN 0-87954-398-1 : $24.95
  1. Hispanic Americans—Societies, etc. 2. Charities—United
States. 3. Voluntarism—United States. I. O'Neill, Michael.
HS1721.H57 1991
361.7′63′08968073—dc20

91-8123
CIP

CONTENTS

1

Hispanics and the Nonprofit Sector

Herman E. Gallegos and Michael O'Neill

The Hispanic[1] community is one of the largest and fastest growing ethnic groups in the United States. There are an estimated 20 million Hispanics in the mainland United States and another 3 million in Puerto Rico. The Hispanic community is growing five times as fast as the non-Hispanic population, because of family size and migration. The Census Bureau projects that Hispanics may account for one quarter of the nation's growth during the next twenty years (Keane, 1989, p. 532).

Since the 1960s, there has been increasing attention to the Hispanic community in the United States, as the nation grew more attuned to the civil rights of minority groups and as the economic and political impact of Hispanics became more evident. Legal, public-policy, and economic analysis of the Hispanic community increased, as did the recognition that Hispanics have a long, significant history on the North American continent. The linguistic and cultural uniqueness of the Hispanic community has also been explored extensively. The impact of the migration of Hispanics, the educa-

---

[1] *Hispanic* is used in this book to refer to persons of Mexican, Puerto Rican, Cuban, Caribbean, Central American, South American, and Spanish descent. Others may prefer to use such terms as *Latino/a, Spanish speaking, Spanish surname,* and the like. We recognize that there is no perfect term, and that *Hispanic* in some ways covers as much cultural and historical territory as does the word *European.* We have followed the usage of the Census Bureau and other sources and opted for a simple, one-word, and widely used adjective to describe in an admittedly imperfect way a very large and diverse group of peoples who, nevertheless, share some important common bonds of language, culture, traditions, and history. For a further discussion of this issue, see Chap. 7.

tional needs of their children and young people, the increase in their political power, and their growing presence in the business world have all received considerable attention.

Little attention has been paid, however, to the important roles that private nonprofit organizations play within the Hispanic community. Economic development groups, legal rights and advocacy organizations, unions, cultural and educational programs, self-help groups, social service agencies, and other nonprofits have been instrumental in sustaining and supporting the Hispanic community. Hispanic mutual assistance agencies have provided a range of necessary services to Hispanic families. Church-sponsored efforts to aid Hispanic immigrants have furthered their economic and social integration into U.S. society. While there has been some analysis of particular Hispanic nonprofit sector activities, such as health care, social services, arts and culture, religion, and philanthropy, there has been no integrated discussion of the role and impact of nonprofit organizations in the Hispanic community. Thus, while it is clear that Hispanic nonprofits represent an important social, political, and economic force in the Hispanic community and in society at large, the dynamics and extent of that role are far from clear.

A national conference to explore this question was held at the University of San Francisco in November 1988, hosted by the university's Institute for Nonprofit Organization Management and supported by grants from the Ford, Irvine, and Pacific Telesis foundations. Ten papers were presented to approximately 50 invited participants representing the academic community, funders, Hispanic nonprofit organization leaders, policymakers, and others who have played significant roles in the development of Hispanic nonprofits. A full list of the conference participants can be found in Appendix A. The conference papers were revised following written and oral reactions from conference participants; these revised papers are found in Chapters 2–11 of this book.

HISTORICAL DEVELOPMENT OF HISPANIC NONPROFITS

The conference planners agreed unanimously that a careful investigation of the historical development of Hispanic nonprofits would be crucial to the success of the conference and book. Two historical papers were commissioned, one by Albert Camarillo of Stanford University on the history of voluntary and nonprofit agencies in the Mexican-American community (Chap. 2), and one by Carlos Rodríguez-Fraticelli, Carlos Sanabria, and Amílcar Tirado of the City University of New York on the history of Puerto Rican nonprofit groups, with special emphasis on New York City (Chap. 3). Unfortunately, it was not possible to commission other papers on the unique history of nonprofit effort within the Cuban-American and Central and South American communities.

In addition to these two general chapters, Chapters 4 and 5 present "personal histories" of two highly important Hispanic nonprofits, the National Council of La Raza and the Mexican American Legal Defense and Educational Fund (MALDEF). Siobhan Oppenheimer Nicolau, the Ford Foundation program officer most closely involved with the establishment of the council, and Henry Santiestevan, the second executive director of the council, tell of the delicate and sometimes explosive events that marked the origin and early years of the National Council of La Raza (Chap. 4). Vilma Martinez, president of MALDEF for nine years, describes some of the history and effect of that organization (Chap. 5). More generally, both chapters also discuss the roles that Hispanic nonprofits played in the public policy and legal arenas.

The history of Hispanic nonprofits is a fascinating and complex story. As Camarillo points out, although many think that these groups began relatively recently—in the 1950s and 1960s, and especially as a result of the Johnson administration's Great Society programs—in fact the Mexican-American *mutualistas* of the middle and late nineteenth century anticipated most of the later issues that Hispanic nonprofits would face—economic security, political rights, equal educational opportunity, and cultural identity. As Camarillo concludes, "Though the names and styles of organizations serving the Mexican American people have changed over time, the fundamental objectives have not."

The *mutualistas* were almost the only opportunity Mexican-Americans had for effective group action. Following the 1848 Treaty of Guadalupe Hidalgo ending the war between Mexico and the United States, Mexican-Americans in the Southwest suddenly became minorities in their own land as the Anglo immigrants to that region assumed economic, social, and political power. Positions of influence in business and government were closed to the new resident minorities; even agencies such as the church, the incipient labor movement, and the public-school system were paternalistic and often discriminatory. The *mutualistas* provided opportunities for economic and political action and also helped maintain the cultural, ethnic, and linguistic identity of Mexican-Americans—in much the same way that Irish, Jewish, Polish, and Italian mutual assistance agencies were at the same time serving those ethnic immigrant communities in the large cities of the East and Midwest. The "multiservice" characteristic of these *mutualistas* (providing insurance, death benefits, cultural events, economic and political advocacy, protection of individual rights) anticipated the complexity of Hispanic nonprofit organizations of the 1960s and later.

The Puerto Rican experience followed a somewhat different course. Whereas Mexican-Americans originally had simply remained in the rural, small-town Southwest as the Anglos moved in, Puerto Ricans emigrated from an economically devastated homeland to the United States and stayed mostly in major urban areas like New York, Newark, and Chicago. Also, residents of Puerto Rico had U.S. citizenship by virtue of a federal law passed in 1917. Nevertheless, both groups quickly found themselves at the bottom of the U.S. socioeconomic and political ladder, and there were many similarities in the development of voluntary and nonprofit agencies within the two communities. Chapter 3 describes organizational complexities in New York's Puerto Rican nonprofits—especially the combination of advocacy, service, and cultural efforts—that are highly reminiscent of the Mexican-American *mutualistas*.

Both communities saw gradual development of these mutual assistance agencies and clubs into labor organizations, social service organizations, and other, more formalized nonprofits during the twentieth century; in both cases there was a rapid period of growth and development in the aftermath of World War II, the civil rights movement of the 1950s and 1960s, and the intervention of a few large foundations and the federal government in the 1960s and after. This growth was not always easy. For example, although there was much cooperation between blacks and Hispanics during the 1950s and 1960s, competition for resources generated by federal antipoverty programs of the late 1960s and 1970s led to tensions between the two groups. As Paul Ylvisaker notes in the final chapter, "the eternal tendency of minorities to fight over crumbs" seriously complicated the general struggle for justice and equality. Also, government and foundation supporters frequently did not have the experience and insight to deal effectively with the Hispanic community, as Nicolau and Santiestevan document in their "insider" story of the Ford Foundation's support of Mexican-American organizations in the Southwest. And there were crisis times ahead in the social service and legal advocacy cutbacks of the Reagan years.

Hispanics entered the 1980s filled with optimism and a newfound sense of confidence. But the 1980s proved at least partly a disappointment. Some gains from earlier decades were short-lived. Racism, although often more subtle, persisted in many segments of the population. The mood of the U.S. public had changed: Many Americans felt that the country had reached an era of unlimited claims and limited resources, and that the government was the cause of, not the answer to, many of the nation's dilemmas. Nevertheless, the four decades following World War II had seen remarkable growth in the number, resources, and impact of nonprofit organizations in the Mexican-American and Puerto Rican communities.

The Cuban-American community presented yet another story. The Cuban presence in the United States was very small until Fidel Castro took power in Cuba in 1959. A large number of Cubans emigrated to the United States, primarily to Miami and a few other cities on the eastern seaboard. Unlike their Mexican-American and Puerto Rican counterparts, Cuban-American immigrants were characterized by relatively high levels of economic, professional, and educational status; they were politically more conservative; and they had a much less complicated relationship with their historic church, one

reason being that both the Cuban emigres and the Catholic church were res-
olutely anticommunist. Whether these and other factors created a situation
in which nonprofit organizations were less important in the Cuban than in
the Chicano and Puerto Rican communities is a question that merits further
investigation.

This conference and book were also unable to explore the important role
played by voluntary and nonprofit agencies within the Central American,
South American, and other Hispanic communities in the United States; there
may well be some significant differences. Central American immigration con-
sists in large part of political refugees from El Salvador, Nicaragua, Guatemala, and other countries where political and military turmoil are at least as
important as poverty in causing migration. Also, each of these groups brings
a different historical and cultural tradition. Finally, Central and South American immigration comes at a period in U.S. history when the rights of minorities and immigrants are better protected than was the case in the nineteenth
century and first half of the twentieth century. The significance of these differences for the development of nonprofit activity is a subject that invites
further research.

What clearly emerges from the historical discussions in the following
chapters is that voluntary and nonprofit agenices have played a highly significant role in the development of the Hispanic community in the United
States. The complexities and diversity of that role constitute the focus of
several other chapters in this book.

THE CURRENT ROLES AND IMPACT OF HISPANIC NONPROFITS
Legal, Political, and Policy Advocacy

Hispanic nonprofit agenices have, in one way or another, been involved in
protecting the legal and political rights of their constituents at least as far
back as the *mutualistas* of the midnineteenth century, as Camarillo documents. This effort, however, moved into a new phase with the return of Hispanic GI's to a still discriminatory society after World War II, the civil rights
movement of the 1950s and 1960s, and the passage of the Civil Rights Act
of 1964 and the Voting Rights Act of 1965. Although largely the result of
pressure from black. Americans, these two landmark laws had profound significance for Hispanics and Hispanic nonprofits. This period saw the development of national Hispanic nonprofits—principally concerned with legal,
political, and policy advocacy—to add to the local and regional Hispanic
agencies, which often were necessarily absorbed with providing social services and other such functions. With particular attention to the Mexican-
American community, Martinez and Nicolau/Santiestevan document the
impact of MALDEF, the National Council of La Raza, and other nonprofits
on legislation; court decisions; administrative regulations; and policies at the
national, state, and local government levels, from correcting the gerryman-

dering of Los Angeles political districts to promoting bilingual education. Rodríguez-Fraticelli et al. discuss the parallel efforts of the Puerto Rican Legal Defense and Education Fund (PRLDEF), the Institute for Puerto Rican Policy, and other groups primarily serving the Puerto Rican community.

Social Services

Like all members of immigrant and minority groups in U.S. society, Hispanics have found that creating indigenous social service agencies is often the best and sometimes the only way to meet human needs that go beyond the capabilities of the family or extended family. Thousands of Hispanic nonprofits in Los Angeles, New York, Miami, Chicago, Phoenix, San Francisco, and various cities in Texas and other parts of the country illustrate the importance of nonprofit social service delivery within the Hispanic community. While some of these are a direct result of the Johnson administration's War on Poverty, others can be traced back to the *mutualista* days of the last century. These agencies provide counseling, drug and alcohol rehabilitation, job assistance, educational assistance, basic welfare support, and a host of other services for Hispanic families. All the following chapters discuss, from various perspectives, the vitally important social service work of Hispanic nonprofit agenices.

Religion

Few groups in U.S. society have such deep ambivalence about their historical religious affiliation as do Hispanics. There is much less tension of this kind in the Jewish community. Irish, German, Italian, Polish, and other European Catholics historically have had strong identification with their church, even if they currently vary from committed to "lapsed" (or "relaxed") Catholics. The varieties of Protestant religious experience make any summary impossible, but while there is great tension between *groups* such as fundamentalist Christians and Unitarians, there is not widespread collective tension among individuals about Protestantism as such. Christianity in the black community has played a vitally important role in the civil rights effort and the advancement of blacks generally. Hispanics, however, often have a deep love–hate relationship with their historic religion, Roman Catholicism. For some Hispanics, religion in general and Catholicism in particular is a concomitant of the oppressor class, and certainly some of the history of Mexico and other Latin American countries would bear this out. For other Hispanics, "the church" is a rich and powerful symbol mixing liturgy, art, history, piety, and the entire cycle of life, death, and rebirth. For still others, Catholicism is a revitalized force using "liberation theology" to cure some of the social and political ills of Latin America. Finally, some Hispanics view Catholicism as an important emotional and spiritual reality but one that is largely tied to non-Hispanic leaders and role models, since few Catholic religious leaders in the United States are Hispanic. William McCready, in Chapter 6, discusses the complex relationship of Hispanics to their religious experience, including not only the historical and still dominant Catholic connection but also the large (20 percent) and increasing affiliation of many Hispanics with various Protestant sects. He analyzes the power of the culture–religion–ethnicity interaction, including its potential for social change. Since religion is the largest, oldest, and probably still most influential part of the nonprofit sector (Hodgkinson, Weitzman, and Kirsch, 1988; O'Neill, 1989; Wuthnow, Hodgkinson, and Associates, 1990), and since Hispanics have had an unusually strong affiliation with one major religion, the connection between religion and Hispanic nonprofits is an important area of investigation.

Artistic, Cultural, Educational, and Linguistic Services

U.S. society is dominated by northern European and especially English culture, values, laws, and language. Although there were three Spanish universities in the New World when Harvard College was founded in 1636, and although a Spanish school was operating in St. Augustine, Florida, 40 years before the Mayflower landed, the dominant culture, language, education, religion, and worldview of Americans became that of the English rather than the Spanish, French, Dutch, or German colonists. Hispanics have typically been expected to adopt, without variation or complaint, this English–U.S. culture. Many Hispanics have been unwilling or unable to do so, partly because of the geographical proximity of their home countries.

Consequently, one of the major functions of Hispanic nonprofits has been to preserve, protect, and strengthen the linguistic and cultural uniqueness of Hispanic communities in the United States. For over a century, Hispanic agencies have sponsored parades, artistic and dramatic events, and religious ceremonies dedicated to these objectives; Hispanic nonprofits have also fought to protect schoolchildren from becoming second-class educational citizens because they come from Spanish-speaking homes and neighborhoods. Margarita Melville, in Chapter 7, discusses the cultural values that permeate Hispanic communities and the role that Hispanic nonprofits play in the protection and enhancement of these values. She discusses the problems in using one construct such as "Hispanic" to describe the great diversity of culture and experience among Latino peoples, and she applies cultural analysis to issues such as the role of Hispanic women and the nature of leadership in the Hispanic community.

SPECIAL ISSUES

Management and Leadership

One of the principal themes of the conference and book is that of leadership and management in Hispanic nonprofit organizations. The Hispanic nonprofit world has had gifted and powerful leaders, some of whom were present at the conference. The historical chapters give many examples of such leadership: Maria Borrero, in Chapter 8, analyzes several key issues concerning the management of Hispanic nonprofits, and Leo Estrada, in Chapter 9, discusses organizational coping styles and funding strategies past, present, and future. Some of the major questions emerging from these and other chapters, and from the conference discussion, include the following:

- Have Hispanic nonprofit board and executive staff members reached adequate levels of leadership and management skills? What does careful evaluation of the management of Hispanic nonprofits show?

- Since young Hispanics now have leadership opportunities that were not available to their parents and grandparents, will this younger generation gravitate toward the business and government sectors rather than staying in Hispanic nonprofits? Are younger Hispanics being motivated and trained to take over the roles of members of the older generation who created and led the Hispanic nonprofits of the 1950s through the 1980s?

- What are the most effective and efficient ways to identify, support, and develop leadership and management talent? What kinds of leadership programs should there be? Should there be special programs for Hispanics, or should Hispanic nonprofit leaders and managers take part in programs aimed at the general populace?

- What needs to be done to attract good board members and volunteers to Hispanic nonprofits? How does one develop volunteer as well as paid staff leadership?

- What effect will the "mainstreaming" of the Hispanic community have on the leadership issue? The Nicolau/Santiestevan chapter and the Puerto Rican history chapter illustrate the tensions between "radical" and "establishment" leadership: Is this still an issue, and will it be in the future?

- What will be the funding structure of Hispanic nonprofits in the future, and are current leaders and managers prepared to meet this challenge? Hispanic nonprofits, many of them heavily dependent on government programs, have experienced sharp funding changes in recent years, and many organizations have ceased to exist. To what extent is the management and leadership of Hispanic nonprofits responding adequately to this challenge?

The Role of Women

Hispanic nonprofits, like black nonprofits, have been a largely male-dominated enterprise. While there have been significant exceptions, such as Vilma Martinez at MALDEF and Antonia Pantoja at Aspira, most managers and leaders of Hispanic nonprofits have been men. Melville and Nicolau/Santiestevan point out that this is due not only to the general position of women in U.S. society but also to *machismo* within the Hispanic community. Significant advances in the role of women in Hispanic nonprofits have taken place in the last twenty years, but there is still a major imbalance between men and women in leadership roles. The gender issue is one of the most important challenges facing Hispanic nonprofits.

The Need for Research Related to Policy and Action

Michael Cortés, in Chapter 10, presents the case for more applied research on philanthropy and Hispanic nonprofits and gives many examples of research questions that need to be addressed. He suggests a research agenda of seven principal topics, including analysis of the relatively unexplored area of individual giving within the Hispanic community and the potential for self-sufficiency among Hispanic nonprofits. Cortés also reviews the research on foundation, corporate, and government funding of Hispanic nonprofits, as well as the fundamental reasons for funding Hispanic efforts.

THE FUTURE OF HISPANIC NONPROFITS

Somewhat paradoxically, the conference planners' concern with the history of Hispanic nonprofits came largely from their concern about the future. The conference planners and participants frequently expressed the feeling that Hispanic nonprofit organizations were at something of a crossroads: The decades of gross discrimination were over, the initial shock of the civil rights movement had ended, and the glory days of the War on Poverty and the Ford Foundation's first involvement were gone. Hispanic nonprofits, like other nonprofits, are now coping with the cutbacks of the Reagan administration in social and legal assistance programs, struggling to diversify their funding base, competing for ever tighter foundation and corporate dollars, and looking for ways to increase constituent support. But more than anything, Hispanic nonprofits are reexamining their mission, their original ideas and ideals, their heart and soul as well as their balance sheet.

Hispanic organizations learned a great deal in the last twenty years. They came to understand their overall goal: seeking the development of a healthy and well-educated Hispanic population that the larger society views as an asset rather than a problem to be dealt with. Hispanic organizations have drawn upon the strength and resources of mainstream organizations, often performing their work through or with the cooperation of established institutions. Despite xenophobic responses such as the "English only" movement and the persistence of racism among some Americans, the Hispanic community continues to work through the democratic system. These relationships with mainline institutions form the basis for continued cooperation and accelerated progress. Hispanic organizations have learned much about maximizing governmental and philanthropic support. Although tempered by demographics and the new financial realities of the 1980s, Hispanic nonprofit organizations and leaders have become proactive and are making the future happen.

In Chapter 11, Paul Ylvisaker, who had much to do with the inauguration of Hispanic programs at the Ford Foundation, discusses the future of Hispanic nonprofits. He emphasizes the larger social framework of migration—the "massive swirls of human movement on a global scale"—within which the question must be considered. Hispanic migration has been complex: In the Southwest, the Anglos came to the Mexican-Americans rather than vice versa; Puerto Ricans were already U.S. citizens before they came to the mainland United States; Cubans, Salvadorans, and Nicaraguans came here largely because of revolution and war in their homelands. But the migration experience has deeply shaped Hispanic nonprofits and will continue to do so. Only a thorough understanding of this phenomenon, and the response of the nonprofit sector to it, can lend clarity to the future of Hispanic and other nonprofits, since the "massive swirl" of migration is, if anything, increasing.

Ylvisaker argues that Hispanic nonprofits will increasingly move from advocacy to service without giving up the former. He also argues that Hispanics will become increasingly effective in the growing competition for resources, that the growth of the Hispanic population will necessarily increase Hispanic nonprofit services, and that the future of Hispanic nonprofits depends to some important degree on the success of Hispanics in finding remedies for education and research deficits.

Adding to these thoughts, we wish to propose some strategies for Hispanic nonprofits in the 1990s and after. These are a mix of time-tested and new strategies.

Strategies that have worked well include organizing, voter registration and political empowerment, and pressuring government to help meet the needs of the Hispanic community. Organizing for community action is the basic building block. Saul Alinsky (1946, p. 64) once noted, "In the last analysis of our democratic faith, the answer to all of the issues facing us will be found in the masses of the people themselves, and nowhere else." Closely related to organizing is the effort to turn out the vote. A high priority must be given to increasing Hispanic empowerment by encouraging eligible Hispanics to register and vote.

Emerging strategies include efforts in research and leadership development. Hispanics in Philanthropy (HIP), a national organization dedicated to promoting responsive philanthropic policies and practices on behalf of Hispanics, is currently developing a research agenda to encompass a broad array of related issues. The Inter-University Program for Latino Research, a national consortium of research centers, seeks to address institutional, root causes of the most pressing needs facing Hispanics and other minorities.

Other groups are pursuing specific research interests in poverty and education. Nationally, the tragedy of Hispanic high-school dropouts—36 percent in 1988, triple the rate of whites and double the rate of blacks—is being dramatically profiled by organizations like the Hispanic Policy Development Project. Research by the Hispanic Coalition on Higher Education, an association of 40 California organizations, is aimed at ensuring that Hispanic students achieve educational equity in higher education. The National Council of La Raza has documented the fact that well-intended programs like the Job Training Partnership Act are shortchanging Hispanics; these findings are being used in an effort to revise that legislation. The council also tracks overall trends regarding Hispanic education and provides advocacy for needed programs. Research on poverty indicates that, despite the lowest levels of unemployment in modern U.S. history, a greater number of Hispanic children and their families are materially poor. Hispanics living below the poverty line increased from 21.6 percent in 1980 to 28.2 percent in 1987 (Southwest Voter Research Institute, 1988, p. 2). Today, several Hispanic research and policy centers are actively addressing the need to strengthen data collection, research, and dissemination of information to cultivate public support and understanding about the problem of persistent poverty among Hispanics. The issues will change as time goes on, but the capacity to conduct quality research directed at social action is critically important for the health of the Hispanic nonprofit sector.

Another important activity is that of developing future leadership. Report after report continues to document what California State Senator Art Torres referred to as "our empty pipeline into the graduate and faculty ranks" (remarks at the Second Annual Chicano/Latino Consortium, Los Angeles, February 22, 1989). This lack of educational achievement and opportunity seriously hampers the development of Hispanic leaders. The need for leadership development is symbolized by the fact that in the 1980s, the Hispanic community lost by death Maclovio Barraza, Ernesto Galarza, Ralph Guzman, Enrique "Hank" Lopez, Graciela Olivarez, Gil Pompa, Tomás Rivera, Willie Velasquez, and other major leaders.

New strategies of resource development are imperative. The Reagan administration cuts particularly affected job training, legal assistance and advocacy, and aid to the poor, areas in which Hispanic nonprofit work was highly concentrated. Because of their historical dependence on government funds, many Hispanic nonprofits suddenly found themselves struggling for survival. Fundraising is now a primary challenge for Hispanic staff and boards. Hispanic nonprofits must seek more diverse sources of funds beyond government, corporations, and foundations. Some are experimenting with fees for service, membership dues, third-party payors, endowment/investment income, and for-profit subsidiary ventures. Even so, some organizations are barely surviving, and survival does not necessarily mean quality performance. Few Hispanic organizations enjoy the benefits of an endowment, assured sources of core operating support from the private sector, or the highly trained and paid development staff required to raise adequate funds. Survival budgets create job uncertainty, heavier work loads, few fringe benefits, and poor prospects for sustaining the quality and level of services. Without adequate resources, Hispanic voluntary organizations can become vulnerable and lose credibility.

For those organizations that provide direct service, the immediate, tragic result is that fewer people receive appropriate help. There is a more subtle effect: Greater demand for direct service diverts funds from research, planning, and demonstration programs, activities that potentially promote the long-range development of these organizations. These cuts, although not as immediately noticeable as the cuts that put the homeless on the sidewalks, will have a long-term, ripple effect throughout the Hispanic community for years.

Hispanic organizations need to align themselves with mainline nonprofit efforts, such as Independent Sector's "Give Five" campaign, an effort to increase giving and volunteering by all Americans. Independent Sector asks Americans to donate 5 percent of their income and give five hours of volunteer time each week. Hispanic nonprofits need to instill such goals in their members, volunteers, and the broader Hispanic communities they serve. Considerable new financial and personnel resources could be generated by such an effort.

Hispanics must also be more aggressive about urging foundations, corporations, and wealthy individuals to be bolder in their giving patterns, more pluralistic in the composition of trustee boards and staff, and more proactive in adopting external affirmative action programs. There is still great need to raise the consciousness of funding organizations, and ethnic diversity can strengthen the philanthropic process.

The final strategy is that of strategically broadening horizons. The immigration issue provides a good example. The condition of Hispanics living in the West continues to reflect the pressures of population and poverty in Mexico as well as the effects of war in Central America. Mexicans and Central Americans leave their homes for the same reasons that have brought immigrants to the United States for decades: the opportunity of a better life for themselves and their families. According to an international commission report, "Violence has uprooted between 2 and 3 million Central Americans—up to 15 percent of the total population—from their homes and communities, leaving most without jobs, adequate income or health services" (International Commission, 1989, p. 1). In Mexico, where 50 percent of the population is under fifteen year of age, the labor force, already underemployed, will double within twelve years, and high fertility rates are expected well into the next century (Rockefeller Foundation, 1988). Unless the consequences of political unrest and economic decline are addressed, the United States will continue to serve as an escape hatch. On the other hand, many potential immigrants would remain at home if peace and a program of recovery and economic development were in place. Hispanic nonprofits, which have had considerable experience influencing domestic policy, must become more involved in influencing foreign policy, since that is the most direct way to influence the *root causes* of U.S. immigration problems. As Hispanic political influence increases, so should its involvement in those institutions that speak for and about Latin American foreign policy.

This book is an attempt to begin and focus a discussion, not to end it. The reader will find that few definitive answers are included, but hopefully the book will show how important the questions are. Hispanics form a large, growing, and highly significant segment of the nation's population. Nonprofits have played a major role in the development of this Hispanic community, and there is every reason to believe that they will continue to do so. We hope that this book will clarify some of the main dimensions of that interaction, as well as the role of nonprofit organizations within other ethnic and minority groups in U.S. society.

2

Mexican-Americans and Nonprofit Organizations An Historical Overview

Albert Camarillo

Among many policymakers and the public in general, a common misconception exists about Mexican-Americans and their attempts to create effective self-help organizations. According to this widely held assumption, only since the 1960s and the establishment of federal War on Poverty programs have Mexican-Americans developed community-based and national organizations promoting the well-being of their group. Indeed, the Johnson administration contributed significantly to the development of dozens of new organizations serving Mexican-Americans and other historically poor sectors of the U.S. population. However, to attribute primary responsibility to Great Society programs for the development of effective nonprofit organizations within Mexican-American communities is to distort history and to obscure the influence of a variety of factors that are critical for explaining the history of Mexican-American organizations. Most importantly, a broader context for understanding the role of nonprofit, voluntary organizations is necessary in order to portray accurately how Mexican-Americans themselves developed their organizations and how other institutions in society—corporate and private foundations, labor unions, citizen action groups, and so forth—assisted in the establishment of hundreds of different types of organizations.

This chapter outlines the historical development of Mexican-American voluntary and nonprofit organizations since 1848, the year people of Mexican origin became a regional minority in the newly acquired southwestern part of the United States. This overview is organized using themes as well as chronology to summarize the development of organizations in Mexican-American history. The thematic approach permits an analysis that reveals continuities as well as change across various periods in the Mexican-American experience. This approach differs from that of many scholars who have assigned to particular periods a general theme, such as the 1920s and 1930s as a period of accommodation and assimilation, or the 1940s and 1950s as the period of the "Mexican-American generation" (Barrera, 1985; Navarro, 1974; Tirado, 1970). The problem with this approach is that it limits our understanding of the evolution of Mexican-American organizations by associating particular eras of Mexican-American history with overgeneralized characterizations. The thematic/period approach, however, allows us to assess the impact of major events during various periods on the development of Mexican-American organizations while understanding how the continuing factors of poverty, social disadvantage, struggle for equality and social mobility, economic and racial discrimination, and advocacy for educational and political rights have influenced Mexican-American organizations over time. These and other factors account for the primary themes characterizing the historical development of Mexican-American nonprofit and voluntary organizations over the past 140 years.

The following themes, set within three broad historical periods (1848–1899, 1900–1939, and 1940–present), provide a basic understanding of the development and multifaceted roles of nonprofit organizations within Mexican-American communities: (1) socioeconomic mutual aid, (2) civil rights advocacy and protection against discrimination, (3) political representation and power, (4) cultural promotion and production, (5) protection of workers, (6) educational equity, and (7) community economic development. These themes change over time, yet they are the principal ones that highlight Mexican-American organizational history.

THE MAKING OF A NEW MINORITY: MEXICAN-AMERICANS: 1848–1899

During the half century following the war between the United States and Mexico, the fate was sealed for Mexicans who opted to remain in their homeland after it was ceded to the United States by the Treaty of Guadalupe Hidalgo in 1848. Mexicans in Texas had already experienced this fate since 1836, when Americans were successful in the Texas Revolution and created an independent republic. Throughout most of the new U.S. Southwest, the rise of Anglo society and institutions caused the demise of their Mexican counterparts. Although the treaty guaranteed Mexican residents in the region constitutional rights as citizens of the United States, the history of the period is filled with violations of those rights.

The circumstances that prevailed during the decades following the U.S.-Mexican War set in motion the socioeconomic and political conditions that would stamp the Mexican-American reality. For the most part, dispossessed of their lands through legal and extralegal means, disenfranchised from the new political institutions brought by Americans, relegated to the lowest class of workers in the new labor market, and maligned socially and culturally by Anglo newcomers to the region, Mexican-Americans emerged as a racial/ethnic minority with attendant negative associations. A response of Mexican-Americans to their decline was the development of a variety of organizations that reflected their new status (Camarillo, 1979; De León, 1982; Del Castillo, 1979; Montejano, 1987; Sheridan, 1986).

By the last quarter of the nineteenth century, dozens of mutual aid associations had been founded across the Southwest. These organizations in many ways mirrored the reality of the majority of Mexican-Americans who were cut off from the direct influences of Mexico as they struggled to maintain their cultural foundations. The mutual aid associations provided some semblance of cultural continuity and ethnic identity as well as economic security for increasingly impoverished Mexican-American communities during a period of dramatic and traumatic change. La Sociedad Hispano Americano de Benfecio Mutua in Los Angeles, founded in 1875, was one of many *mutualistas* established that promoted festivities to commemorate Mexican national holidays. In a similar way, beginning in 1894, La Alianza Hispano-Americana served the cultural and social needs of the Tucson Mexican-American community. For Mexicans in Arizona, however, the Alianza also served a variety of other functions typical of mutual aid organizations of the period. For example, the Alianza actually was founded as an association of Mexican-Americans to combat the political maneuvering of Anglos who were attempting to usurp Mexican-American political representation in Tucson. The Alianza was also an insurance-providing organization that offered sickness and death benefits to 10,000 members associated with lodges established throughout the Southwest during the early twentieth century. The popularity of La Alianza attested to the need of a multifaceted mutual aid organization for working class Mexican-Americans (Briegel, 1974; Del Castillo, 1979; Hernandez, 1983).

Mutual aid associations were not peculiar to the Mexican-American experience. In fact, these organizations were common especially among new immigrants to the United States during the second half of the nineteenth century. Like Mexicans, European immigrants struggled to establish some measure of social and economic security through mutual aid associations and other organizations. The fundamental difference, however, between Mexican-Americans in the Southwest and European immigrants in other regions was that Mexicans had gone through a period of socioeconomic decline as the "natives" of the area, while white Americans, in a real sense, were the immigrants to the Southwest.

The mutual aid associations among Mexican-Americans were necessarily multifaceted organizations that provided a margin of economic security in times of financial crisis or served as advocacy groups to protect the community from abuses in a hostile society. Consequently, organizations such as La Alianza or La Sociedad Hispano Americano—and dozens of comparable *mutualistas*—selected from agendas that included economic benefits, cultural activities, political advocacy, and protection of civil rights. The *mutualistas* played a crucial role during the second half of the nineteenth century by providing Mexican-Americans a modicum of stability during a period of rapid change.

Other types of organizations developed as a result of loss of land, economic decline, political powerlessness, and the general instability brought about by the introduction of U.S. capitalism into the Southwest. For example, Mexican-Americans in New Mexico were compelled to respond in united fashion to halt the destruction of their traditional ways of life. Increasingly pushed off their ancestral land grants by U.S. speculators and hemmed in by barbed-wire fences introduced by Anglo farmers and ranchers, and by owners of the railroads, northern New Mexican villagers banded together in 1889 to form Las Gorras Blancas ("White Caps"). As a secret group of nightriders, Las Gorras Blancas cut fences and tore up railroad ties. An important offshoot of the White Caps was El Partido del Pueblo Unido. This group developed in response to the changing political conditions at the local level and the decline in grass roots representation of the Hispanos. Neither Las Gorras Blancas nor El Partido succeeded long in their efforts to curtail the advance of Americanization (Rosenbaum, 1981).

The emergence of mutual aid associations, political advocacy groups, and incipient labor organizations (e.g., Los Caballeros de Labor in New Mexico and sheepshearers' unions in California and Texas) of Mexican-Americans during the late nineteenth century laid the foundations for the rapid expansion of these and other voluntary organizations that served Mexican-Americans during the early twentieth century, especially the hundreds of thousands of Mexican immigrants who entered the United States to escape the Mexican Revolution.

MEXICAN IMMIGRATION AND ORGANIZATIONAL EXPANSION: 1900–1939

While conditions facing Mexican-Americans during the second half of the nineteenth century gave rise to their first organizations, the conditions that the group experienced during the first four decades of the twentieth century explain the current proliferation of local and national organizations. Mexican-Americans entered the new century as a group that had survived—although at great cost—a radical transformation of their society. Isolated in their urban barrios and rural *colonias,* they were, for the most part, separated from mainstream Anglo society by race, class, language, and culture. The tension between Anglos and Mexicans that was manifested in racial antagonisms during the previous century had reached a level of biracial accommodation by 1900, although social distance between the two peoples continued to characterize race relations. In the early 1900s, Mexicans no longer constituted a political or economic obstacle to Anglos and were, in fact, increasingly becoming an essential part of the Southwest's labor market.

Any possibility for a peaceful and amicable coexistence between Mexicans and Anglos was shattered during the early twentieth century as a result of intensified anti-Mexican attitudes. These attitudes were based on long-held negative feelings about Mexicans and fueled by fears of mass immigration from Mexico. Indeed, the first great wave of immigration from Mexico, a result of the Mexican Revolution, brought nearly one tenth of Mexico's people (perhaps as many as one million people) north across the border. The reactions of Anglos to large-scale immigration was ambivalent: On the one hand, they became dependent on the low wage labor the Mexicans provided, but on the other hand, they decried the problems Mexicans supposedly created. Among the reasons articulated by those who advocated restricting immigration from Mexico in the post-World War I era, the complaints cited most often included the following: Mexicans could not be assimilated into U.S. society because they were so different (e.g., they lacked motivation to succeed, they demonstrated no interest in democratic government, their culture made them unable to integrate into society), their children created problems in the public schools and made the educational process more difficult for Anglo students, they caused public health problems because of their propensity to live in overcrowded conditions and spread contagious diseases, and they took jobs away from U.S. citizens. Those who supported unrestricted immigration from Mexico (e.g., agriculturalists, mine operators, railroad corporations) argued, on the other hand, that Mexican immigrants provided an indispensable source of manual labor throughout the Southwest. By 1930, the arguments of the antirestrictionists were silenced, however, as the economic turmoil of the Great Depression played havoc with the national and regional economies (Camarillo, 1984; Romo, 1983).

To explain why during this period there occurred a significant expansion of organizations serving the needs of Mexican-Americans and immigrants, one must understand not only the prevailing racial attitudes but also the socioeconomic conditions—some new, many old—that prompted organizational development. First, an enormous proliferation of mutual aid-type organizations went hand in hand with mass immigration from Mexico. In adjusting to life in the United States, Mexican immigrants organized hundreds of new *mutualistas* to meet their needs for sickness and death benefits and, in a broader context, to recreate their social networks in a new environment. Many of these mutual aid associations were founded as strictly local groups, while others, such as La Sociedad Benito Juarez and La Union

Patriotica Benefica Mexicano Independiente, had dozens of chapters in the various states of the Southwest and later in the Midwest (Camarillo, 1979; Hernandez, 1983).

The mutual aid societies, much like their predecessors of the previous century, often played a variety of roles in Mexican-American communities. They not only provided insurance benefits for members but also were typically among the main organizations that promoted social and cultural festivities. The *mutualistas* often joined in sponsorship of sociocultural events with groups that were organized specifically to maintain Mexican cultural traditions. Many of these clubs and groups instructed youngsters about folk dances and songs in efforts to promote the cultural traditions of Mexico for those growing up as the first generation of Mexican-Americans. From Chicago to San Antonio to Tucson to Los Angeles, the *mutualistas* and other organizations during the period contributed in fundamental ways to the sociocultural maintenance of expanding Mexican-American communities (Hernandez, 1983).

The multifaceted mutual aid organizations also contributed in several cases to the well-being of Mexican workers through unionization. It is no surprise that many *mutualistas* were responsible for the development of Mexican-American labor unions throughout the period, especially during the 1920s and 1930s. The major U.S. labor unions had made it quite clear that they had no intention of organizing Mexican workers, and some unions were adamantly opposed to the large-scale use of immigrant workers in the Southwest labor market. With little help from the major unions, Mexican-Americans were particularly vulnerable to exploitation. The list of discriminatory and exploitative practices used against Mexican immigrants and Mexican-American workers in the mining, food processing, construction, and transportation industries and in agribusiness have been well documented by scholars: racial wage differentials, contract labor, wages paid in script for purchases only at company stores, jobs designated only for "Mexicans," deportation of union leaders, and so forth. These and other conditions forced many mutual aid associations to take the lead in organizing Mexican-American workers into unions. For example, in 1927 a federation of mutual aid societies from throughout southern California gathered in Los Angeles and formed the first Mexican-American labor union in 1928, La Confederacion de Uniones Obreras Mexicanas (Acuña, 1981; Barrera, 1985; Camarillo, 1984).

Although the mutual aid societies were often involved in important ways to stimulate unionization of Mexican-American workers, during the 1930s two other groups were concerned about the plight of Mexican workers and acted to help organize them. Beginning in the early 1930s, the U.S. Communist Party attempted to organize Mexican and other agricultural workers through the unions they established, especially the Trade Union Unity

League and the Cannery and Agricultural Workers Industrial Union. After the demise of both the Mexican-American labor unions and the communist party-supported unions, which were effectively squashed by growers in California, the upstart Congress of Industrial Organization (CIO) began organizing food processing workers—a great number of whom were Mexican women–during the late 1930s and 1940s. Although the United Cannery, Agricultural, Packing, and Allied Workers of America (UCAPAWA)—the CIO's fifth largest union—experienced early success in unionizing Mexican-American and other workers in California and Texas, it too was suppressed by growers, management, and local law enforcement agencies. The efforts of UCAPAWA and the Mexican-American labor unions to advance the status of workers were modest at best. So too were a variety of other scattered unionization attempts aimed at the Mexican-American working class. From the Japanese-Mexican Sugar Beet Workers' Union in Oxnard in 1903 to the efforts of the Western Federation of Miners in Arizona to the union of pecan shellers in Depression-era San Antonio, Mexicans were involved in the formation of unions in virtually every industry in which they were employed, including the garment, steel, furniture, shipping, and construction industries (Acuña, 1981; Reisler, 1976; Ruiz, 1987).

Although the period from the turn of the century through the Great Depression was one marked more by failure than success for unionization among Mexican-American workers, it nevertheless was a period in which foundations were laid for more significant union victories during the post-World War II era. More than anything else, the unionization efforts of the early twentieth century reflected the dire circumstances that confronted Mexican-Americans and their need to join together in organizations to protect their rights and interests as workers.

The protection of workers' rights was in many ways inseparable from efforts to protect basic civil rights, a reality most Mexican-American labor unionists faced during the period. Mexican-Americans struggled to civil and legal rights through a variety of local groups and, later in the period, through their first national civil rights advocacy organization.

Although civil rights advocacy of Mexican-Americans was something articulated by community leaders and spokespersons since the mid-nineteenth century, the first formal organizations to include protection of civil rights in their agendas were products of the early twentieth century. For example, in 1911 Mexican-Americans in Texas organized El Primer Congreso Mexicanista, a statewide meeting of local organizations, to unite for action against discrimination and repression by Anglos. The Congreso also identified a variety of other issues with regard to racial equality, in particular the educational segregation of Mexican-American children and violation of citizens' legal rights in the political/judicial system in Texas. Another example of a civil rights defense organization was La Liga Protectora Latina, formed in Phoenix in 1914 to oppose state legislation that would have forbidden corporations and other employers from hiring Mexican-American workers beyond a 20 percent ceiling. La Liga was successful in rallying Mexican-Americans against this proposed discriminatory law directed at restricting the number of Mexican workers in Arizona's mining industry. The group later served as a state lobby in support of legislation to improve conditions for Arizona Mexican-Americans (Hernandez, 1983; Limón, 1974).

The culmination of civil rights advocacy for Mexican-Americans and other Latinos occurred in 1939 with the formation of the Congreso de Pueblos de Habla Espanola (Congress of Spanish Speaking People). Indeed, in many ways the Congreso represented the amalgamation of the *mutualista,* labor, and civil rights advocacy movements for Mexican-Americans during the first four decades of the twentieth century. The Congreso was initiated by Luisa Moreno of UCAPAWA and supported broadly by hundreds of local mutual aid organizations, Mexican-American and other progressive U.S. labor unions, California-based progressive political groups (e.g., the Women's Committee of the American League for Peace and Freedom and the Hollywood Anti-Nazi League), and the Confederacion de Sociedades Hispanas, an organization that represented some 200,000 Puerto Ricans and other Latinos in New York. The Congreso convened in Los Angeles in 1939, and two local leaders, Eduardo Quevedo and Josefina Fierro, were selected as president and secretary, respectively. Delegates attending the meeting represented Mexican-American and other Latino groups with a combined dues-paying membership of 874,000 people. In addition to advocacy and protection of civil rights for Latinos and opposition to racial and class discrimination, the Congreso offered Latinos a broad platform for action: political advocacy condemning legislation adversely affecting Latinos; promotion of labor unionization; promotion of the health, education, and welfare of Latinos; and protection of the foreign born. The Congreso was the first broad-based civil rights national organization for Latinos. It achieved a degree of cooperation among Mexican-Americans across the Southwest and Latinos in other parts of the nation never attained before or since. Although it did not survive much beyond 1945 for a variety of reasons (deportation of key leaders, induction into the armed forces of young male leaders, and surveillance by the FBI because of its alleged communist orientation), it mirrored the need for civil rights protection for Latinos and signaled a new period of increased political action among Mexican-Americans during the post-World War II period (Camarillo, 1984; Meier, 1988). Importantly, the Congreso illustrated the leadership roles that women assumed on an increasing basis after 1940. Although Mexican-American women were involved in many, if not most, organizations prior to 1940, since World War II more women have emerged as key leaders in a variety of organizations (some of these leaders are cited in the pages that follow).

The Congreso was a significant development in the organizational history of Mexican-Americans; it boldly ventured into a regional effort to unite Mexican-Americans for concerted action. It did not, however, unite all existing organizations in the Southwest; this fact illustrated differences in strategy and ideology that existed among Mexican-American organizations. Conspicuously missing from the list of organizations supporting the efforts of the Congreso was the League of United Latin American Citizens (LULAC). Founded in Texas in 1929, LULAC was concerned about the socioeconomic and cultural status of Mexican-Americans; but unlike the Congreso, it was opposed to direct political action. Rather, LULAC strategy was to promote good citizenship among Mexican-Americans and thereby change the image of Mexicans in U.S. society. Started by more middle-class-oriented Mexican-Americans, LULAC early on organized dozens of local chapters throughout Texas and later throughout the Southwest. Although assimilationist in nature, LULAC organizing principles revolved around Mexican-Americans accommodating themselves to U.S. culture and institutions through gradual integration. This orientation, however, did not prevent LULAC from becoming an important advocate in support of Mexican-American legal and educational rights during the 1940s and later (San Miguel, 1987).

LULAC's early integrationist aims characterized a dimension of the Mexican-American population already evident during the 1900–1940 period and revealed a development particularly obvious in the post-World War II period: the diversity within the ethnic group. Although increasingly diverse across region (differences among Mexican-Americans in the various states), across generations (foreign born vs. native born), and across classes (an emerging middle class within the large working class), the problems that characterized the population and galvanized organizational efforts during the first third of the twentieth century continued to shape the development of newer organizations after 1940.

NEW ORGANIZATIONAL OPPORTUNITIES: 1940 TO THE PRESENT
Although one could make the case for dividing the years since 1940 into two separate chronological periods in the historical development of Mexican-American organizations, it is perhaps more instructive to view the continuities and changes characteristic of Mexican-American organizations during this period rather than interpret the period from 1940 to 1960 and the decades since 1960 as distinctly different. The organizations that blossomed during the past five decades were responses to new and different opportunities available to Mexican-Americans. During this era of organizational expansion, new influences—especially foundation support, federal programs, and the civil rights movement in general—factored into a dramatic increase in the number of nonprofit, voluntary organizations serving the group after the mid-1960s. Newer organizations as well as longstanding groups took advan-

tage of new resources. What was not new about the period since 1940 were the reasons that compelled Mexican-Americans and their supporters to organize. To be sure, conditions have changed in recent decades, but in viewing the recent history of Mexican-American organizations, one is struck by the continuity of purpose: the striving for equal opportunity. New organizations have arisen while others have declined during this period, but the great majority may be explained by the same themes that characterized most organizations in the prewar era: social and economic advancement, civil rights advocacy, political representation, cultural promotion, and educational equity.

Continuity and Change Among Organizations

What motivated Mexican-Americans in the immediate post-World War II decades to organize actively and to create newer institutions? Most historians agree that returning Mexican-American GIs expected and demanded more from U.S. society after risking their lives to defend the United States. Yet, when most returned to their barrios and *colonias,* they found conditions little changed since they had left for overseas. Many of these returning GIs became convinced that political power was the key to creating more and better opportunities. Several of the most important postwar organizations founded by Mexican-Americans illustrated this new preoccupation with political representation and the potential influence of the Mexican-American electorate.

Two of these organizations, the Community Service Organization (CSO) and the Unity Leagues, were founded in the Los Angeles area shortly after the war. Initially, both were organized to provide more political leverage for Mexican-Americans who continued to face institutionalized forms of discrimination and who were unrepresented in local politics. The Unity Leagues later merged their local efforts with CSO, a group whose original purpose was to elect the first Mexican-American to serve on the Los Angeles City Council in over 80 years. After helping to direct voter education and registration drives that greatly aided the election of Edward Roybal to the council in 1949, the CSO—as a nonpartisan and "nonpolitical" organization—served the Los Angeles community in a variety of ways, including civil rights advocacy in police brutality cases, lobbying for state legislation that benefited Mexican-Americans, and participation in civic improvement programs. For the most part, CSO settled into a mutual aid mode after being red-baited during the McCarthy period of the early 1950s. Importantly, both the Unity Leagues and CSO were influenced by Saul Alinsky's Industrial Areas Foundation of Chicago and Fred Ross, Sr., of the American Council on Race Relations, groups that promoted the development of grass roots organizations by providing technical assistance to disadvantaged populations (Acuña, 1981).

Two other new organizations established during the late 1950s and early 1960s further illustrated the concern for direct political action as well as the persistent lack of representation of Mexican-Americans in the political process. The Mexican American Political Association (MAPA) in California was established in 1959 as a nonpartisan group to leverage the Democratic Party using the increasing influence of the Mexican-American vote. MAPA endorsed candidates, articulated policy issues of concern to Mexican-Americans, and served as an effective lobby in California local politics before its decline during the 1970s. MAPA's counterpart in Texas, the Political Association of Spanish-Speaking Organizations (PASSO), sought to serve as an umbrella group for a variety of Mexican-American organizations in the state; its agenda, like MAPA's, was intently political. Unlike its California cousin, however, PASSO failed to have a significant impact on Texas state politics (Barrera, 1985; Camarillo, 1984; Meier and Rivera, 1981).

MAPA, PASSO, and CSO were all more overtly political than their predecessor organizations; in this sense, they represented links between many pre-1940 organizations and those that became identified as "Chicano movement" organizations beginning in the late 1960s. Certain other groups active during the 1940s and 1950s also may be described as links between past and contemporary organizations. For example, the Asociacion Nacional Mexico Americana (ANMA) was formed around 1950 to protect the civil rights of Mexican workers who faced harassment and deportation by the Immigration and Naturalization Service; several chapters were started in cities throughout the Southwest. Although shortlived, ANMA was one of the few organizations that resisted the repression directed at Mexican-Americans involved in progressive community and labor unions during the early 1950s (Gonzales, 1985; Urrutia, 1984).

Another example of a prototype organization that expanded significantly during the 1970s and 1980s was the Council of Mexican American Affairs (CMAA), founded in Los Angeles in 1954. Started by a group of professionals as an umbrella association for a variety of local organizations, CMAA's purpose was to facilitate leadership and serve as a catalyst for addressing issues critical to the well-being of Mexican-Americans. Although the council did not exist very long, it pointed to a future direction of organizational development among various professional groups in the fields of legal services, education, health, community economic development, and promotion of the arts (Meier and Rivera, 1981).

The concern over educational opportunities increasingly became a top priority among several organizations in the postwar decades, again illustrating how certain organizations and issues of the period served as springboards for more contemporary groups. The leader for advocacy of Mexican-American educational rights was not a new organization, but one that had existed for over two decades—LULAC. This group was instrumental in several successful court cases that struck down the legality of educational segregation of Mexican-American children in California and Texas public schools during the 1940s. Although LULAC engaged in other types of advocacy work in the postwar period, its greatest contributions were related to work in education (San Miguel, 1987).

Another group that promoted educational opportunities for Mexican-American youth was the American GI Forum. The organization was founded in Texas as a response to racial discrimination involving the refusal of a local south Texas funeral home to bury the body of a Mexican-American war hero in the town's Anglo cemetery, but later the GI Forum evolved into a multifaceted organization of veterans. By the early 1950s, the GI Forum had become one of the largest Mexican-American groups in the country, with over 100 local chapters. In addition to its concern with educational rights and opportunities, the forum's chapters were also active in local politics and continued to fight discrimination against Mexican-Americans (Allsup, 1982).

The Rise of the Chicano Movement

Most of the organizations active during the 1940s and 1950s continued their work through subsequent decades. By the 1970s, however, the more established groups, such as LULAC, CSO, MAPA, and the GI Forum, were eclipsed by a new generation of Mexican-American groups that took their cue for activism and service from what became known as the Chicano Movement. Whether identified or not as products of the movement, the enormous proliferation of organizations that developed during the late 1960s, 1970s, and 1980s constituted a new phase in Mexican-American organizational history. Although many of these organizations had different styles and structures than their counterparts before the 1960s, the fundamental issues around which they organized were essentially those that had long been on the agenda.

Earlier generations of Mexican-American activists had described their organizational efforts as "movements" for change (e.g., the labor unionization movement of the 1930s or the movement for new opportunities during the 1940s and 1950s), but the one that was labeled the Chicano Movement in the late 1960s was different for several reasons. The Chicano Movement was not a unified organizational development, but rather was composed of a variety of ideologies, objectives and purposes, and organizational initiatives; it was an ethnic phenomenon that served as a catalyst and new point of departure for Mexican-Americans. The movement involved far larger numbers of activists, leaders, and organizations than any previous period of history. The resolve to create social change was unprecedented. Also unprecedented was the support provided to organizations by foundations and government agencies.

Influenced significantly by the civil rights, antiwar, and black power movements of the 1960s—and buoyed by an attitude in U.S. society supportive of historically disadvantaged groups—hundreds of organizations formed in the wake of the Chicano Movement. The new organizations were inspired partly by events during the 1960s that ushered in an unprecedented era of advocacy for civil rights and social change, but they also drew inspiration from previous struggles by Mexican-Americans and from new charismatic leaders who burst onto the scene in the 1960s (such as Cesar Chavez and Dolores Huerta of the United Farm Workers Union in California, Reies Lopez Tijerina in New Mexico, Corky Gonzales in Colorado, and Jose Angel Gutierrez in Texas). New symbols—such as the concept of "Aztlan" as the mythical homeland of the Aztecs and, as claimed by some, the spiritual/geographic origins of Chicanos—and new slogans such as "Chicano power" and "Viva La Causa" reflected a greater sense of unity and mobilization among Mexican-Americans everywhere (Meier, 1988).

These newer organizations, however, were not very different in fundamental values from their predecessors. Central to most organizations established since the late 1960s were the recurring themes that had served as the basis for the development of dozens of Mexican-American groups. Many older themes were given new vision and meaning by leaders and organizations during the 1960s and 1970s: opportunities for educational and socioeconomic advancement, Chicano political power, cultural self-expression through the arts and letters, civil/legal rights advocacy, and the development of services and programs for local communities. The principal objectives that emanated from these themes set the context for a host of newly established organizations.

Although many continuities existed among the reasons why Mexican-Americans carried on the tradition of organizing nonprofit groups and voluntary organizations, two newer influences further contributed to Mexican-American organizational development in the 1970s and 1980s. Although some precedents existed in earlier decades, beginning sometime in the late 1960s, corporate and private foundations—especially the Ford Foundation—and federal government agencies generated resources rarely available previously to Mexican-Americans. These new economic resources were utilized effectively by Mexican-American leaders—new leaders as well as established leaders—who were energized through their involvement in the Chicano Movement.

Major Themes of Organizations and Some Examples

Perhaps the best way to characterize most of the organizations developed since the late 1960s is to categorize groups by their function and intent, or by the themes each represented. In this way, one can plainly see how recent organizations have reflected the historical as well as the contemporary reality of the nation's second largest ethnic minority population. It is difficult to separate organizations into categories, for like Mexican-American organizations of the past, many of those operating today are multifaceted.

Protection of legal and civil rights, and public policy advocacy, on behalf of Mexican-Americans continues to be a rallying point for organizations. Mexican-American leaders supported by various foundations have helped establish some of the most effective organizations protecting the group's rights. The Mexican American Legal Defense and Educational Fund (MALDEF), funded initially by the Ford Foundation, has for twenty years played a critical role in support of the educational, civil, occupational, and voting rights of Mexican-Americans throughout the nation. Headquartered in Los Angeles, MALDEF maintains several regional offices and continues to be the principal legal advocacy organization for Mexican-Americans. It is supported broadly by foundations, corporations, and private donations. Vilma Martinez, one of MALDEF's most able leaders, guided the organization during most of the 1970s; she contributed to the long-standing role of women serving in leadership positions in Mexican-American organizations over time (Gonzales, 1985; Meier, 1988; Meier and Rivera, 1981).

Advocacy concerning public policy issues affecting Mexican-Americans and other Hispanics was a role assumed by another organization established the same year as MALDEF. The National Council of La Raza (known as the Southwest Council of La Raza before 1972) is based in Washington, D.C., and serves as an advocacy and issues-analysis organization on matters of national importance to Hispanics (such as employment opportunities, educational attainment, and governmental resources for poor communities). The National Council acts as a liaison in Washington for over 100 affiliated local Hispanic community organizations (Gonzales, 1985; Meier and Rivera, 1981).

Although different in many ways from either MALDEF or the National Council, the Southwest Voter Registration Education Project—developed by the late Willie Velasquez—became an effective organization that dramatically elevated the political clout of Mexican-Americans in Texas. The groups often worked hand in hand with MALDEF in cases involving violation of the federal Voting Rights Act. It, too, has developed an issues-analysis approach to press for greater political representation of Hispanics in the Southwest (Gonzales, 1985; Meier and Rivera, 1981).

Organizations in the 1960s and 1970s that were concerned more with direct partisan politics than with advocacy per se played important roles in furthering the political agenda of Mexican-Americans. The La Raza Unida Party is a good example of how Mexican-Americans in Texas organized themselves as a political third party out of frustration with both the Democrats and Republicans in local politics. Although not the first formal political party established by Mexican-Americans, it was by far the most successful, even if its success was modest and short-lived. Inspired by young Chicano activists and led by Jose Angel Gutierrez, La Raza Unida Party was founded in 1970 and within a few years had succeeded in electing a slate of Mexican-American officeholders in small south Texas towns; especially noteworthy was its success in Crystal City. La Raza Unida attempted expansion to other states and cities in the Southwest but never duplicated the temporary gains it had made in south Texas. Nonetheless, La Raza Unida Party symbolized the political aspirations and radical politics of the Chicano Movement during its heyday of the early 1970s (Foley, 1977; Gutierrez and Hirsh, 1974; Shockley, 1974).

In addition to new groups that formed around the issues of political advocacy and party politics, a much larger number of organizations developed around special issues and as professional associations. Examples abound: A group of young Chicano attorneys established the Raza Bar Association in Los Angeles in 1972; health care service providers and practitioners started that same year the National Chicano Health Organization in Oakland, California; Mexican-American priests organized their own group (Padres Asociados para Derechos Religiosas, Educativos, y Sociales, or PADRES) to promote ethnic leadership within the Catholic Church and to promote social change within the communities they served; in the field of education many groups developed during the 1970s, prominent among them is the Association of Mexican American Educators, the National Association for Chicano Studies, and the National Chicano Council on Higher Education (Gonzales, 1985; Meier and Rivera, 1981).

Dozens of other organizations focusing on specific concerns were developed during the 1970s and 1980s by professionals and lay persons. For example, aspiring Mexican-American artists established several groups that promoted public art (mural art) as well as gallery art produced by Chicanos. A group of Los Angeles women, headed by Francisca Flores, created La Comision Femenil Mexicana Nacional in 1970 to assist in job training and leadership among Mexican-American women. Mexican-American cultural centers were founded in most towns and cities where Mexican-Americans were concentrated; these centers actively sponsored a host of social and cultural events for the community in the tradition of the earlier *mutualistas*. Community economic development corporations and employment service organizations, funded largely by federal or state sources, were also important groups in local communities. For example, The East Los Angeles Community Union (TELACU), founded in 1968, focused its efforts on political–economic developments in the largest Mexican-American community in the nation. Likewise, a service organization by the name of SER (Service, Employment, and Redevelopment) that was administered by LULAC and the GI Forum was concerned primarily with job training in high unemployment areas where Mexican-Americans were concentrated.

Another important type of Mexican-American organization developed primarily during the late 1960s and 1970s was that of the community-based group, which served a variety of functions and often changed its orientation over time. Among the most important of these groups were Crusade for Justice in Denver, Centro de Accion Social Autonoma (CASA) in Los Angeles, Alianza Federal de Pueblos Libres of New Mexico, and Communities Organized for Public Service (COPS) in San Antonio. Although each had a different agenda related to its particular locale, each shared the goal of facilitating socioeconomic and political change in the communities. The Crusade for Justice, headed by Corky Gonzales, was founded in 1967 as a broad-based civil rights group that demanded changes in educational, employment, and local political opportunities for Mexican-Americans; it became one of the principal Chicano Movement organizations on the national scene during the early 1970s (Marin, 1977). CASA was cofounded in Los Angeles during the late 1960s by longtime activists Bert Corona and Soledad Alatorre; it focused originally on issues concerning the rights of undocumented workers. Before it changed into a leftist organization advocating political education toward social revolution, CASA set the precedent for organizations that later concentrated their efforts on the plight of Mexican immigrants (Gutierrez, 1984). COPS began in 1974 primarily as a political pressure group in San Antonio and represented various Mexican-American local interests attempting to influence city politicians to serve better the large Mexican-American population; it functioned in much the same way that the CSO had operated during its early years in Los Angeles (Gonzales, 1985). The Alianza Federal de Pueblos Libres differed dramatically from most other local community organizations in that its sole purpose was to advocate the return of northern New Mexican land grants that Reies Tijerina and his followers declared were stolen from their rightful Hispanic owners; the Alianza began its work in 1967 but met stiff political and law enforcement resistance before its decline by the early 1970s (Blawis, 1971; Nabokov, 1969).

The list of organizations developed since the late 1960s is a long one. This chapter makes no pretense about including organizations of all types that were established during the period. Those mentioned earlier are merely examples of some of the major categories of organizations that reflected the many themes of nonprofit and voluntary groups created by and for Mexican-Americans.

CONCLUSION

Although the names and styles of organizations serving the Mexican-American people have changed over time, the fundamental objectives have not. Whether it was 100 years ago or yesterday, a compelling objective for Mexican-Americans has been representation in the political process; from La Gorras Blancas of the late 1890s to the Southwest Voter Registration Education

Project of the late 1980s, access to political power continues to be a key organizing principle. Defense of Mexican-American legal and civil rights is also a legacy handed down over the decades by organizations such as La Alianza Hispano Americana, the Congreso de Pueblos de Habla Espanola, and the Mexican American Legal Defense and Educational Fund. The goal of providing self-help continues today in ways similar to the first mutual aid associations founded by Mexican-Americans during the second half of the nineteenth century. Although the *mutualista* declined dramatically after World War II, the idea of mutual aid and economic stability of Mexican-American communities is still at the core of many contemporary groups like the Comision Femenil Mexicana or The East Los Angeles Community Union (TELACU). The struggle for educational rights and equality also continues as a rallying point for professional organizations such as the Association of Mexican American Educators, the National Association for Chicano Studies, and student organizations like Movimiento Estudiantil Chicano de Aztlan (MEChA). And those groups today that focus their efforts promoting the visual and performing arts among Mexican-Americans do so in the same vein that similar folkloric groups did over 100 year ago.

Of course, particular circumstances facing individual communities of Mexican-Americans have changed over time, and correspondingly, so too have the organizations serving these communities. And although there are no doubt dozens of organizations serving Mexican-Americans today that defy categorization, it is safe to say that the large majority of contemporary Mexican-American organizations may be identified with one or more of the objectives/themes noted in this essay.

The history of voluntary and nonprofit organizations developed by and for Mexican-Americans over the past 140 years reflects the material conditions, aspirations, and struggles for equal opportunity and equality in U.S. society. Historically, a broad range of organizations developed to meet the needs of a Mexican-American population characterized as poor, underrepresented in the political arena, plagued by discrimination and lack of opportunities, and in search of a better living. The themes that help us explain the historical development of Mexican-American organizations are still very much a part of the Mexican-American reality today. The needs of Mexican-Americans during the last decade of the twentieth century and into the next century will no doubt provide the backdrop for the evolution of newer organizations, some of which will conform to the types already established, while others will develop innovative approaches in response to new needs and demands.

The future success of Mexican-American organizations will also depend in part on how they continue to adapt to changing circumstances at the local, state, and national levels and how they respond creatively to opportunities as well as to problems. Also important will be the partnerships that must emerge between local, state, and national interests of Mexican-Americans and other Hispanics. And key to any future development and success of organizations will be the support they receive from corporations, foundations, and government agencies. To be sure, the future growth and status of the Mexican-American population will be influenced significantly by the role of nonprofit and voluntary organizations during the near future.

3

Puerto Rican Nonprofit Organizations in New York City

Carlos Rodríguez-Fraticelli, Carlos Sanabria, and Amílcar Tirado

This chapter is an attempt to develop a history of Puerto Rican nonprofit organizations in New York City. It traces their organizational development in the context of the origins and growth of the Puerto Rican community, the ongoing colonial relationship between the United States and the island, and the social, economic, and political transformations experienced by U.S. society during the period from the late nineteenth century to the present.

Our decision to concentrate on the Puerto Rican experience in New York City is based on the following reasons. First, New York City is the oldest, largest, and most important center of Puerto Rican activity in this country. At present, there are two million Puerto Ricans in the United States of whom over 860,000 live in New York City. Second, some of the main patterns established in New York City were repeated in other areas. Finally, Puerto Rican New Yorkers today are suffering the worst effects of the decline of manufacturing in a major employment sector and the reduction of social and educational services. In this context, Puerto Rican community-based and nonprofit organizations face their greatest challenge.

The Puerto Rican experience in the United States is unique. Because of the political relationship between the island and the United States, Puerto Ricans have come to this country as citizens since 1917 and have had an established right of free entry into the country since 1904. Yet because of their cultural and racial background, Puerto Ricans have been relegated to second-class status. Today, Puerto Ricans, like other "nonwhite" racial–eth-

nic groups—blacks, Chicanos, and Native Americans—occupy a place at the
bottom of the U.S. socioeconomic and political ladder.

In this chapter, we examine the role played by Puerto Rican nonprofit
organizations in the process of adapting to and surviving within U.S. society.
Some of the main themes explored are the role of politics in the formation
and development of Puerto Rican community organizations, the important
function of culture and ethnicity in sparking organizational efforts, and the
influence of class interests in shaping these organizational experiences. This
discussion focuses on those organizations that have played major roles and
have developed new approaches in response to the continuous challenges
confronting Puerto Ricans in the United States.

For analytical purposes, we use a broad definition of nonprofit organizations. Nonprofit Puerto Rican organizations are defined as nongovernmental
associations established by and for Puerto Ricans for the specific purpose of
delivering services—social, economic, and cultural—and/or acting as advocates on behalf of the community. Since these organizational endeavors often
reflect the struggle of the Puerto Rican community or sectors of that community for empowerment, it is also necessary to consider broader political
dimensions.

Indeed, one of the main threads in this history is the ongoing tension
between service delivery and advocacy—a tension that has affected the internal functioning of organizations as well as relations among them and with
the larger community. This tension has been intensified as organizations
have become more dependent on outside funding sources. Today, the search
for independence and self-sufficiency remains a central concern of Puerto
Rican nonprofit organizations. In this chapter, we discuss how organizations
have historically tried to cope with this issue.

We have divided the history of Puerto Rican nonprofit organizations into
five main stages. The first stage extends from the nineteenth century to
World War I and covers early Puerto Rican migratory movements and
organizational efforts. The second phase covers the period from 1917 to
1948. During these years, Puerto Rican neighborhoods emerged as distinct
communities, and Puerto Ricans began to develop organizational structures
to respond to their needs as a community. A third phase stretches between
1948 and the early 1960s. These years marked the growth and expansion of
Puerto Rican community organizing outside the traditional neighborhoods
and the emergence of a second generation of Puerto Rican leadership with
a distinctive worldview and organizational approach. The fourth period,
from the early 1960s to 1975, covers Puerto Rican organizational responses
to the War on Poverty and the effects on Puerto Rican organizations of
growing dependence on outside funding. The last stage, from 1975 to the
present, coincides with the crisis of the U.S. economy and the organizational
attempts by Puerto Ricans to deal with this worsening situation.

FROM THE NINETEENTH CENTURY TO WORLD WAR I

Puerto Ricans have been settling in the United States since the nineteenth century. The earlier immigrations were composed mostly of merchants and students who came to study in U.S. colleges and universities (Sánchez-Korrol, 1983, p. 11). By the 1860s the class composition of the immigrants began to change. The expanding U.S. economy, especially the cigar-making industry, increasingly attracted skilled workers from Puerto Rico. At the same time, growing political unrest on the island, along with repressive Spanish colonial policies, forced separatist leaders—predominantly middle-class profession-als—into exile. Most of these immigrants came to New York City, the nation's main manufacturing and trading center, where they integrated themselves into the small but growing Spanish-speaking colony.

In New York, Puerto Rican workers joined existing mutual aid societies or established new ones to address their social, economic, and spiritual needs. Crossing class lines, supporters of Puerto Rican independence along with Cuban exiles set up revolutionary organizations to further their common struggle against Spanish colonial rule. Representing the better-educated and most radical sector of the Cuban and Puerto Rican working class, artisans and *tabaqueros* (tobacco workers) organized clubs that served as information and fundraising centers for the revolutionary cause (Vega, 1984, pp. 39–79).

As a result of the Spanish-American War (1898), Spain transferred control of Puerto Rico to the United States. Under U.S. rule, the island rapidly became a large sugar plantation controlled by U.S. capital. The process of land accumulation and the displacement of Puerto Rican peasants acceler-ated the formation of a large surplus labor force (Centro de Estudios Puer-torriqueños, 1979, Chap. 4). As living conditions deteriorated, migration rap-idly became one of the few alternatives for the impoverished Puerto Rican working class.

Since the early days of military occupation, U.S. industries began to look at the new possession as a potential source of cheap labor. Labor agents from the United States initiated the practice of contracting Puerto Ricans to work in the agricultural sector in different parts of the mainland (Centro de Estu-dios Puertorriqueños, 1982). In the meantime, an increasing number of Puerto Rican workers migrated of their own volition to the industrial urban centers, especially to the northeastern region.

FORMATION AND GROWTH OF THE PUERTO RICAN
COMMUNITY: 1917–1948

After World War I, most Puerto Rican migrants came to New York City, where the demand for unskilled, inexpensive labor continued unabated. A clearly defined Puerto Rican community with its own organizational and institutional life began to crystallize. Puerto Rican-owned businesses, such as *bodegas,* barber shops, lawyers' and physicians' offices, and storefront churches, began to appear during the 1920s to cater to the needs of the immigrants.

Yet the *colonias* (settlements) remained fundamentally working class. The small Puerto Rican upper class and professional element usually settled outside the established barrios. Very few participated actively in community struggles (Chenault, 1970, p. 47).

The principal Puerto Rican *colonias* were located in East Harlem and the Navy Yard section of Brooklyn. As in the earlier days, Puerto Rican skilled workers' organizational lives continued to revolve around their crafts. But as the *colonias* grew in numbers and as the composition of the migration became more heterogeneous, new forms of organizational activity began to emerge during the 1920s and 1930s. Of greatest importance were the hometown clubs such as the Club de Caborrojeños, the Mayagüezanos Ausentes, and the Hijos de Peñuelas. These clubs served as meeting places for people from the same towns or regions. Through these associations, the new immigrants developed social and cultural networks necessary for survival in an alien and increasingly hostile society (Sánchez-Korrol, 1983, pp. 157–158).

Meanwhile, other cultural and civic organizations developed along class lines. On the one hand, professionals and intellectuals established their own clubs, such as the Casa de Puerto Rico (1925), to promote Hispanic culture, customs, and traditions. On the other hand, workers created organizations like the Ateneo Obrero (1926) for cultural and educational purposes and, more important, to address the needs of the second generation (Vega, 1984, p. 144).

The first successful attempt to develop a citywide organizational response to confront the new reality experienced by Puerto Ricans in the metropolis took place in the early 1920s. In 1923, a group of Puerto Ricans living in Manhattan established the Porto Rican Brotherhood of America. Although predominantly a working class organization, the Brotherhood promoted the importance of unity and concerted action to defend the interests of the *colonias*. Equally important, the organization was predicated on the belief that Puerto Ricans themselves had to define their own problems and needs and devise their own solutions (Sánchez-Korrol, 1983, pp. 147–150).

The founding of the Brotherhood was partly a response to the growing awareness that the Puerto Rican community in New York was entering a new phase. The growth of the *colonias* took place at the same time that entry of Europeans was sharply curtailed by immigration law during the early 1920s. This legislation, however, did not directly affect Puerto Ricans, who were technically regarded as migrants as a result of a 1904 Supreme Court decision—a status officially sanctioned in 1917, when the U.S. Congress imposed U.S. citizenship on Puerto Ricans.

The fact that Puerto Ricans, who were considered inferior by the dominant Anglo society because of their racial composition and cultural background, continued migrating exacerbated anti-Puerto Rican prejudice in the city. Furthermore, the encroachment of Puerto Ricans in neighborhoods that until then were controlled by other ethnic groups created friction as the older groups perceived the new arrivals as a threat. Ethnic tensions grew. In the summer of 1926, thugs hired by Jewish merchants attacked Puerto Ricans in East Harlem. Puerto Ricans fought back, and interethnic clashes erupted throughout El Barrio (Vega, 1984, pp. 141–144).

The Brotherhood took the lead in defense of the community. Although directed against Puerto Ricans, the attack posed a potential threat to the general Spanish-speaking population, which could easily be identified as Puerto Rican. To address this growing threat, the Brotherhood sponsored the formation of a more encompassing organization, La Liga Puertorriqueña e Hispana. Composed of representatives of Puerto Rican and other Hispanic groups, the group's objectives were to unite all Spanish-speaking organizations, to represent the community before the authorities, to promote harmonious relations with other ethnic groups, and to educate the city's Hispanic population. As a Puerto Rican-controlled organization, the group also carried out campaigns to urge Puerto Rican participation in the electoral process and worked for the economic, political, and social betterment of Puerto Rico (Sánchez-Korrol, 1983, pp. 153–154).

During the years of the Great Depression, the Puerto Rican *colonias* in New York City became an embattled community as the anti-Puerto Rican campaign reached new heights (Sánchez-Korrol, 1983, pp. 155–157; Vega, 1984, pp. 176–182). Puerto Ricans were portrayed as criminals, carriers of contagious diseases, and social leeches. In this antagonistic environment, the problems of the Puerto Ricans were exacerbated, as many were laid off simply because of their ethnicity. Calls for an end to Puerto Rican migration to the city intensified (New York State Chamber of Commerce, 1935). Puerto Rican organizations, including the Liga, played an important role in the ensuing struggles in defense of the *colonias*.

Concurrently, Puerto Ricans began to participate more actively in politics as a means of dealing with the growing attacks. In Brooklyn, for example, Puerto Rican leaders established political clubs aligned with the Democratic and Republican parties. However, these parties proved to be unresponsive (Vega, 1984, p. 111; interview with Celia Vice, June 6, 1988; interview with Gilberto Gerena Valentín, June 6, 1988). Besides being "nonwhite," the community was numerically too small and poor to have any political leverage.

It was in the more progressive political organizations, such as the Communist and the American Labor parties, that Puerto Ricans found programs more attuned to their needs. Also, the militant Puerto Rican Nationalist Party gained widespread support in the community at that time. These parties, especially the Communist and the Nationalist, created their own social and cultural groups, such as the Club Eugenio María de Hostos and the Club

Pomarrosas, respectively, which became centers of intense community activity.

In Puerto Rico, the depression was having a similar radicalizing effect on the population. The devastation of the colonial economy created conditions for a political crisis of immense proportions. Anticolonial and antiimperialist movements gained wider support across class lines. By the late 1930s, the federal government had concluded that a redefinition of the colonial relationship was the only way out of the crisis. In the following years, the federal government worked closely with the leadership of the Partido Popular Democrático (PPD) to accomplish this objective, instituting a series of political reforms and a new economic development project known as Operation Bootstrap (Centro, 1979, Chap. 5).

FROM 1948 TO THE EARLY 1960s

The new economic program was based on the attraction of U.S. capital to the island through the creation of a highly favorable investment climate—cheap labor, tax exemptions, and political stability—and the exportation of the surplus labor force to the United States. The latter would forestall the growing political pressure on the new colonial arrangement and assist in the stability needed for economic progress. As a result of these policies, cheaper and more efficient transportation, and the postwar economic expansion in the United States, Puerto Rican migration grew at a phenomenal pace. Between 1940 and 1950, the Puerto Rican population in the United States rose from 69,967 to 301,375. Of these, over 80 percent resided in New York. Ten years later, in 1960, the U.S. Census Bureau reported 612,574 Puerto Ricans living in the city (Wagenheim, 1975, pp. 71, 74).

The mass migration of Puerto Ricans to New York City coincided with a similar migration of thousands of blacks from the southern states. Like the Puerto Ricans, blacks came to the city in search of work. These "new" migrations spurred the intensification of racial tensions, specifically the anti-Puerto Rican campaign (Mills, Senior, and Goldsen, 1950; Senior, 1965). Public officials became increasingly concerned with the rapid growth of the Puerto Rican population and its spread to the other boroughs of the city. They charged that Puerto Rico's migration policies were exacerbating the city's problems. The government of Puerto Rico responded that it did not encourage or discourage Puerto Ricans regarding migration to the United States but simply facilitated their movement.

After some discussion, several important agreements were reached between the two governments. First, a coordinated effort to channel Puerto Rican migration to other regions of the country was initiated. Second, the New York City administration created, in 1949, a Mayor's Committee for Puerto Rican Affairs. Composed of the directors of the public departments and leading Puerto Rican government officials, the committee's purported charge was to ease the integration of Puerto Ricans in the city (New York

City, 1953). Its goals included the development of a politically "acceptable" Puerto Rican leadership, not identified with progressive or militant struggles and organizations. Furthermore, the political agenda of the Mayor's Committee was to draw the rapidly growing Puerto Rican population into the Democratic Party (Wakefield, 1959, pp. 264–265). This took place at the same time that a large-scale campaign at the federal, state, and city levels was launched by conservative political forces working against radical groups, especially Communists. Left-leaning Puerto Ricans community leaders were targeted by this campaign.

The body responsible for assisting the development of Puerto Rican organizations was the Migration Office (later the Commonwealth Office) (Fitzpatrick, 1987, pp. 50–52). Established in New York in 1948, the office's responsibility was to assist all Puerto Ricans living in the United States to adapt to their new reality. To accomplish its objective, the office hired community organizers to work closely with existing groups and assist in the creation of new ones. Among the organizations that received the support of the Migration Office was the Hispanic Young Adult Association (HYAA) (interviews with Antonia Pantoja, June 8 and 13, 1988; interview with Josephine Nieves, June 1, 1988).

Established in the early 1950s, HYAA was formed by a group of concerned Puerto Rican college students and young professionals. Its membership consisted mostly of second-generation Puerto Ricans trained in social work. The group was influenced by the dominant assimilation paradigm—the melting pot theory—and by the idea that science and effective social intervention could eventually solve society's ills. Finally, the group shared a faith in education as "the great equalizer."

HYAA regarded existing organizations, epitomized by the hometown associations and their leadership, as still culturally and ideologically centered on the island. In HYAA's view, these groups were mainly social clubs with a short-range vision and little concern for the needs of the community as a whole. Hence, these organizations were not adequately prepared to undertake the difficult task of guiding the integration of Puerto Ricans into the mainstream. Therefore, it was the responsibility of socially minded, educated professionals such as those in HYAA to fill the void in leadership. HYAA began its own training sessions in leadership and initiated a series of community projects, including a housing clinic in the Migration Office and a voter registration campaign in East Harlem, which would sharpen and test skills of potential leaders.

As a result of an intense process of intellectual and practical education, HYAA matured quickly. The initial resistance among some of its members to identifying the organization as strictly "Puerto Rican" was soon overcome. In 1956, after intense debates over Puerto Rican identity, HYAA became the Puerto Rican Association for Community Affairs (PRACA).

In 1959, following the same principles that guided HYAA in the past,

PRACA initiated a series of annual Puerto Rican Student Leadership Conferences. The objective was to develop leaders so that the Puerto Rican community might become an influential group within the city's power structure. These conferences brought together for the first time thousands of Puerto Rican youth—high-school and college students and professionals—to share and discuss their experiences as new New Yorkers and their roles in the process of community empowerment.

Meantime, the issue of the Migration Office's role in the development of a Puerto Rican leadership began to surface. The office had appropriated the right to represent officially the community before government agencies. Critics argued that the office's main responsibility was to the PDD, the party in power on the island, and not to the Puerto Rican community in New York (Glazer and Moynihan, 1963, p. 110). Soon a group within PRACA began increasingly to regard the office as an obstacle to the development of an independent Puerto Rican leadership. The group revolved around a newly formed organization called the Puerto Rican–Hispanic Leadership Forum (interviews with John Carro, May 25 and June 3, 1988).

Incorporated in 1957, the forum followed the existing ethnic organizational models—the National Association for the Advancement of Colored People (NAACP) and the American Jewish Committee. Like PRACA, the forum's main objective was the development of a new Puerto Rican leadership. It insisted on the need to create financially sound and well-organized Puerto Rican nonprofit organizations, with full-time personnel and support from outside sources, such as philanthropic foundations and government funds. A network of organizations dealing with the concerns of the community as a whole—delinquency, housing, economic development, and education—would serve as the basis for empowering the Puerto Rican community. The forum also conceived itself as the power broker between the city and the Puerto Rican community.

One of the forum's first projects was a census of existing Puerto Rican/Hispanic organizations in New York. This would allow for an assessment of the strengths and weaknesses of these organizations and their potential for leadership. The forum also started a program to place potential Puerto Rican leaders in government and private agencies, and launched an antijuvenile delinquency campaign (Herbstein, 1978, pp. 131–139). The forum's effectiveness in projecting its members as responsible and educated New Yorkers rapidly paid off.

Government agencies and the Democratic Party began to regard them as the representatives of the Puerto Rican community. In 1961, in exchange for the forum's support for Robert F. Wagner's reelection as mayor, several forum members were appointed to top city administrative posts. These included Herman Badillo, deputy commissioner for Relocation of the Department of Real Estate; John Carro, special assistant to the mayor; Luis

Hernández, city tax collector; and Max González, deputy commissioner of the Department of Market (Gotsch, 1966, p. 39). New York Puerto Ricans were finally being accepted into the city's political structure.

The forum's most ambitious project was the establishment of Aspira, an educational organization aimed at forming the future leadership of the New York Puerto Rican community. Conceived as a nonprofit bilingual counseling agency, Aspira was to assist Puerto Rican youth in pursuing careers in professional, technical, and liberal arts fields. This was to be accomplished through counseling about existing educational and job opportunities while providing technical and practical training in community organizing. The idea was that these young professionals would return to their community and assist in its social, economic, and political advancement (Aspira, 1959). The forum presented the project to several philanthropic foundations.

Until the early 1960s, foundations had paid little attention to the Puerto Rican community. Most of the foundations were concerned mainly with the conditions of blacks in the United States, while Puerto Ricans were regarded as a regional problem. Furthermore, the Puerto Rican population was relatively small when compared to the black and Mexican-American populations. The rapid growth of the Puerto Rican community and the acknowledgment that Puerto Ricans were an integral part of U.S. society led foundations to respond to the forum's proposal. Initial funding for Aspira came from the Taconic Foundation, Nathan Hefheimer Foundation, New York Foundation, New York Fund for Children, the Rockefeller Brothers Fund, and the Field Foundation (Herbstein, 1978, p. 133).

Incorporated in 1961, Aspira became the first Puerto Rican agency in New York City to be funded by outside monies. The project generated immense enthusiasm among the Puerto Rican student population. For the first time, an organization was to assist in developing its full potential without the prejudice and racism so entrenched in the school system. Students themselves took the initiative and began to establish clubs in their high schools. By 1963, there were 52 Aspira clubs functioning throughout the city. Two years later, in 1965, Aspira was firmly established. That year it broke away from the Puerto Rican Hispanic Leadership Forum and became an independent agency.

Meanwhile, in the mid-1950s, other citywide Puerto Rican nonprofit organizations began to emerge. One of the most visible was El Desfile Puertorriqueño (Puerto Rican Day Parade) (Herbstein, 1978, pp. 182–197). The original purpose of Desfile, a coordinating council, was to further organizational activities in the community, strengthen Puerto Rican identity, and struggle for Puerto Rican civil rights. This was to be accomplished by a massive cultural demonstration, which would serve as a show of unity while highlighting the growing numerical importance of Puerto Ricans in the city. Although the first two parades were billed as la Parada Hispana (1956), by

1959 the event was renamed the Puerto Rican Day Parade. This was the result of the process of ethnic affirmation experienced by the community in the mid-1950s. By the late 1960s, the Desfile had lost much of its original purpose, becoming a showcase for politicians from Puerto Rico and New York City. Still, it remains to this day an established Puerto Rican tradition in the city.

Another key organization created during this period, in 1956, was El Congreso del Pueblo (Council of Hometown Clubs). Unlike HYAA and its off-shoots, the Congreso was primarily comprised of working-class migrants. Rooted in the community, this organization regarded Puerto Rican cultural tradition as an important force in the struggle for civil rights. Using the already existing hometown groups as its organizational model, the Congreso fostered the formation of such groups throughout the city. At the same time, it helped newcomers find shelter, housing, and jobs and occasionally provided emergency financial assistance (interview with Gerena Valentín, June 6, 1988).

The Congreso del Pueblo soon developed as a broad-based organization in the Puerto Rican community, comprising approximately 80 clubs throughout the city. During the 1960s, its activity was intense. The Congeso mobilized the community in the struggle for civil rights, working in all vital areas affecting Puerto Ricans. It was at the forefront of the struggle for better housing and led protests and demonstrations against police brutality, racism, and discrimination. In education, the Congreso worked closely with other organizations, such as Aspira and United Bronx Parents, in the struggle for better facilities and programs, including bilingual education. It also actively participated in the battles for decentralizing the city school system waged in the late 1960s. The Congreso also played a key role in organizing El Desfile Puertorriqueño, the Fiesta Folklórica, and other community-based organizations, such as the Organizaciones Unidas del Bronx. Although it was a New York-based group, the influence of the Congreso went well beyond the city's boundaries. Serving as a model, it spurred the formation of organizations in other urban centers.

Like the great majority of existing Puerto Rican groups, the Congreso was a self-supported, voluntary organization. The situation, however, began to change in the mid-1960s when it (as well as many of its member organizations) started to receive antipoverty funds.

THE WAR ON POVERTY AND THE NEW YORK CITY PUERTO RICAN COMMUNITY: 1960s TO 1975

In the 1960s, mass mobilization and pressure on the state and federal governments led to the passage of the Civil Rights Act (1964) and the Voting Rights Act (1965), to protect the civil rights and improve the conditions of blacks and other minorities. Concurrently, the federal government passed the

Economic Opportunity Act (1965) and launched an ambitious antipoverty program. Through the latter, federal funds were funneled to community-based organizations for the development of self-help projects that would assist in improving socioeconomic conditions.

Many Puerto Rican community organizations in New York City welcomed the antipoverty legislation. The forum, for example, regarded it as a unique opportunity to "exploit and develop the particular strengths of the Puerto Rican community in fighting poverty and, at the same time, to attack some of the major barriers to the group's emergence as an effective actor in the city's affairs" (Bonilla, 1965, p. 1).

To take full advantage of this juncture, the forum designed, in 1964, a far-reaching proposal for the creation of a Puerto Rican Community Development Project (PRCDP) (Puerto Rican Forum, 1975). As originally conceived, the PRCDP was to serve as a clearinghouse for a variety of self-help programs. Its main objectives were to increase family income; reduce poverty and dependency; raise the educational level of the community; and strengthen family life, cultural institutions, and Puerto Rican organizational life throughout the city. The plan envisioned public funding for over 60 community-based groups represented in the project, including Aspira, PRACA, and the Puerto Rican Family Institute, a nonprofit organization created in 1963 to assist recent migrant families to acclimate to the new environment. A Puerto Rican college and a research center were also projected.

The idea received the support in principle of most of the city's Puerto Rican nonprofit groups, including the Congreso del Pueblo, which joined in the enterprise. The PRCDP, however, was not implemented as originally conceived. On the one hand, elements within the city government were extremely reluctant to fund this kind of comprehensive approach. The project presented a potential danger, since it could be the basis for the formation of a solid Puerto Rican bloc that could seriously challenge the established political structure. Thus, city officials opposed it on the grounds that Puerto Ricans were not a majority in any of the existing city districts.

Within the PRCDP itself, there were also serious differences over control of the organization and disbursement of funds. Furthermore, within the professional sector there were two diverging views concerning the functions and administration of the project. One position, represented by the forum and Aspira, upheld a long-range perspective that stressed educating youth and training professionals to serve the community. It also advocated setting up a centralized administrative structure. The other position prioritized the development and strengthening of social service delivery agencies. It argued that although education was an important tool for socioeconomic and political advancement, the vital problem faced by the community was the lack of jobs and economic opportunity. Advocates of this point of view stressed the need for more job training and consumer programs, and a more militant stance on civil rights. Administratively, they supported a decentralized system structured from the bottom up. An impasse ensued, which ended only when the forum and its supporters resigned from the project (Herbstein, 1978, pp. 150–153).

Those who remained rewrote the proposal to reflect their concerns and priorities. In the new version, the community action approach dominated. The city funded the PRCDP, which in turn subcontracted with local agencies to provide community organizing, tutoring, job training, and addiction prevention programs. The block program, the stronghold of PRCDP, operated by subcontracting with 100 agencies in poverty areas that offered advice and referral services to other PRCDP-funded programs or to governmental agencies.

During its early years, the PRCDP was a militant organization. It helped organize and worked closely with grass roots organizations, such as the United Bronx Parents, in their struggle for better public services to the community. It also organized and actively participated in mass demonstrations to protest violations of Puerto Rican civil rights in New York City. But by the early 1970s, as a result of another internal split, control of the organization passed into the hands of the less militant faction (Fitzpatrick, 1987, pp. 54–56; Herbstein, 1978, pp. 156–159).

At the same time, the city funded two other citywide projects—Aspira and the Puerto Rican Family Institute. Several other local organizations, the Massive Neighborhood Development, the East Harlem Tenants Council, and the Lower Manhattan Small Business Development and Opportunities Corporation, supervised by the forum, also received antipoverty funds.

The antipoverty programs had a profound effect on the character of Puerto Rican nonprofit organizations. They provided funds for much-needed social services and helped agencies to become firmly established. But at the same time, the funds fostered the bureaucratization of these institutions. Voluntary work was replaced by paid work. Dependent on government funds, many of these groups grew more conservative as their fortunes became increasingly tied to the political power structure.

A few individuals used their control over federally funded programs for personal enrichment and as a tool for political maneuvering. The most glaring example was the Hunts Point Multi-Service Agency, under the auspices of the PRCDP, which was accused of mismanaging funds. Corruption charges were also leveled against the PRCDP itself. This led to an investigation, and in 1978 the city government ceased funding the PRCDP.

In spite of all the monies invested in antipoverty programs, the socioeconomic conditions of minorities changed little. Dissatisfaction spread among various minority communities. This paved the way for the resurgence of radical movements, which rejected reformist solutions and attacked the motives of those who controlled the substantial economic and material resources of the antipoverty apparatus. In their view, most of the existing organizations had sold out and were misleading the people into believing in false solutions to their situations. The only answer was a total restructuring of the U.S. economic and political systems.

A new radical leadership and mass movement emerged in the Puerto Rican community, as in the black and Chicano communities. This movement renewed the militant tradition of the pre-1950s, linking community work with political activism and linking the conditions of Puerto Ricans in the United States with the island's colonial situation. Organizations such as the Movimiento Pro-Independencia (MPI), transformed later into the Partido Socialista Puertorriqueño (PSP), and El Comité/Movimiento de Izquierda Nacional Puertorriqueña, gained widespread support, especially among the younger generation. At the forefront of this struggle was the Young Lords Party (YLP).

The Young Lords grew out of the ghetto experience of Puerto Ricans (Young Lords Party and Abramson, 1971). Originally a Chicago street gang, the Young Lords became politicized under the influence of the Black Panthers Party. In the summer of 1969, it established a chapter in New York City. More politicized than the Chicago branch, the New York chapter soon broke away and transformed itself into the YLP. The organization called for the people's control of all community institutions, including the police, health services, sanitation, schools, housing, transportation, and welfare. It launched several important campaigns in the Puerto Rican community: It established a free breakfast program for children in East Harlem, initiated preventive health care programs such as anemia and tuberculosis testing and lead-poisoning detection programs, and participated in various events, including the takeover of Lincoln Hospital in the Bronx. The YLP was also influential in the development of a militant Puerto Rican student movement through the Puerto Rican Student Union, which played an important role on its own in the campaign for open admissions and the establishment of Puerto Rican studies programs in colleges and universities in the city.

But in the process of becoming a Marxist–Leninist political party, the YLP turned from community-based activities to organizing at the workplace. By the time of its dissolution in 1977, the YLP, by then called the Puerto Rican Revolutionary Workers Organization (PRRWO), had lost most of its influence in the community. However, its impact was long lasting. It raised political consciousness among second-generation Puerto Ricans. Furthermore, many of its members continued Young Lords' objectives on other fronts and in other organizations.

In the early 1970s another organization—the Puerto Rican Legal Defense and Education Fund (PRLDEF)—was created to challenge systemic discrimination against Puerto Ricans. Founded in 1972 by a group of Puerto Rican lawyers, PRLDEF was modeled after the NAACP Legal Defense Fund. Its initial sphere of action was New York City, and its first legal battle revolved around the issue of bilingual education.

In 1972, it filed a class action suit against the New York City Board of Education on behalf of Aspira and other organizations. As a result, in 1974 the board signed the Aspira Consent Decree, agreeing to provide bilingual education for all Limited English Proficient (LEP) Hispanic students in the city schools. PRLDEF continued to oversee the process, and in 1975 and 1977 filed contempt proceedings against the city government for its failure to fully comply with the agreement (Santiago, 1978, pp. 47–98). PRLDEF also became involved in class action suits around other issues, such as employment discrimination against Puerto Ricans and violation of voting rights in New York City (Fitzpatrick, 1987, pp. 57–58).

1975 TO PRESENT

During the 1970s, the socioeconomic conditions of the Puerto Rican community in the United States, and specifically in New York, continued worsening. By 1976, Puerto Ricans not only trailed far behind whites on key socioeconomic indicators but were also below other major Latino groups. In large measure, the deteriorating conditions of Puerto Ricans in New York can be attributed to structural economic changes. With the decline of manufacturing as the main source of employment, large numbers of Puerto Rican workers, the majority of whom were concentrated in this sector, were displaced from the job market.

Fiscally conservative initiatives by federal, state, and city governments to deal with this crisis exacerbated the plight of the Puerto Rican community. The limited but important advances in the public service sector, as well as in health, education, and housing, were turned back, leaving the community more vulnerable to economic policies over which Puerto Ricans as well as other poor people had little control.

Puerto Rican nonprofit organizations that are heavily dependent on public funds have been strongly affected by conservative fiscal policies. Some organizations have ceased to exist; others have seen their activity sharply curtailed. PRACA, for instance, has become essentially a foster care agency. The National Puerto Rican Forum has limited its work to administering several employment training and job development programs.

As they did in the past, Puerto Ricans created new organizations to deal with changing conditions. For instance, the Institute for Puerto Rican Policy (IPRP), incorporated in 1981, attempts through research, advocacy, and networking to develop new problem-solving strategies for the Puerto Rican community in New York City. To maintain its independence, the institute refuses government funds, instead relying on private foundations, corporations, and individuals for support (interview with Angelo Falcón, n.d.). The IPRP has served as a watchdog, making effective use of the mass media to highlight the lack of defined public policies that address the problems faced by the community. One of its main areas of concern since the beginning has been Puerto Rican patterns of political participation and their implications for community empowerment. In recent years, the IPRP has developed the New York City Project, an attempt to present a comprehensive analysis of the impact of New York City policies on the community in four areas: education, employment, housing, and city charter revision. Besides policy analysis, the project involves conferences and public forums geared at educating the community and facilitating the development of common strategies.

In 1981, Puerto Rican community activists, many of them seasoned in the struggles of the 1960s and 1970s in New York City, organized the National Congress for Puerto Rican Rights (NCPRR) (interview with Richie Pérez, June 28, 1988). The New York City chapter of NCPRR has worked to end discrimination, oppose the English only movement, and defend the rights of Puerto Rican workers to organize for better pay and working conditions.

During the 1980s, Puerto Ricans were also involved in coalition-building endeavors with other racial/ethnic community organizations, especially with the rapidly growing Latino population. For example, in the educational sphere, several Puerto Rican organizations, including Aspira, the Puerto Rican Educators Association (PREA), the NCPRR (NYC), and the Centro de Estudios Puertorriqueños, participated in the formation of the Puerto Rican/Latino Education Roundtable. Established in 1983, the roundtable advocates and organizes around educational issues, including parent involvement and community empowerment, bilingual education, student retention, and opposition to the English only movement.

In a similar vein, to deal with the intensification of racial attacks against minorities, other Puerto Rican groups such as the Puerto Rican Committee Against Repression, the NCPRR (NYC), and PRLDEF joined in 1986 with other Latino groups to establish the Latino Coalition for Racial Justice.

More recently, many Puerto Rican organizations have been exploring other potential funding sources, such as foundations and, increasingly, the business sector, to deal with the critical fiscal problem. Corporations that do business with Puerto Rican communities, the argument goes, have a responsibility toward them. But efforts to obtain major funding from corporations have proven to be very difficult. Furthermore, many of these corporations demand that the organizations expand their programs to serve Hispanics in general, and, in some instances, corporations have sought to redefine the agenda of the organizations (interview with Marta Garciá, n.d.).

CONCLUSIONS

According to traditional interpretations, popularized by Glazer and Moynihan in their influential book *Beyond the Melting Pot* (1963), the deplorable conditions experienced by Puerto Ricans in New York City are to a great extent determined by a weak organizational tradition. In our opinion, the history of Puerto Rican community organizations in the city contradicts this notion. Instead, a combination of other factors—such as the class character and the timing of the migration, transformations in the city economy, and the pervasiveness of ethnic and racial prejudice—explain the lack of progress of the Puerto Rican community. Also, the lack of political and economic power are elements that need to be taken into consideration.

To survive and grow in a hostile society, Puerto Ricans have created myriad organizations. These organizations have undertaken many forms of activity, from a strictly service delivery approach to advocacy and, in some instances, to radical action. Throughout the history of the community, the defense of the Puerto Rican ethnic group has been a central issue in the organizational endeavors of Puerto Ricans.

As in the past, Puerto Rican nonprofit organizations continue to play an important role in ameliorating socioeconomic problems and advancing the aspirations of the community. Declining socioeconomic conditions and the rising conservative trend in the country make even greater the need for organizing at the community level.

4

Looking Back: A Grantee–Grantor View of the Early Years of the Council of La Raza

Siobhan O. Nicolau and Henry Santiestevan

In the formative stages of the Southwest Council of La Raza—later the National Council of La Raza—Siobhan Nicolau was the Ford Foundation program officer in charge of Hispanic grants, and Henry Santiestevan was the executive director of the council. During those often turbulent years, Ernesto Galarza, one of the founders of the Chicano Movement in the United States and a founder of the council, urged the authors and others who were deeply involved to keep copies of everything that passed through their hands and to record their days in diaries. Ernesto was a firm believer in preserving history; he repeatedly announced that a movement that does not know where it has been can easily lose its way.

The authors heeded Ernesto and kept records on paper. This chapter grew out of a review of the contents of dusty boxes of memos, letters, notes, and yellow newspaper clippings—out of recollections and out of conversations with others who participated in the events we recount. It is not an entirely objective analysis. First, we aren't entirely objective types. Second, even if we were, our involvement was too close to qualify us as disinterested critics. This chapter is a memoir—a narrative composed from personal experiences supported by a considerable body of primary material, much of which has never before been made available. It is our intent to present a serious historical account, *from our points of view,* of the forces inside and outside the Mexican-American community that contributed to the establishment of several major nonprofit advocacy and service institutions, an account of the developmental stages the council passed through on the road from relative dependence to independence, and an account of how those who became Chicano leaders were nurtured and prepared within those nonprofits to play significant roles on the Mexican-American and national stages. Our story details internal and external struggles, and its celebrates the triumph of survival and the fact of progress.

At the same time, our story raises some basic questions regarding the role and conduct of government and philanthropy in social action. It sets the stage for discussion about the options open to emerging groups that want to carve niches for themselves in the context of a pluralistic society, and it clearly illustrates how trade-off and compromise function and affect the course of events in a pluralistic society. Perhaps most importantly, it paints a picture of the short-term nature of most public-policy directions, a reality that should stimulate consideration of how emerging groups can develop experienced leadership, broad networks of contacts, and resources sufficient to assume major responsibility for their own destinies.

THE BACKGROUND

The birth and development of the Mexican-American nonprofit institutions that emerged in the late 1960s must be viewed against the reality of the Mexican-American condition of that period. In the 1960s, Mexican-Americans in the Southwest had far fewer resources at their disposal than did blacks, and they had further to go than blacks because their movement got underway later. The early agenda required massive organization, the creation of stable institutions, and the preparation of a large cadre of leaders experienced and sophisticated in advocacy, fundraising, and institutional management. None of that could take place without resources—and resources were a scarce commodity.

Most private foundations in the 1960s said, "Come back when you have experience." Most corporations said, "We don't support ethnic organizations." And in the early days, federal officials tried to look the other way so that they would not offend the governors and mayors in the Southwest, many of whom were none too pleased with the rising tide of Mexican-Americans who wanted full societal participation. In addition, the liberal, professional whites who had played a significant role in supporting the black movement were in short supply in the Southwest.

Labor liberals, however, were not so scarce, and they—assessing their own vested interest—had developed and nurtured a generation of Hispanic leaders. The early stirrings that led to *the movement*—the action that preceded formation of the United Farm Workers and the emergence of the angry young men—were initiated and kept alive by people who had their roots in labor or grass roots organizing: Maclovio Barraza, Ruben Valdez, and Paul Montemayor of the Steelworkers; Bert Corona of the Longshoremen; Herman Gallegos and Cesar Chavez of the Community Service Organization in California; Henry Santiestevan of the United Auto Workers (UAW); and Ernesto Galarza of the National Farm Workers Union. These men, together with the angry youths who were coming together in the colleges and barrios, joined ranks to organize for justice. They lacked the strong network of religious institutions that had nurtured black leadership, they lacked visibility outside the Southwest, and they lacked a history of slavery, a powerful tool that had galvanized white guilt and support for the black civil rights movement. In the beginning, almost all the support for the Southwest Council of La Raza and its subsidiary organizations came from labor and the Ford Foundation.

The funding picture improved in the mid-1970s. Mexican-Americans began to get a limited share of Great Society money. But the programs being funded were not always the programs Mexican-Americans needed or wanted. They were, to a large extent, programs geared to the black reality. The priorities of government funders interested in minority issues had been established with little attention to stages of Latino institutional development or uniquely Hispanic needs.

At the same time, the private philanthropic sector (which always likes to think of itself as part of the cutting edge) began to dip its toes cautiously into the Hispanic waters. It took business longer. Corporations didn't pay attention until the 1980s, when the strength of the national and local Hispanic markets and the demographic projections of the twenty-first century workforce triggered their consciousness.

But Mexican-American leadership prevailed and matured over two decades, despite the neglect, anguish, unwanted intervention, unrelenting chase for dollars, and internal tensions inherent in all organizational development. Stable institutions were established, their leaders learned how to pass on the mantle of power, constituencies were created, many of the more blatant injustices were corrected, Mexican-Americans became a factor at the polls, the invisible minority assumed a national presence, and, by 1988, it was clear that La Raza was here to stay. Certainly the need for advocacy and special services has neither evaporated nor diminished, but in some areas Mexican-Americans are now dismantling barricades and developing strategies to get themselves and their children through newly opening doors of opportunity.

IN THE BEGINNING

The Ford Foundation's support of the National Council of La Raza, Aspira, eight locally based community development corporations, the Mexican American Legal Defense and Educational Fund, the Puerto Rican Legal Defense and Education Fund, the Southwest Voter Registration Education Project, and a variety of research and specially targeted projects undoubtedly enabled Hispanics to develop permanent institutions that survive today and form a firm base for expanding social, economic, and political influence on a national scale. There is also no doubt that Ford's large-scale support had its disadvantages and created some large-scale problems. But without the Ford Foundation's commitment to a strategy of national and local institution building, the Chicano Movement would have withered away in many areas, unable to overcome a desperate lack of resources and often savage attacks by hostile external interests.

Crucial as was the Ford Foundation's support, historically it was not the first foundation to commit assistance to Mexican-Americans. That honor belongs to the Rosenberg Foundation of San Francisco, which, from its inception in 1935, placed a high priority on rural areas and children. Long before the civil rights movement, the Chicano Movement, the War on Poverty, or the Office of Economic Opportunity (OEO), the Rosenberg Foundation made philanthropic and social history with small but critical grants relating to migrant farm workers and their children. Rosenberg and Ford, both mainstream, established, philanthropic institutions dominated by Anglos, took the initiative in reaching out to Hispanics. It is instructive to examine how the Ford Foundation became interested in Hispanic issues at a time when most policymakers, philanthropists, and political leaders understood "minority" to mean black.

Two of the unsung heros of the early Chicano Movement in this country are Paul Ylvisaker and S. M. Miller. They worked within Ford to change the perception that blacks were the only disadvantaged group warranting special attention. The funds finally allocated to Hispanic programs by Ford—the only significant support available at the time—resulted from the concern and actions of these two men.

In 1964, Ylvisaker, then Ford's director of public affairs programs, contracted with the University of California at Los Angeles to produce a study of the status of Mexican-Americans that would be widely accepted by mainstream policymakers and funders, and that would raise their consciousness about the existence of serious problems in the Mexican-American community. This extensive and scholarly work, known as the Grebler Report, was highly academic and long-range. Ylvisaker realized from the beginning that work directed to immediate problem solving was needed. To get a sense of what was happening, he began to explore existing organizations as well as the many new groups that were emerging throughout the Southwest. After a period of what Ylvisaker referred to in conversation with the authors as "trolling the waters broadly and deeply to educate myself," he opened negotiations in 1966 with two Mexican-American scholars, Ernesto Galarza and Julian Samora, and a respected Chicano activist and writer, Herman Gallegos, to undertake further investigations and to make recommendations for an effective Mexican-American program at Ford. Gallegos recalls that Ylvisaker, in poetic language most uncharacteristic among workers in philanthropy, exhorted the trio of consultants "to go out and dream your dreams."

When Ylvisaker left the foundation in 1966, he turned the "dreams" over to S. M. Miller, who shared the conviction that the problems of blacks and other disadvantaged groups would not receive sustained attention unless the political base for the disadvantaged were broadened. Miller pressed the newly installed Ford president and vice president, McGeorge Bundy and Mitchell Sviridoff, to expand the definition of "disadvantaged." At the time, neither Sviridoff nor Bundy knew much about Chicanos, but to their credit they were willing to learn. Miller overcame Bundy's initial reluctance to "plunge into a whole new minority," and plunge the Ford Foundation did.

Mike Sviridoff is an intuitively brilliant man with a keen political sense. In the 1960s, Sviridoff led New Haven's Grey Areas program, the Ylvisaker/Ford initiative that served as a model for programs like Headstart and Legal Services that eventually became associated with OEO. Sviridoff came to Ford in December 1967 from New York City, where he had first designed and then administered the superagency for social services, the Human Resources Administration. But his roots were in the union movement, specifically the UAW. His overall experience and especially his early union involvement caused him to respond with sympathy and sensitivity to the Galarza/Samora/Gallegos recommendation that Mexican-Americans needed organization on the local and national levels.

On the other hand, Sviridoff had experienced "up close and personal" the most tumultuous period of New York's war on poverty—petitions, sit-ins, and riots. He was remarkably understanding of the extravagant passion of youth, but he also knew that passion unchecked or passion without substance can be formidable obstacles to the achievement of noble goals. The young Chicano activists who visited Sviridoff in 1968 did not leave him feeling confident that they were sufficiently experienced or prudent to lead a successful organizing effort. Sviridoff takes risks, but he has always been strongly committed to the principle of "the good start." His rule was that premature explosions can kill the best of dreams, and he feared—not without reason, as it turned out—that the young activists might blow themselves up.

The proposal that Miller brought to Sviridoff for the establishment of the Southwest Council of La Raza resulted from a planning process instituted by Galarza, Samora, and Gallegos. With foundation approval, they had formed a group of approximately 25 Mexican-Americans to discuss goals and design an organization. Jack Conway, acting on behalf of the Industrial Union Department of AFL–CIO, made a planning grant to support the effort. Conway was joined by the National Council of Churches and later Ford, both of which made grants to the Organization for Business, Education and Community Advancement (OBECA) of San Francisco, a group with which Gallegos had been closely associated.

Conway assured Sviridoff that the activists would be balanced by Galarza, Gallegos, and other experienced and cooler heads. Conway related the council's effort to similar and successful union-supported initiatives in the black community, such as the Watts Labor Action Council and the East Los Angeles Community Union.

The initial proposal submitted to Ford was drafted by Miguel Barragan of the Bishops' Committee of San Antonio. Whereas Conway's support soothed Sviridoff, Barragan's proposal only reactivated his concern. In Sviridoff's words, quoted in the September 1969 Ford Foundation internal assessment of the foundation's grant to the Southwest Council of La Raza, "It was all so mushy, words without meaning, therefore without substance. There was a lot of passion but no definite idea where it would all lead." There were meetings and redrafts, and finally the goals and priorities were defined—if not to Ford's liking, at least to what Sviridoff found acceptable.

And so, as a result of Ylvisaker's early concern; Miller's sustained pressure; the recommendations of Galarza, Samora, and Gallegos; Conway's intervention; and Sviridoff's willingness to gamble, on June 10, 1968, the Ford Foundation made a $630,000 grant "to develop a regional Chicano organization" and "to develop Chicano leadership capabilities at the local level."

THE EARLY YEARS

The initial board of the Southwest Council represented a mix of union people, young activist organizers, and a sprinkling of professionals and academics—all male, with the exception of Audrey Kaslow, a Los Angeles community activist who later became the first Hispanic woman to serve on the U.S. Parole Commission. Eighteen of the 25 board seats were distributed among the Southwest states on the basis of population. Seven seats were designated at large. Gallegos assumed the executive directorship, with the agreement that he would serve only two years. Maclovio Barraza of the Steelworkers Union was installed as chairman of the board. An office was established in Phoenix because it was considered neutral territory by the California and Texas delegates, who were squaring off in the war for control, and where there was virtually no organization in place to protest the new kid on the block. Thus, the process began to forge a strong civil rights institution that could speak for the Chicano citizens of the United States.

Meanwhile, back at the Ford Foundation, Miller left philanthropy to return to his first love, academia, and Siobhan Oppenheimer Nicolau arrived from a background of organizing Hispanics on the local level and administering poverty programs, first in the Northeast with OEO and later as assistant to the commissioner of New York City's poverty program, the Community Development Agency. Quite by chance, the two principal factions coming together to build the Chicano Movement in the Southwest, labor and civil rights, mirrored the Ford Foundation's staff most directly charged with the implementation of the Hispanic grants. In "foundation land," Sviridoff and Nicolau were a very unlikely pair—the ex-labor organizer and the middle-aged Turk.

The process of achieving consensus among old-line labor types, young Turks, and rising professionals almost destroyed both grantee and grantor. The concept of a strong civil rights organization was new to the Mexican-American community, the charge was an ambitious one, and this kind of cooperative endeavor was a new experience. The early days were times of struggle and dissension. Various factions maneuvered endlessly to obtain power rather than to define or develop it. The Texas contingent confronted the California contingent, the young radicals schemed against the older conservatives, the urbans and rurals bickered, and the women demanded equal representation with the men.

While the council was struggling to come to grips with its internal balance of power, an incident occurred that almost ended Ford's support of the Chicano Movement. In the spring of 1969, as Congress debated the role of foundations and other tax-exempt organizations, the Ford Foundation was denounced on the floor of Congress by a liberal San Antonio congressman, Henry B. Gonzalez. The Southwest Council had granted funds to the Mexican American Unity Council (MAUC), which made a subgrant to the Mexican American Youth Organization (MAYO), a community organizing group. MAYO supported a slate of candidates in its newspaper, *El Delguello*. (Support of political candidates is forbidden under the tax act regulating nonprofits.) Representative Gonzalez was outraged and went on the offensive, accusing the MAYO/MAUC groups of being dangerous radicals and the foundation of being irresponsible and unknowledgeable. The Ford Foundation then told MAUC it could not give any further money to MAYO. Ford also promised Gonzalez that it would keep a careful eye on the Southwest Council, its subgrantees, and other Hispanic grantees, such as the Mexican American Legal Defense and Educational Fund (MALDEF).

This is a sequential description but not an explanation of these events. There is no concise way to present the incredible complexity of politics, history, and personal relationships that led to the MAYO crisis. In our files we have a chronological account made in 1969 of what happened and who did what to whom. The information and interviews with local businessmen, political leaders, and Chicano leaders may be the only in-depth account extant. Our files also contain copies of all the correspondence between Representative Gonzalez and the Ford Foundation, all the memos that relate to "Situation Mayo," copies of the newspaper articles that ran in San Antonio, and the correspondence between the Ford Foundation and the Southwest Council.

How did Gonzalez, a liberal champion of his people, get himself in a battle to the death with a group of college-educated young men who clearly had the potential to be tomorrow's leaders?

The St. Mary's College students who formed MAYO in 1967 were Juan Patlan, William Velasquez, Richard Jasso, Juan Torres, Ignacio Perez, Mario Compean, and Jose Angel Gutierrez. They felt that the traditional Mexican-

American organizations were ignoring young people and weren't sufficiently interested in organizing the community to produce social change. MAYO devised a program that focused on education, economics, and politics. Compared to black organizations of the time, MAYO's agenda and rhetoric were rather mild. For example, MAYO's first statement of purpose, written in 1967, includes the following words: "There are two types of elements in every society, one element is the Gringo and the other is the Anglo. The Gringo is racist. The Anglo is the opposite, working with La Raza to remove the shackles of oppression that bind them."

But MAYO was in Texas, which wasn't prepared for Mexican militancy no matter how mild. Texas Anglos were not about to put up with the kind of "nonsense" their peers in San Francisco and New York were suffering at the hands of "so-called civil rights activists."

MAYO began organizing in the areas around San Antonio, signing up young people and proclaiming the need to work for change. In fall 1967, MAYO decided that the movement required an organization that would function in the barrios and would include adults as well as young people. So MAUC was born, and Willie Velasquez, then an administrative assistant to the Bishops' Committee for the Spanish-Speaking, became the first director. At about the same time, Velasquez met Gallegos, who filled him in on the plans he was making to establish the Southwest Council of La Raza. Velasquez was impressed, and in 1968, Velasquez organized a conference sponsored by the Bishops' Committee that drew almost 1,500 Chicano activists from all parts of Texas and the rest of the Southwest. Its purpose was to demonstrate solidarity for "the movement." Representative Gonzalez did not attend the conference; he said he was not properly invited, and claimed the conference had communist overtones.

From then on the lines were drawn. The struggle involved the local community action program, a Vista minority program, county commissioner Albert Peña, state senator Joe Bernal, and most importantly, Henry Gonzalez. Gonzalez considered Peña and Bernal his enemies and Velasquez his protegee. Gonzales had brought Velasquez to Washington as a summer intern. Velasquez later reported to the authors that Gonzalez warned him not to associate with Peña and Bernal. Velasquez, however, had found Peña and Bernal sympathetic to his organizational interests and refused to disassociate himself from them.

The young leaders did not negotiate with Representative Gonzales or pay him the respect he felt he deserved. Gonzales, on the other hand, chose not to exert influence on the young leaders but rather to use his considerable power to get rid of them. Velasquez and the others countered by fielding a slate of political candidates and running a voter registration campaign. After much protest and maneuvering, including the mock funeral of a dead rabbit named "Justice," OEO reluctantly agreed to remove the Vista program. By this time, Jose Angel Gutierrez had called the governor a "son of a bitch." Gonzalez was enraged, but many others rallied to the cause of "Justice," and MAYO organized a broadly supported demonstration to honor the Vista members. Two thousand people took part in the peaceful Palm Sunday Del Rio march. The Del Rio manifesto concluded, "On this day, Mexican Americans commit themselves to struggle ceaselessly until the promise of this country is realized for us and our fellow Americans, one nation, under God, indivisible, with liberty and justice for all."

It is difficult to see revolution in those words, but Gonzalez and Mayor MacAllister of San Antonio did. The respectable showing of the Chicano candidates in the elections further agitated them. Gonzalez went on the attack. He attacked OEO, the staff of the U.S. Civil Rights Commission, CBS, and the Ford Foundation. In his attack on Ford, he joined Wright Patman (D-Texas), who was looking into tax reform and foundations. Gonzales claimed that MAYO was spreading racial hate and supporting political candidates with Ford funds, that Ford was funding groups that were terrorizing neighborhoods, and that Gallegos had last been seen publicly at the height of the rioting at San Francisco State College.

On April 10, 1969, Gutierrez called a press conference to answer the charges against MAYO and to explain the MAYO philosophy regarding gringos versus Anglos. The conference was taped. Gutierrez handled himself with great maturity. The press kept pushing him, but he resisted giving them the sensational headline they wanted. Finally, a reporter asked what he would do if his family were attacked, and Gutierrez fell into the trap. He said he would kill the gringo, a statement that resulted in banner headlines. Gonzalez read his shock into the *Congressional Record*. Ford was bombarded with letters. Sviridoff sent Nicolau to the neutral city of Phoenix to meet "the dangerous radicals," Willie Velasquez and Jose Angel Gutierrez.

Nicolau reported back from Phoenix that they were neither radical nor dangerous. What was dangerous was the situation:

> They (MAYO/MAUC) presented their case and frankly, they aren't doing anything they ought not to be doing. They are undertaking non-violent, non-racist activities in fields that correspond directly to our budget priorities. We may feel that Congressional sentiment compels us to desert the pursuit of these priorities for the present, but I think we must be clear in our minds that the Chicano programs are not the problem. (memo from Nicolau to Sviridoff, April 18, 1969)

Gonzalez had the foundation and the council in a difficult position, even though MAYO had not used Ford money to support the particular issue of the newspaper, *El Delguello,* that carried the endorsement of candidates. Strong congressional factions were looking for reasons to get foundations out of social action programming. Ford had to clear the air without sinking the entire Mexican-American initiative and undercutting the leadership structure it had helped establish. Heavy negotiations ensued with all parties. In the end, Ford made a tough, painful, pragmatic decision and announced to the press that MAYO would no longer be supported. This produced the predictable and understandable cry of outrage on the part of the young leadership and Commissioner Peña. The council was instructed to embark upon "hard programming." (Foundation staff were unsure what that meant in practice, but they rolled into high gear looking at substantive projects in the fields of education, housing, and economic development.) Program officers Nicolau and David Carlson were detailed to watch things carefully, and consultants Bill Grinker and Hank Lopez were hired to watch *them* and the programs. Velasquez went to the council staff, Patlan moved into the top spot in MAUC, and Gutierrez, who had been doing field organizing for the Mexican American Legal Defense and Educational Fund, was eased out and back to Wintergarden, Texas, where he came from.

In Wintergarden, Jose Angel organized the La Raza Unida Party. The remarkable success of La Raza Unida made the major political parties take notice that the Chicano voter was here to stay and had better be considered in party planning. La Raza Unida came to exert significant influence in the region.

AFTER MAYO—THE NEW COUNCIL

When the MAYO matter had been "handled," if not forgotten, the council turned its attention back to helping the barrios help themselves. There was consensus among the SWCLR originators that the council should help barrios change repressive and oppressive conditions. In the early stages, there was great enthusiasm but few clear plans of how that would be accomplished. Many—including Santiestevan, who was a member of the council board—believed that the best way to build power was through political action, which meant giving priority to registration drives and "get-out-the-vote" campaigns at the grass roots level. Encouraged by a small grant from the UAW, the council set up an internal committee to develop a political action program. And then a blow fell. In 1969 the council was informed by Ford that newly enacted congressional legislation had placed severe restrictions on the use of funds by 501(c)(3) nonprofit organizations for voter registration. The council was instructed to cease voter registration and to devote the majority of its attention to the hard programming agenda, that is, substantive programming directed to housing, education, and economic development.

The council confronted the issue in a watershed meeting held in Asilomar, California, on July 19–20, 1969. There was sharp debate, but a policy resolution approving a hard program agenda was adopted. The voter registration effort was spun off but survived, with historic results, in what was to become the Southwest Voter Registration Education Project (SVREP). Labor support, especially from the UAW and the Steelworkers, was crucial to the founding and survival of SVREP. The early funding that the council had used to set up its internal voter registration committee came from the UAW. After spin-off, that council committee became SVREP, with Willie Velasquez as its head. But the hostile Nixon administration repeatedly blocked its efforts to obtain tax-exempt status from the Internal Revenue Service (IRS), despite the fact that SVREP had met all the complex regulations applying to organizations that seek to fund voter registration programs through charitable grants. It was not until the Watergate scandal broke and the Nixon administration actions became public knowledge that SVREP finally was granted the requested status by the IRS. During this long struggle for survival, SVREP was kept alive by funding from the Steelworkers. As soon as Velasquez had the IRS charter, he broadened SVREP's constituency and funding base. During the next fifteen years, SVREP literally changed the political map of Texas. With the cooperation of MALDEF, it challenged in court and eliminated Texas at-large local and legislative districts, destroyed the gerrymandering that had frozen Mexican-Americans out of elective public office, and through registration drives brought Latino voters to the polls in large numbers.

The adoption of the housing, education, and economic development agenda assured continuation of Ford funding and the survival of the council, but it fundamentally changed the type of organization the council was to become. Indeed, change was in the air when the dust of the Asilomar decision was still settling. Word reached Santiestevan that Ford was poised to make a second grant of more than $1 million to the SWCLR and that Sviridoff was insisting on a "seasoned organizer," preferably one with union experience, to replace Gallegos, who had agreed to serve for no more than two years. The MAYO incident gave Sviridoff reason to press for a smooth leadership transition. That transition was achieved when Santiestevan voluntarily took early retirement from the United Auto Workers after 22 years in the labor movement to accept the directorship of the council in March 1970. Ford then made an additional grant of $1,303,700 to strengthen the SWCLR's ability to undergird the activities of affiliated groups, each of whom had 501(c)(3) IRS status, as did the SWCLR. These were the original affiliates of the SWCLR and their executive directors:

Mexican American Unity Council (MAUC), San Antonio, Juan Patlán

Chicanos Por La Causa (CPLC), Phoenix, Ronnie Lopez

Mexican American Community Programs Foundation (PF), Los Angeles, Tony Hernandez

The East Los Angeles Community Union (TELACU), Los Angeles, Esteban Torres

Spanish Speaking Unity Council (SSUC), Oakland, Arabella Martinez

Mission Development Council (MDC), San Francisco, Shone Martinez

OBECA/Arriba Juntos Center, San Francisco, Lee Soto

Under the conditions of the grant, the SWCLR was to serve as a conduit for subgranting funds specified by Ford for the affiliates; to act as a monitor of affiliate programs and fund expenditures; to provide technical assistance to staffs of affiliates in education, housing, and economic development; to develop leadership; and to act as an advocate for Latino causes.

Looking back, the authors feel that it was too much to pile on one dish from which to serve a hungry throng of young militants, union veterans, rising professionals, ambitious political hopefuls, and sophisticated administrators—not to mention power-minded machos and strong-willed La Raza women demanding their well-earned share of leadership.

In truth, there were earthquake faults embedded in the very foundation of the council structure. One was the notion shared by the council and Ford that a strong national organization and strong local organizations that would function as a constituency for the national organization could be created simultaneously and harmoniously. Neither the council founders nor the foundation realized the potential for tension and competition inherent in the fact that the emerging local community leadership and the emerging council leadership were being drawn from the same groups. Tensions arose over who should control the politics on which level. By giving the council the power to make local subgrants and provide technical assistance to local groups in the hard programming areas, Ford essentially put the council "in charge" of the operation. But problems arose when the council was unable to convince Mexican-Americans who had the experience to provide high-level technical assistance to work for a new organization whose board members and affiliates were involved in an ongoing series of power struggles. The council was groping to define its mission and establish a base of stable leadership; Mexican-American professionals saw little advantage in being caught in the cross fire or affiliated with an organization that might not be able to offer them career opportunities. Indeed, as late as 1974, when Raúl Yzaguirre was asked to apply for the directorship of the council, he viewed the opportunity with little enthusiasm. In a May 8, 1989, letter to Nicolau he states, "My initial reaction was negative . . . my own analysis was that one of the main reasons for the imminent demise of the organization was board self-indulgence and board leadership that catered more to parochial concerns than to the common good."

Because professionals were reluctant to involve themselves, Ford staff played an increasingly direct role in assisting the local CDCs. Dave Carlson became the housing guru, Eamon Kelly took over many of the economic development duties, Nicolau orchestrated technical assistance, and Ford's education division staff looked over the shoulder of the council's education director. Allan Talbot, a consultant employed by Ford to evaluate the Southwest Council of La Raza, commented on Ford staff and the CDCs in his April 1972 report to the foundation:

> The dependent relationship on the Foundation, particularly on program officers Siobhan Nicolau and David Carlson, may have no parallels with other grantees. Carlson, not Fernandez, in effect became the housing officer and Mrs. Nicolau is Santiestevan's Frances Perkins. As Mrs. Martinez-Springer [Director of the Spanish Speaking Unity Council in 1972] puts it: "Oh, Oppy and David are part of the staff."

The arrangement was a "workable," short-term solution to the technical assistance problem, and, in some respects, Carlson and Nicolau helped Santiestevan maneuver around some potentially sticky political situations by taking the heat for unpopular decisions; but by 1972, Ford, the CDCs, and the council found themselves mired in some awkward situations. Chicano groups not associated with the council—particularly those in California— were declaring that the council was a tool of the Anglo establishment. At the same time, the council's dependents, that is, the CDCs, had become more competent in the hard programming areas than the council itself because they were the ones receiving the benefit of the technical assistance. The parent–child relationship was out of balance, and the fragile coalition of power on the council board was beginning to feel pressure from a new faction, the executive directors of the CDCs, who had only one vote on the council board and deeply resented the limit placed on their decision-making participation.

In order to deal with outside criticism of the close council–foundation relationship and the mounting and vocal discontent of the executive directors, Ford took two actions, with Santiestevan's agreement. First, Ford encouraged—indeed, insisted on—the council's entering into relationships with other funding institutions and agencies. Ford and the CDC directors urged the council to move to Washington, D.C., and begin to play the role of broker and advocate for Chicano organizations with the federal agencies. Not all council board members looked with favor on such a move. Those whose vision of the council was based on the creation of a political force in the Southwest were particularly opposed. Those who wanted the council out of the local scene thought it was a grand idea. The board voted to move to Washington, and a small field office staffed by Polly Baca and Miguel Barragan was left in Phoenix to soothe the opposition.

Second, with great reluctance Ford agreed to fund the CDCs directly. Sviridoff's vision of the council had been that of a strong national membership organization supported by local affiliates, essentially a union model. He repeatedly pressured the council to develop membership to provide credibility and visibility for its work. The council repeatedly went through the motions of "exploring" membership but dragged its feet in implementing any membership plan. Off the record, the council board admitted that they feared loss of control. That control was alienating the CDCs, all of whom were performing well programmatically, all of whom were in a position to identify and hire their own technical consultants except as such assistance related to large-scale real estate development, and all of whom wanted and were demanding an independent funding relationship with the Ford Foundation. Sviridoff recognized that independence of the CDCs and lack of a membership base could fatally weaken a council that was still experiencing difficulty agreeing on its agenda. But the CDCs had grown and matured and were beginning to have significant effects on their communities. Sviridoff felt that direct foundation funding was in their best interest.

Council leadership, on the other hand, evidenced little cohesion. Barraza's agenda was essentially a labor agenda. As a consequence, by his own admission he was comfortable with the labor representatives and the young activists on his board, but he had problems with the academics who didn't, in his words, play by the rules. As council chair, Barraza was strong, decisive, and sometimes stern and overbearing. He felt that the young, emerging leadership should be handled firmly, and he was much less patient with the younger generation than Santiestevan was. Barraza's "firm handling" contributed to the CDCs' demand for liberation. On the other hand, Barraza knew how to be flexible and reasonable and how to use the art of compromise to achieve his goals, and he understood well the imperative of unity in leadership. On tough issue after tough issue, he stayed with Santiestevan. For example, when the move to Washington was on the table, Barraza supported Santiestevan's position even though his heart was in the development of a strong political base in the Southwest. When board member Graciela Olivarez, later to become director of the Community Services Agency in the Carter administration, precipitated a sharp split in the board by demanding that it adopt a policy creating a 50–50 balance of men and women, Barraza supported Santiestevan and Olivarez even though he clearly did not like the proposal. Both the older male board members and the young ones were products of their tradition and socialization; it was not easy for them to accept women in public roles. In fact, the proposal was approved by only one vote.

Although the women were seated in 1973, they struggled long and hard thereafter to be treated as equals. Barraza imagined that his support for the women would place them firmly in his camp. He discovered otherwise. They had very independent ideas of what the council's priorities and agenda should be, and they had no intention of being railroaded by anybody.

NEW AGENDAS—NEW LEADERSHIP

In 1974 it became increasingly clear that the council was entering a new stage of development. Although it had survived turbulent seas for some six years, the frail craft continued to show strains. They were similar to strains experienced in the development of countless other organizations—staff inadequacies, leadership quarrels, money-raising difficulties, political pressure,[1] attacks from disaffected organizations cut out of Ford's funding pattern, fears about survival, jealousies, and the interpersonal complications and power struggles made more complex by the introduction of women.

Some of the women and young Turks didn't think that Santiestevan was promoting enough action; none of either group felt that Barraza was taking them seriously or was disposed to share power with them. As they became increasingly vocal, Barraza recognized that his days at the helm were ending and that his labor agenda would not prevail. Other community agendas were bubbling to the surface.

The threat to Barraza's position was developing at a time when he was leading an inner AFL–CIO effort to form an organization of Hispanic union members, which was to become the Labor Council for Latin American Advancement (LCLAA). He knew that he had to deal for a top spot in LCLAA from a position of strength, not as the deposed chair of the council. Matters were complicated by the fact that Barraza was competing with a fellow Steelworker and council board member, Paul Montemayor, for influence in LCLAA and for control of the Steelworker support for Mexican-American initiatives. It was Barraza's perception that he was fighting for his position in the labor movement, and he responded to the call for his resignation from the council chair by drawing upon his years in the tough school of union survival. He bargained with the opposition. As Marta Sotomayor, a board member at the time and later council chairperson, recalls, "Maclovio offered Henry's head immediately in return for another year in the Chair." (personal conversation with Nicolau, November, 1988).

Santiestevan had little choice. Resigning was the only way to bring about the smooth transition that assured council survival. Certainly it was not when Santiestevan planned to leave, and the manner of his leaving was not to his liking, but in retrospect he has come to believe that it was the right time. The council was reasonably well established in Washington, D.C. Santiestevan had groomed some outstanding young CDC leaders, who felt frustrated and powerless. It was time to let them lead.

Raúl Yzaguirre, who had administered migrant programs and directed a successful consulting firm, succeeded Santiestevan in 1974 as council director. Ronnie Lopez, not Raúl, was Barraza's candidate; Raúl was Paul Montemayor's somewhat reluctant candidate. Both Barraza and Montemayor understood that an Yzaguirre council victory would support a Montemayor

---

[1]During the highly political year of 1972, the SWCLR had wrestled with and successfully resisted pressures to trade off its independent integrity for favorable grant consideration from certain elements of the Nixon administration. The SWCLR's refusal to yield to such enticements was later documented during the Watergate hearings.

victory within LCLAA. Raúl won the election by a single vote—even though
he made no more than a halfhearted try for the post. He recalls:

> Paul Montemayor and Alex Mercure conspired with some of my former associ-
> ates who were still working at my old consulting firm and lured me into a hotel
> room. They locked the door and would not let me out until I agreed to submit
> an application. Paul in particular accused me of turning my back on the move-
> ment by refusing to heed a call for help from my friends. . . . Paul assured me
> that the votes on my behalf were there and that the only issue was the terms of
> my employment. . . . When I arrived at the board meeting, I quickly realized that
> a very well organized campaign was in place to elect Ronnie Lopez. . . . During
> the board interview I indicated that I could not guarantee that I would take the
> job . . . to my eternal surprise the board called us in [Ronnie Lopez and Raúl]
> and announced that I was the new director. . . . As you may recall, Maclovio
> flew out of the meeting in a rage. (letter from Yzaguirre to Nicolau, May 8,
> 1989)

Yzaguirre's selection was as much about another organization, LCLAA,
as it was about the council, and not all those who voted fully understood
what was going on. Some voted for Yzaguirre, others against Barraza, some
in support of Montemayor, others—strongly lobbied by Alex Mercure—for
other reasons. Yzaguirre's victory essentially extinguished Barraza's influence; he served out his twelve months in an uncharacteristically low-key
manner. The following year, Juan Patlan, executive director of the Mexican
American Unity Council and Raúl's fellow south Texan, assumed the chair-
manship of the council.

When Yzaguirre arrived at the council, he was neither old enough nor
self-effacing enough to assume the Santiestevan role of patient mentor and
groomer. Yzaguirre was filling a leadership gap, and the manner of his selection did not send him down the road with any clear board direction. In the
process of consolidating his control and establishing an agenda, he antago-
nized the young, urban CDC leaders, who viewed the council as an institution that would articulate and serve *their* needs. The conflict led to the
replacement of Patlan by Marta Sotomayor. Patlan recalls, "It was the problem of two young machos locking horns." Another outcome was the resignation of the major urban CDC executives who chose to pursue independent
paths when they recognized that they were not going to be the central focus
of the Yzaguirre council.

When Yzaguirre took over in 1974, he replaced almost all of the staff and
began to build his own network of affiliates, some of which had roots in the
rural constituency he had established during his years with the OEO Migrant
Division. Yzaguirre, a skilled grantsman, obtained an impressive number of
federal grants through which he serviced the needs of the urban and rural
groups, increased their number, and solidified their loyalty. The staff
increased from thirteen to 110, and council branches were opened in Albu-

querque, Chicago, San Francisco, and the Texas Valley. During this period of remarkable growth, the council developed a program to help rural communities obtain housing grants and rural-venture grants. The council was involved in migrant education, published the magazine *Agenda,* played an important role in bringing together the organizations that were being created around specific issues, and launched a program of legislative analysis.

Yzaguirre, a forceful proponent of Chicano rights, worked strenuously to keep that council goal alive. However, in the early years of his directorship, he largely turned the council into a technical assistance agency for emerging local groups because advocacy and policy funding was in short supply. The 1970s were good years for the council, and Yzaguirre experienced little Ford interference in his reorganization. Since the foundation was in fact trying to reduce council dependency on Ford funds, it drew into the background and stayed there.

SURVIVAL IN THE 1980s: NEW CHALLENGES

In the 1980s rough seas rose again for the council with a change in the federal administration. Significant federal programs were transferred to the states. As a consequence, the council found itself once more struggling to redefine its mission. Sharp cutbacks in staff and programs were required. Labor support, which might have provided a stable base, had evaporated with the rejection of Barraza and Santiestevan and the labor agenda. Yzaguirre made adjustments: Under his leadership, the council moved to broaden its constituency to include representatives from other Hispanic groups. It brought the urban CDCs back into the fold, and it reached out to corporate America. Perhaps the most striking accomplishment was the visibility and credibility the council achieved as an advocate for Hispanic issues.

The council was less successful in other areas. Its attempts to achieve financial self-sufficiency through council-operated businesses failed. Like many other unendowed nonprofits, the council has never been able to solve its basic problem of funding instability. And the Yzaguirre reign has not enjoyed unrelieved serenity. There have been several challenges to Yzaguirre's leadership, which he and others closer to the council in recent years are better able to recount than we.

But all organizations suffer problems, particularly in their formative years. Institution building is not free of trouble. A national vision and a sense of the common good are not arrived at easily. It would be pleasant to imagine that we all enlisted in the battle for justice and marched with unity and pride to victory, but such was not the case. We struggled long and hard—just as all other groups do—to achieve internal unity. We chipped away at monumental outside ignorance, and we fought against forces that did not want us to succeed. The miracle is that the council survived in the face of serious internal tension, recurring external attack, neglect and indifference, and

periodic sharp U-turns in government and philanthropic policy. As Yzaguirre wrote to Nicolau:

> In terms of organization development lessons, it is precisely those years [1974–
> 1989] that are the most instructive. The lessons regarding the broadening of our
> funding base, the definition of missions, the changes in board culture, the ten-
> sions between trying to be a professional organization and a movement vehicle,
> the role we played in coalescing the Hispanic organizations, the difficulties in
> dealing with both friendly and unfriendly administrations—these and other top-
> ics remain to be explored and are so important in terms of the maturation pro-
> cess of an organization. (letter from Yzaguirre to Nicolau, May 8, 1989)

The National Council of La Raza, SVREP, and the CDCs—along with
many other organizations of equal importance—played key roles in the maturation process of the Chicano Movement and participated in the drama
that attended the Chicano struggle for justice and opportunity. The authors
hope that this personal account illuminates the early history of the movement and inspires others to share their experiences. And we hope that it helps
new leaders chart new courses for the future.

5

Hispanic Advocacy Organizations

Vilma S. Martinez

This chapter reflects my experience as a board member and as president of the Mexican American Legal Defense and Educational Fund (MALDEF) for over ten years and as an active participant with other organizations in the struggle for civil rights for Hispanics. MALDEF has not been the only legal advocacy organization for Hispanics: The National Council of La Raza, the Puerto Rican Legal Defense and Education Fund, the Southwest Voter Registration Education Project, and others have played important roles in this struggle. Based on the amount of activity, resources employed, and results obtained, however, it is clear that MALDEF has been and continues to be the principal such organization.

Prior to joining MALDEF, I worked for three years at the NAACP Legal Defense Fund in New York, the legal arm of the black civil rights movement. Much of MALDEF was modeled after the LDF. But it soon became clear to us that the role of MALDEF had to be different from that of the model. The LDF was able to rely on other well-established black, community-based organizations to do educational policy and community advocacy work. The lack of such established organizations in the Hispanic community has meant that Hispanic advocacy organizations have had to fulfill many additional functions besides that of bringing lawsuits.

The following relates some of my experiences during the last twenty years with MALDEF and other organizations. But to put this subject into context, one must go back much farther than the reach of personal memory.

THE BACKGROUND

In the years between the world wars, much of the Southwest was a segregated society in which Mexican-Americans were, at best, second-class citizens and, at worst, pieces of property. Schooling for Mexican-Americans was segregated and of very low quality, and in many cases was unavailable after the seventh grade. Most public facilities—including restaurants, swimming pools, public schools, public parks, bathrooms, and even cemeteries—were segregated, by rule or by practice.

Congressman Henry B. Gonzalez of San Antonio, Texas, was one of many Mexican-Americans refused service at a public restaurant. Thanks to the efforts of then-Governor John Connally, the Head Start program was kept out of Texas. The Mexican-American school dropout rate was extremely high all over the Southwest. There was practically no access to higher education. Mexican-Americans were denied the right to vote through the use of "literacy" tests, poll taxes, outright intimidation, and bureaucratic refusal. There were practically no Mexican-American elected officials. Police violence toward Mexican-Americans was notorious, and abuse by police continued through the 1930s. As late as 1967, when the United Farm Workers struck in South Texas, Texas Rangers led by Captain A. Y. Allee harassed and brutalized the strikers. When news reached Allee that an injunction had been filed against him, he bragged that he had been sued many times but had never received an official reprimand. Of the Mexican-Americans born in the 1940s, as I was, few made it to college, and most of the rest of us dropped out of school shortly after the sixth grade. As late as the 1970s, the publisher of the *Los Angeles Times* stated on television that there was little reason for his newspaper to cover issues pertaining to minorities. These people did not read the *Times,* he said, because it was too complicated.

But these years were not barren in the struggle for equal rights. The post-World War II period saw the first effective use of the courts as a means of gaining equality for Mexican-Americans. In the late 1940s, Carlos Cadena, a Mexican-American attorney in San Antonio, won a lawsuit that stopped the use of "restricted covenants" that had prevented land in Anglo neighborhoods from being sold to Mexican-Americans or blacks. Cadena and Gus Garcia, another Mexican-American attorney, brought a suit against segregration in public schools. Segregation of Mexican-American students was not stopped, but the suit caused state authorities to repudiate the practice on an official level.

The crucial case, however, was *Hernandez v. Texas,* argued before the U.S. Supreme Court in 1954 by Cadena and Garcia. The defendant, Pete Hernandez, had been convicted of murder in Jackson County, which had a population that was about 15 percent Mexican-American. There was no Mexican-American person on the jury. In fact, there had not been such a person on *any* jury in *any* case in Jackson County for 25 years. *Hernandez* was the first Mexican-American discrimination case to reach the U.S. Supreme Court and the first case in that court to be argued by Mexican-American attorneys. It was also a victory.

During these years, one of the major arguments used by Texas authorities was that Mexican-Americans were not a distinct race or class of people. Therefore, they argued, Mexican-Americans were not entitled to the special protections of the Fourteenth Amendment. Speaking for the Court, Chief Justice Warren wrote that the Texas Court was incorrect when it limited the scope of that amendment to the white and negro classes and that "... persons of Mexican descent were a distinct class."

The legal implications of *Hernandez* were profound. The nation's highest court had finally recognized Mexican-Americans as a separate class of people who were discriminated against and who, as a class, could seek redress under the law. It opened the door for class action lawsuits against the ills besetting the Mexican-American community.

ESTABLISHMENT OF HISPANIC ADVOCACY ORGANIZATIONS

In the 1960s, the response of the Hispanic community was, for the first time, confrontation. In 1963, Cesar Chavez, an Arizona-born farmworker, started a drive to organize farm laborers. In the same year, Reies Lopez Tijerina founded La Alianza Federal de Mercedes to demand that the lands of northern New Mexico be returned to the Mexican-American people. In 1967, Jose Angel Gutierrez founded the Mexican American Youth Organization in San Antonio. This union of Latino students, through a series of transformations, became La Raza Unida, the first Latino political party. In 1968, the Mexican American Legal Defense and Educational Fund opened its doors in San Antonio and Los Angeles. In 1968, the National Council of La Raza was formed. In 1969, Corky Gonzales, a former boxer, poverty program director, and founder of the Crusade for Justice, established La Raza Unida in Colorado. In 1972, the Puerto Rican Legal Defense and Education Fund was formed in New York.

The Nature of Hispanic Advocacy Organizations

There are many active organizations that work for the benefit of Hispanics through political, social, or economic means. These include the League of United Latin American Citizens (a number of whose members founded MALDEF), the American G.I. Forum, the Mexican American Political Association, the Hispanic Bar Associations, and many others too numerous to list. Narrowly defined, for the purposes of this chapter, a Hispanic advocacy organization seeks to change law and public policy (and the distinction between these is frequently unclear) not only by legal process, but also by many other methods. This is due partly to the costs in time and resources of bringing a case from pretrial discovery through posttrial appeals and partly to the fact that there are frequently more effective methods. Thus, when a Hispanic advocacy organization is faced with widespread discrimination in a large school system, it may seek to force federal or state authorities to expend their own substantial resources to enforce the antidiscrimination law. In this way, the organization limits its expenditure of resources to that of monitoring, and it may achieve a tactical advantage in a courtroom by having a controversial case brought by a more "neutral" plaintiff.

Advocacy Through Legislation

In the early 1970s, MALDEF representatives provided information to opponents of a bill in the Texas legislature that would have permitted local school districts to charge tuition to undocumented children. The bill was enacted over the opponents' objection that the bill was unconstitutional, and at least one school district implemented a tuition charge. MALDEF then fought the constitutionality issue in federal court. More recently, in Texas, MALDEF successfully sued the state for unfair allocation of education resources to minority children. The order of the court will require a legislative response, and MALDEF hopes to work with legislative and administrative groups to fashion new methods of funding and allocation that both satisfy the law and are politically practical.

At the federal level, all Hispanic advocacy organizations have worked extensively on two major areas of concern to Hispanics, the Voting Rights Act and the immigration statute. The Voting Rights Act has been probably the most significant factor in bringing black Americans into the political process, especially in the South. But in its original form, *it did not deal with the voting rights of Mexican-Americans.* The act was expanded to cover all Hispanics only through the efforts of such organizations, which have defended and helped preserve the act in its expanded form ever since. At the federal level, these groups were also active in trying to prevent enactment of unfair immigration legislation. Failing that, they worked to include in such legislation provisions against unfair job discrimination and provisions for a legalization program.

MALDEF and other organizations currently maintain an information center available to those opposing English only and similar discriminatory measures by state and local government bodies.

Advocacy Through Administrative Agencies

Hispanic advocacy organizations have worked to monitor the performance of administrative agencies charged with enforcing the law where the inaction or wrongful action of these agencies has a disproportionate effect on Hispanics. Work of this type has included assisting the U.S. Census Bureau to achieve a more nearly accurate count of Hispanics, forcing state and local health agencies to provide adequate prenatal care to poor Hispanic women, monitoring the employer sanctions of the Immigration and Naturalization Service (INS) and their effects on unlawful discrimination against Hispanics, getting the National Park Service to alter its hiring and promotion policies for Hispanics and to provide Spanish-speaking guides in areas where many of the visitors speak Spanish, and working to change federal civil service tests found to have a disproportionate adverse effect on Hispanics and blacks.

Education and Publicity

Frequently, the most effective role of the Hispanic advocacy organization is to educate both Hispanics and the general populace on the nature and extent of a particular form of discrimination. Properly monitored, the efforts of existing agencies and the force of public opinion can often achieve major successes. For example, MALDEF action helped create centers in California to counsel Hispanic community college students to plan their studies to enable them to transfer to four-year colleges. MALDEF's Washington-based policy analyst keeps track of all "English only" measures nationwide and helps coordinate the effort of opponents. Since the enactment of the Immigration Reform and Control Act (IRCA), MALDEF has provided information not only to individuals affected, but also to employers seeking to comply in a nondiscriminatory manner with the act.

Research and Conferences

Hispanic advocacy organizations have sponsored conferences of Hispanics and non-Hispanics to deal with a broad range of issues affecting the Hispanic community. They offer briefings to newspaper editorial boards, participate in research with university groups and private think tanks, secure funding for research by experts on critical issues, and work directly in the Hispanic community to help create new organizations. For example, MALDEF helped organize the first statewide Hispanic women's network in Texas.

Lawsuits

The core activity of many Hispanic advocacy groups has been legal process, principally but not only in education, political access, and employment. Thus, in 1988, MALDEF enjoined the judges of a local municipal court in California from enforcing an "English only" rule on court clerks. In 1982, MALDEF sued to prevent seven California counties from providing the INS with names of citizens who requested Spanish-language ballots. In 1988, MALDEF sued to enjoin the INS from its practice of using general (i.e., without specific names) warrants to conduct sweeps of work areas. Also in 1988, an Arab plaintiff alleged that his employer, a college, had denied him tenure on the basis of "race" (the standard in the applicable statute). Because of the potential effect on Hispanics, MALDEF intervened; ultimately, the U.S. Supreme Court held that the statute covers discrimination on the basis of ancestry or ethnic differences.

SUBJECT AREAS OF HISPANIC ADVOCACY ORGANIZATION ACTIVITY

Employment

Access to equal employment opportunity is one of the most critical rights for Hispanics. All advocacy groups have devoted significant resources during the last twenty years to force private corporations, unions, governmental agencies, and universities to alter discriminatory hiring and promotion practices.

Although the provisions of Title VII of the 1964 Civil Rights Act seem straightforward, changing business practices and the emergence of more subtle forms of discrimination have required more sophisticated and creative responses by Hispanic advocacy organizations. Thus, a suit brought in the 1960s might have asked for back pay for the plaintiffs (both for individuals and for members of a class) and a mandated schedule for hiring and promotion of Hispanic workers. In more recent years, the organizations have sought access to training programs, overhaul of personnel review procedures, and elimination of discriminatory testing standards.

The impetus for the enactment of the 1964 Civil Rights Act derived from an understanding by Congress of the scope and variety of discrimination against blacks. Even though the act prohibited abuses on the basis of "national origin," there was little, if any, focus by national politicians on the pervasive abuses of the rights of Hispanics or those of other minority groups. In addition, Hispanic advocacy organizations, along with other advocacy groups, resorted to the 1866 Civil Rights Act, whose procedures were more flexible and whose remedies were broader, to seek redress for employment discrimination against Hispanics. Much of the early work of Hispanic advocacy organizations focused on litigation to establish that Hispanics were properly treated as a separate "race" for purposes of the 1866 Act. In these early years of group activity, one of the principal tasks was that of education of both Hispanics and non-Hispanics. Hispanics had to understand that, regardless of its history, the civil rights legislation was there for their protection. And government administrators had to learn how to implement the legislation in situations of discrimination against Hispanics. As a result, much of the organizational litigation in these years was brought against government entities themselves. In this manner, advocacy groups quickly put everyone on notice that Hispanics were entitled to protection under both the 1866 and the 1964 acts and that the groups intended to enforce that protection.

Major litigation was brought against private companies, principally in cases of egregious discrimination. The issues in those years included proof of coverage under the two federal acts and, frequently, the validity of the ill-defined "BFOQ" ("*bona fide* occupational qualifications") defense that could be asserted in cases alleging national origin or sex discrimination but not in cases alleging race discrimination. In the BFOQ defense, an employer admitted discrimination (based on national origin or sex) but argued that it was justified in view of the reasonable requirements of the job. Arguments that would seem ludicrous today were taken seriously by many courts and worked to retard progress against employment discrimination.

By the 1970s, employment litigation had become one of three major areas of concentration by Hispanic groups. It offered the potential of direct economic benefit to Hispanics. It also lent itself well to class action suits brought on behalf of hundreds of individuals.

The accumulation of political skills by Hispanic advocacy organizations and changes in presidential administrations permitted the organizations to leverage their resources by assisting, inducing, and prodding governmental agencies to enforce federal statutes rather than await the results of time-consuming and costly lawsuits. The Equal Employment Opportunity Commission, the Office of Federal Contract Compliance, and the Civil Rights Division of the Justice Department all played a part in this cooperative process.

During these years, MALDEF started the first advocacy center to focus exclusively on the rights of Hispanic women, and advocacy groups helped write into the Comprehensive Employment and Training Act (CETA) the special funding for Operation SER, which works to train Hispanics for available jobs.

A decision in Colorado gave Hispanic children the direct right to sue a school district for discriminatory hiring practices if the Hispanic students were being hurt by a lack of Hispanic teachers. These teachers had often been hesitant to act as plaintiffs in discrimination suits against what might be their only possible employer.

A suit against the board of trustees of the California State College system established the right of plaintiffs to use the employer's own personnel files as evidence of patterns of discrimination in hiring and promotion practices.

A suit against the Contra Costa County Community College in California resulted in a settlement that mandated hiring of Hispanic teachers and administrators not only to correct past employment discrimination but also to provide Hispanic students with appropriate opportunities for tutoring, counseling and educational support. Similarly, action by a coalition of Hispanic advocacy organizations in San Francisco resulted in a federal government study that concluded that in 1978 Hispanics were the most underutilized group in the city for municipal employment, that those employed by the city were concentrated in low-level jobs, and—most significantly—that the underemployment of Spanish speakers had the effect of cutting off public social services to the same group in the city.

By the 1980s, suits had become even more complex and comprehensive. Advocacy litigation was often targeted at entire industries and was assisted by the knowledge on the part of employers that Hispanic population growth, both as a labor market and as a consumer market, would make significant changes inevitable. An example was a discrimination suit against Lucky Stores that resulted in a ten-year hiring and promotion schedule that took into account the projected rather than the current labor market. In a suit against the city of Tucson, still pending, plaintiffs alleged that the police department relied exclusively on Hispanic civilian and officer employees to provide services to those residents of the city with limited or no English, a practice that had the effect of limiting those employees' opportunity for promotions, shift changes, and advanced training.

At the request of the Hispanic Advisory Council to the Los Angeles Police Commission, MALDEF analyzed the hiring and promotion practices of the Los Angeles Police Department over a ten-year period, documenting significant discrimination against Hispanics and others. The Police Commission subsequently adopted nearly all the study's recommendations and is in the process of implementing them.

The enactment of the Immigration Reform and Control Act of 1986 (IRCA) raised a new type of employment discrimination, termination based on incorrect interpretations of the act. Congress recognized that one of the many drawbacks of the statute was that some employers might use it to justify discriminatory termination and hiring practices. Advocacy groups have fought these practices in court and have instituted education programs to assist employers in complying with IRCA without unlawfully discriminating against Hispanics. In 1988, MALDEF hired a full-time attorney to monitor discrimination resulting from enforcement of IRCA's employer sanctions. In a recent Texas case, *LULAC v. Pasadena Independent School District,* four undocumented Hispanic workers were wrongfully terminated even though they were permitted, under the IRCA grandfather provision, to continue working. In this first test case of immigration-related discrimination, MALDEF obtained a preliminary injunction calling for reinstatement, payment of back pay, and payment of attorneys' fees.

Equal Educational Opportunity

During the past twenty years, Hispanic advocacy organizations have sought relief in the courts from discriminatory practices affecting placement of Hispanic children in schools. Second, they have fought for the right of children who speak limited English to obtain effective training in that language and, during that training period, to be taught substantive subjects in their native language. Third, advocacy groups have sought to protect the rights of Hispanics who are not U.S. citizens.

The Language Issue. At the outset, advocacy groups realized that achieving equal educational opportunity for Hispanics required new methods. For over ten years after the 1954 *Brown v. Board of Education* decision, blacks had demanded desegregation of public schools in order to obtain equal education for their children. But many Hispanic children not only attended segregated schools but also were confined to barrios where they spoke mostly Spanish. Simply placing them in integrated schools without dealing with the language issue was no solution.

The remedy sought by MALDEF and other groups was a form of bilingual teaching, where the children were (1) trained thoroughly in the English language, and (2) taught substantive courses in Spanish during the period in which their English was less than fluent. In this manner, the children not only learned English as quickly as possible but also "kept up" with their peer groups in the substantive topics, thus making the transition to an all-English curriculum as effective and painless as possible. In this manner, MALDEF hoped to avoid the closed-door atmosphere that alienated many Hispanic children from school at an early age. A second remedy employed by Hispanic advocacy organizations was to establish that fair hiring standards for teachers in an ethnically and racially diverse environment necessarily included an ethnically and racially diverse faculty.

During this period, bilingual education for Hispanic children was mandated in the State of Texas; two landmark cases, *Lau v. Nichols* and *Serna v. Portales,* established the right of non-English-speaking children to receive instruction in a language they understood. MALDEF successfully challenged state laws in Idaho and Texas that provided that children could be educated only in English. One example is *Gomez v. Illinois State Board of Education,* where the Seventh Circuit Court of Appeals held (in January 1987) that the board is required to implement the Transitional Bilingual Education Act in a manner to provide full educational opportunity to limited-English-proficient children. MALDEF has continued to press the board to establish effective administrative remedies. In spite of these successes, bilingual education remedies have run afoul of funding problems, opposition from teachers unions, and periodic xenophobic politics (such as the English only movement), and litigation continues to this day.

The Residency Issue. MALDEF challenged a Texas statute that permitted local school districts to charge tuition to undocumented children in primary and secondary schools. The challenge prevailed at the Federal District Court, the Fifth Circuit Court, and the U.S. Supreme Court. The problem of residency qualification never arose in California primary and secondary schools because Wilson Riles, then state superintendent of education, after discussions with MALDEF, decided that all of California's children should and would be educated, without distinction. In a related area, Hispanic advocacy groups have recently challenged the practice by some state colleges of denying the benefits of in-state tuition rates to state residents who do not hold permanent resident visas. In 1987, after lawsuits by MALDEF, several universities in Illinois and California changed this practice.

Allocation of Funds. In recent years, advocacy groups have focused on what many believe is the most critical need for Hispanics and other minorities, fair and adequate allocation of tax revenues to areas where concentrations of minorities are high. Historical discrimination by administrative agencies and the use of real property as the basis for allocation have worked to minimize public-school services for taxpayers who need them most in order to participate fully in society. The most striking example has been the *Edgewood* case, where MALDEF successfully challenged the entire system of school financing in the state of Texas. Although the case will ultimately be decided by the Texas Supreme Court (the case was based on the Texas State Constitution), alternate methods of school funding are already being analyzed in the Texas legislature.

MALDEF has sued the Los Angeles Unified School District for inequitable allocation of its resources between minority and nonminority areas. In that district, many schools in Anglo neighborhoods are underpopulated, while many in Hispanic and black neighborhoods are overcrowded and forced to operate twelve months a year. This case is still in its early stages.

Finally, in what could become a landmark case, MALDEF has sued the University of Texas for failing to establish regional campuses in areas of heavy Hispanic population, effectively depriving Hispanics of local, state-supported colleges and graduate schools. At this writing, a settlement seems to be possible.

Voting Rights

From the beginning, Hispanic advocacy organizations have engaged in litigation to preserve voting rights and access to the political process for Hispanics. Subjects of litigation included the use of property and poll taxes and the abuse of "literacy tests" that effectively limited Hispanic voting power. In *Garza v. Smith,* MALDEF won the right of illiterate voters to bring someone into the voting booth with them.

Redrawing of Districts. One of the most important areas of action by advocacy groups involved redrawing of voting districts. Not only were Hispanic voters typically devalued by the use of gerrymandered districts, but in many areas of the Southwest, large concentrations of Hispanic voters were lumped with even larger groups of Anglo voters in counties where all the representatives were elected at large. The mathematics alone effectively prevented most Hispanics from having any chance of election. In addition, the cost of campaigning over an entire county eliminated many potential Hispanic candidates. The remedy proposed by MALDEF was the creation of smaller, single-member districts within a county. In *White v. Regester,* this became the accepted corrective method. Shortly after *Regester,* San Antonio elected three additional Hispanics and one black to the Texas state legislature. Challenges to at-large voting systems have continued during the last twenty years, covering state legislatures, municipal bodies, and school districts. In a challenge against the city of Los Angeles' 1982 redistricting plan for its city council seats, MALDEF was able to create a new, largely Hispanic seat in northeastern Los Angeles and to consolidate Hispanic voting strength in the San Fernando Valley.

The Voting Rights Act. The key to much of the voting rights activity was, of course, the extension of the Voting Rights Act of 1965. This statute was designed to increase voting among southern blacks by stopping abusive practices by governmental officials. The act is credited with having led to the registration of over one million blacks and increasing the number of black elected officials from 100 to 1,000. In 1975, the act, which originally had a ten-year life, was to be extended. Hispanic advocacy organizations worked hard to convince Congress that the abuses in the Southwest against Hispanic voters more than warranted inclusion of Hispanics as a protected class under the act. The groups were able to draw on extensive documentation of these abuses by the U.S. Commission on Civil Rights. In August 1975, the new act was passed, together with the "Hispanic" amendments. Henceforth, many election districts in the Southwest were under official scrutiny of the U.S. Justice Department. Bilingual ballots were required in those areas.

Hispanic advocacy organizations have had great success in the area of voting rights. There has been a dramatic increase in the number of Hispanic voters and in the number of Hispanics elected to public office. Between 1976 and 1984, thanks largely to the efforts of the Southwest Voter Registration Education Project, the number of Hispanic voters in Texas increased by more than 50 percent, rising to a total of more than one million. This, in turn, has meant an increase in solicitation of Hispanic voters. The 1988 Democratic Party presidential primary in Texas was fought and decided in largely Hispanic south Texas.

The Rights of Chicanas

The discrimination problems of Hispanic women were frequently similar to those suffered by Hispanic men, but their manifestation was often different. Hispanic women workers were more vulnerable to artificial height, weight, and other physical requirements for hiring and promotion. Hispanic women were also more affected by the unavailability of adequate care centers for small children. The problems of Hispanic women were often different from those suffered by Anglo women. The mainstream women's movement was fighting for the right of each woman to have unfettered freedom of choice with regard to birth, abortion, birth control, and sterilization. But the poor, limited-English-speaking Hispanic woman often needed outside protection against forced sterilization by governmental agencies. These same women needed access to adequate prenatal and infant care. In 1974 MALDEF began the first specialized program for advocacy for Chicana Rights, in San Antonio. Thirteen years later, in Dallas, MALDEF helped organize the first Texas Hispanic Women's Network.

The Census

In April 1973, MALDEF sued the U.S. Census Bureau for undercounting Hispanics in the 1970 census by at least 600,000. MALDEF lost the suit, but the census bureau publicly acknowledged the undercount, and the president of MALDEF was chosen to serve as a special consultant to the bureau to help prepare it for the 1980 census. MALDEF's efforts to insure a more accurate count of Hispanics in the 1980 census included using churches as disseminators of information, educating the Hispanic community on the importance of filling out census forms completely and accurately, and vigorously protecting the integrity of the census process by suing to prevent the INS from using supposedly confidential census information to make sweeps.

Language

The Spanish language has been a source of great strength to the Hispanic community, but it is sometimes perceived as a political liability. Spanish-speaking Hispanics who want to thrive in the United States must learn English as quickly as possible; those who do not are generally much older or are living, either by choice or circumstance, in areas where little if any English is heard. In this, the experience of Hispanics closely parallels that of other immigrant groups to this country. The differences for Hispanics are twofold: First, the cultural "mother country" is not located across a wide ocean but in this hemisphere, frequently as close as a bus or automobile trip. Second, although the majority of the Hispanic community is English-speaking, immigration continues. Thus, the Hispanic community includes recently arrived immigrants who speak primarily Spanish, permanent residents who speak both Spanish and English, and new generations that speak only English. The vast majority of Hispanics in this country, of course, have been here for many generations.

Hispanic advocacy organizations have two goals with regard to language: first, to prevent governmental and private bodies from using the language factor as a device to subject Hispanics to unlawful discrimination; and, second, to encourage young people to retain their Spanish, which is not only part of their cultural heritage but for many a significant economic advantage. Language discrimination has often manifested itself in school or work rules against the use of Spanish or other non-English languages. Sometimes this form of discrimination reveals itself as a variation of the xenophobia practiced by the Know Nothing Party in the nineteenth century.

MALDEF obtained an injunction against the Huntington Park, California, municipal court judges who had imposed an English only rule on court clerks. The injunction of the Federal District Court was upheld at the Ninth Circuit, which also held that Proposition 63, California's English only initiative, had no effect on this case since it was merely a policy declaration. MALDEF's Washington, D.C.-based policy analyst is spokesperson for "English Plus" and helped create the English Plus Information Clearinghouse for those opposing English only measures.

Other Civil and Constitutional Rights

It is sometimes difficult to predict when and where Hispanics and other minority groups will require the services of advocacy groups to fight discriminatory practices. In a case that became national news and was later the subject of the motion picture *Stand and Deliver,* MALDEF assisted Hispanic students at Garfield High School in Los Angeles in protesting what they considered arbitrary action by the Educational Testing Service (ETS). The students had scored extremely well on a national calculus examination. ETS claimed that there was evidence that the students had cheated, and the scores were disallowed. Others disagreed, arguing that ETS had preconceived notions of how Hispanic students in an inner-city high school should be expected to perform. The students successfully passed a retest.

In 1983, seven California counties attempted to provide the INS with names of all voters who requested Spanish-language ballots. This action was prevented only by a MALDEF lawsuit. In 1988, MALDEF joined an effort by the School of Education at the University of California at Berkeley to study the validity and effect of standardized tests, in particular their usefulness among different ethnic and cultural groups. In the same year, the issue of protected classes under the 1866 Civil Rights Act was finally resolved satisfactorily. An Arab plaintiff alleged that St. Francis College denied him tenure on the basis of "race." The Federal District Court held that this was not "racial" discrimination, that is, that Arabs did not constitute a separate race (nor any other category protected under the act, such as national origin). The Third Circuit reversed this decision, stating that "race" includes mistaken concepts of race. This led to several cases by Hispanics on same issue. Ultimately, the U.S. Supreme Court (where MALDEF filed an *amicus* brief) held that the statute includes discrimination on the basis of ancestry or ethnic characteristics.

HISPANIC ADVOCACY ORGANIZATIONS AND THE HISPANIC COMMUNITY

Hispanic Community Participation

The Hispanic community has always had strong cultural identification and pride. But historically, Hispanics have taken few initiatives to participate in the political system. This has been due partly to ignorance of the system's mechanics but principally to the distrust of Anglo political structures that, over generations, had effectively insulated Hispanics from political power. For example, the population of south Texas is largely Hispanic but because of gerrymandering and other devices, elected officials were mostly Anglo. Hispanics were conditioned to believe that their vote did not make a difference.

The Hispanic community clearly understood that it had been victimized; there was agreement on what needed to be done. There was no need to rally the community; the need was to deal with the actual problems of voting and political access. And when victories were won, both legislative and judicial, these had to be communicated to people, to explain that roads previously closed were now open.

Hispanic Organizations

One of the most striking characteristics of Hispanic advocacy organizations has been their willingness and ability to fulfill many different community functions. Mike Baller, a MALDEF lawyer who worked for many years with the NAACP Legal Defense Fund in New York City, stated in May 1982 that the LDF was able to rely on other black organizations to do educational policy and advocacy work but that MALDEF didn't have that luxury, there were too many unmet needs in the Mexican-American Community. The National Council of La Raza is an excellent example of this phenomenon. It was conceived as a technical assistance organization for fundraising and for supporting grass roots organizations, but it became the Washington voice for all those grass roots groups. In addition, since there were no Hispanic think tanks or colleges (as there were black colleges and a few black think tanks), it fell to the National Council of La Raza to develop much of the theoretical basis for the Hispanic movement, to train many of its leaders, and to serve as a clearinghouse of ideas and information. At an early stage, the National Council provided assistance to Hispanic groups throughout the country, not only Mexican-American groups. It showed them how to raise funds from corporate and foundation sources, how to obtain government assistance, and how to organize themselves effectively. The council's most important function was as an active and effective lobbying arm for all Hispanics.

Hispanic Leadership

One of the major deficiencies in the early years of Hispanic activism was the lack of skilled and experienced community and political leaders, reflecting in part the immense hurdles for Hispanics in U.S. higher education generally and in part the lack of colleges geared to Hispanic students. There was no large college-educated Hispanic talent pool from which one could draw. Advocacy groups recognized this problem and attempted to deal with it in several ways. Scholarships were given by MALDEF to promising Hispanic law students, particularly those who demonstrated past involvement with and future commitment to the Hispanic community. The National Hispanic Scholarship Fund was created to raise money and give scholarships to promising Hispanic students pursuing both undergraduate and graduate studies. One interesting approach has been MALDEF's Leadership Development Program, a twenty-week training course in four areas: personal development, data analysis, management and organizational skills, and community development and networking. MALDEF assists graduates to find places on public and private boards and commissions that make decisions affecting the Hispanic community. The program started in San Francisco in 1980; similar programs were added in Chicago, Los Angeles, Dallas, and San Antonio. About two-thirds of the program graduates have been placed on important decision-making groups.

Hispanic Issues

Determination of the important issues for the Hispanic community is sometimes straightforward. Voting rights, education rights, and equal employment opportunity are obvious. Some issues require a definition of the group to be protected. For example, although immigration legislation is ostensibly aimed at undocumented workers, it is frequently the resident, documented Hispanics and other minorities who suffer the resulting job discrimination. Hispanic advocacy organizations must understand the needs of the Hispanic community in order to fulfill their tasks adequately. Thoughtful research by and for the community should be able to provide guidance. For example, an understanding of the projected demographics of a large urban school district can affect the strategy of an advocacy group in considering different remedies for poor-quality schools: a change in funding patterns, an emphasis on bilingual classes, regional rather than centralized planning, transfers of groups of children within the district, and a greater concentration of adult education resources.

Unfortunately, the Hispanic community does not currently have sufficient resources for this important research and development work. Most of the Chicano studies programs at major universities have not yet defined their roles to include this type of basic research, although there are important exceptions, such as Juan Gomez-Quiñones and Leo Estrada at UCLA, Albert Camarillo at Stanford, Ricardo Romo at the University of Texas, and MAL-DEF's Public Policy program. The Tomás Rivera Center at Claremont College in California has begun several promising areas of research. A new center is to be opened at Trinity University in San Antonio.

CONCLUSION

Many of the factors that lead to success are obvious: (1) adequate funding, which in turn means capable people concentrating on this aspect; (2) talented and experienced staff to perform the "line" functions of the organization; and (3) a solid businesslike structure to make best use of the organization's resources and to protect it from the normal ups and downs of any such endeavor. Each advocacy organization must find its own way, based on its own mission, its own people, and its own place in the Hispanic community. In my view, however, there are certain goals and needs common to any advocacy group that seeks to bring Hispanics to full participation in the mainstream of our society. Such an organization must seek to be both a leader of people and a leader of ideas. Its goals should include (1) the building of respect and trust by Mexican-Americans and the society in general, and (2) the gradual institutionalization of the organization in both Mexican-American society and the broader society.

A Hispanic advocacy organization must understand both how to express the dreams of Mexican-Americans and how to translate these into effective action. Most importantly, it must understand Mexican-American society and our national society well enough to develop and articulate theories and ideas that will provide the foundation for substantive change. Such a group requires not only people with talent for legal advocacy, educational reform, political operation, and fundraising; it also requires people with vision.

Finally, such a group must constantly renew itself by reaching out to every new generation with its ideas and methods, teaching what it knows, and seeking the intellectual replenishment that only fresh points of view can offer.

6

Organized Religion and Nonprofit Activities Among Hispanic People in the United States

William C. McCready

This is a brief investigation of an important issue area about which there is little empirical information: the relationship between people of Hispanic heritage and various forms of organized or institutional religion. This chapter begins with a discussion of the role of religious identity and behavior in the lives of Hispanics and proceeds to an examination of how those patterns may influence the relationships between organized religious groups and other nonprofit endeavors within Hispanic communities. It is important to note at the outset that *Hispanic* is a term designed by the U.S. mainstream culture to encapsulate people from many different Spanish-language and -culture backgrounds; it is not an accurate description of a single, ethnically exclusive group.

Although the religious preference distribution of Hispanics is specified in greater detail in a later section of this chapter, it is useful to note here the common stereotype that Hispanic equals Catholic. In 1980, Hispanics were 73 percent Catholic and 15 percent Protestant. By 1988 they were 70 percent Catholic and nearly 20 percent Protestant. There has always been a minority of Hispanics who were not raised in the Catholic tradition, and increasingly there are more who are leaving that church. This changing profile of religious preference and experience will influence the ways in which Hispanics, churches, and the nonprofit sector interact. The way in which diverse Hispanic communities relate to the nonprofit sector depends, to a degree, on the interaction between Hispanic culture and religious tradition and organizations.

A THEORETICAL FOUNDATION: CULTURE AND RELIGION

It is important to provide a theoretical base for understanding how the culture–religion interaction affects various Hispanic groups. Hispanic culture is much older and more complex than its Christian tradition. Hispanic cultures represent various mixes of pre-Columbian, Spanish, and Indian roots. We must therefore use a definition of religion that reflects and is compatible with this cultural variation and richness.

The definition of religion used here is taken from anthropologist Clifford Geertz (1968, p. 643), who described religion as "a system of symbols which acts to establish powerful, pervasive, and long-lasting moods and motivations in men by formulating conceptions of a general order of existence and clothing these conceptions with such an aura of factuality that the moods and motivations seem uniquely realistic." In other writings, Geertz discusses religion as a model both "of" and "for" reality. This represents the essential linkage between religion and culture. Culture is also a model both "of" and "for" reality. Simply put, a model "of" is something that relates the essential way things are. It is that conviction inside the self that knows, in a fundamental noetic manner, what is real. A model "for" is akin to a pattern or a blueprint. It is the map within the self that tells us which way to go and what to do. It is connected more with the propositional than with the definitional. It is related to the "shoulds" and "oughts" of life rather than to the "passions" and "wants." Religious and cultural forces are more closely intertwined in some cultures than in others; it is foundational, for several reasons, that we understand this aspect of Hispanic life.

First, cultural religion is a defining group characteristic. It prescribes the way life really is and describes the norms for the "way things really are." The models "of" and "for" are clearly expressed in the religious perspectives that people espouse. For example, in Hispanic communities the bondedness of the community is reflected in festival participation in a way that is strikingly different from celebrations in European-derived religious communities.

Second, religion provides a "boundary" between minority cultural groups and the mainstream society. People's religious perspective is part of what makes them different and unique; in some ways it serves a function similar to language.

Third, religion can provide access to some of the resources of mainstream society. Other groups coming to this country have found this to be true, and we shall explore the differences between European migrations and contemporary migrations from Hispanic countries in this regard.

Perhaps most importantly, religion and culture, interacting in individual lives and communities, often provide considerable impetus toward social change. It is within the intersection of religion and culture that people answer the important questions of their lives, such as purpose, worth, and identity. One of the reasons pentecostal evangelical churches are gaining Hispanic members is that they provide better support to an individual's sense of self-esteem and value than do many of the more formal, mainstream churches. Understanding the religion–culture interaction is critical to understanding a people's social context.

The motivating power of religion and culture stems largely from their ability to connect the individual simultaneously to a large group or community and to a transcendent ideal reality. Fitzpatrick (1976), for example, has argued that Puerto Rican religious experience is more a religion of the community than of the organized church or parish.

HISPANIC RELIGIOUS IDENTITIES: AN INTERSECTION OF FAITH AND CULTURE

Hispanics are frequently perceived as being predominantly Catholic in terms of religious preference. It is important to modify this perception with more detail. First, the Hispanic population of the United States has increased significantly during the last decade. Data from the National Opinion Research Center (NORC) General Social Survey indicate that while the rate of increase for the population as a whole between 1980 and 1988 was 8 percent, the increase for persons of Hispanic origin was 34 percent. However, there was a large difference between the rate of Hispanic Catholic increase and the rate for Hispanic Protestants: Catholics increased at 28 percent, while Protestant growth was 78 percent. In estimated raw numbers, there were approximately 10.6 million Hispanic Catholics in 1980 and 13.6 million in 1988. On the other hand, there were approximately 2.13 million Hispanic Protestants in 1980 and 3.8 million in 1988. Analyses of these data show that the proportion of Hispanics raised as Catholics declined from 87 percent to 83 percent between 1973 and 1988, and the proportion of those who are still Catholic as adults remains about the same, at 83 percent. However, the proportion of those who were raised Catholic and who became Protestant doubled from 7 percent to about 14 percent during this period.

People from different cultures have devised many acceptable ways of communicating their religious feelings and sensibilities to each other and their children. Some people may feel that "high expression" signifies an intensity of belief, and, therefore, they have raucous and noisy celebrations at their religious ceremonies. Others may feel that, since religion is so important, a more serious demeanor is required, and they devise celebrations that are temperate, somber, and more majestic than festive.

It is only when cultures are mixed within a society that these differences become relevant to the entire society. We can see the power of such differences when we realize that many conflicts in our modern world are essentially religious in nature. The Middle East, Southeast Asia, Ireland, and many parts of the Indo–Soviet border all attest to the intensity and power of cultural/religious differentiation in a multicultural setting. Religious identity, for some people, becomes a way of identifying with a culture or even with a nation. The strong identity between being Catholic and being Polish is an extremely important part of contemporary Polish society. However, it is not only those who display such an identification who partake of the power contained in this religious/cultural interaction. People who have been socialized into a cultural system with a strong integration of religion and culture also are strengthened in their own personal sense of integration—a sense that can be very useful when one is confronting a new society and a different, unyielding culture. Many Hispanic groups socialize their members in such a way as to emphasize the primacy of familial relationships and obligations as well as the dignity of the individual and the necessity of engaging in personal contact when dealing with others (Doyle, 1982).

Like many immigrant groups before them, Hispanics stress the communal nature of life and the need to belong to a community in some way in order to be fully supported. Just as the individual needs to feel the strength and support that comes from belonging to a family, the family needs to experience the same feelings that come from belonging to a community. To the outsider, immigrants appear to be clannish and secretive. From the inside, however, only membership in the group makes life bearable and worth living.

The Pentecostal evangelical churches provide *iglesias calientes* or "warm churches" where the person feels part of a small, bonded group that sustains and supports self-esteem and self-worth better than do *iglesias frias* or the colder, larger churches common to the northern European experience.

Various sociologists have devised models of the process of assimilation. Their most common themes provide the following description. The first generation is typically closest to the country of origin in terms of culture and lifestyle. Language is still that of the country of origin and communities are close-knit and bonded. The second generation is transitional and stands astride both cultures—the new and the old. Its members are frequently in conflict with both their parents and their children and have little facility with their native tongue. The third and subsequent generations are very comfortable in the host society and move through it at their own determination. Some choose to become reacquainted with their cultural roots and heritage, but this is not seen as necessary. These generations have successfully made it into the mainstream.

Perhaps the most commonly used marker of this process is intermarriage (Alba and Kessler, 1980). Endogamy is most prevalent in the early generations and steadily declines over time. After enough iterations, culture apparently becomes so diluted that it can no longer be found within the society as a distinct entity. Some research has been done that indicates that, even among the third generation, cultural variations can be found that trace back to the culture of origin (McCready, 1976). These studies found that college students could assess their family styles and after analysis could be segmented into discernible ethnic groups, each with its own particular characteristics. It appears that some things disappear with time, while others do not. This is the reason why the interaction of culture and religion is important.

One of the reasons that we conceive of culture as being diluted is that we think of it as it comes from the place of origin. Naturally, after some time the patterns, values, and memories that contain culture will change. However, it has yet to be determined just how this change takes place. Many analogies have been used to depict the experience of generations of immigrants in this society. We have studied assimilation, acculturation, melting pots, mosaics, multiculturality, pluralism, and many other variations on the same theme. While these may be the subjects of valuable discussions, their relevance to policy has yet to be demonstrated firmly. However, a special case of the "dilution" question comes up when we begin examining the cultural persistence of characteristics within Hispanic groups.

The principal difference between Hispanics and others in this regard is the twin impact of their proximity to their homeland and considerable evidence already accumulated that their culture seems to endure longer than most. (Undoubtedly, some of this is due to language, which is dealt with elsewhere in this book, but some of it is also due to the cultural "density" that is provided by the interlocking of culture and religion.) Because Hispanics may modify the host culture as much as they are modified by it, we need to consider the older models of how groups in our society relate to each other and to the common national "culture," if indeed there even is one.

Cultural pluralism is a model that has been successful at explaining the relationships among groups in our society in that it preserves the multicultural nature of reality while enabling groups to form coalitions rather than always competing with one another. The assimilationist asks, How long until we are all alike? and the acculturationist asks, What is the underlying commonality which binds all these various groups together? But the pluralist asks, How does our multiculturality make us a unique society? Differences are strengths rather than weaknesses in this context. Pluralists tend to look for what remains after the passage of time and several generations, while the others tend to look for what has disappeared. Both outcomes do take place, and some things remain while others disappear, but the importance of these different perspectives is more than a matter of research emphasis or taste. Whether we concentrate on what has vanished or what is still here determines how we will frame our policies. The need to focus on what has disappeared also has a converse side in that people feel a need to produce cultural conformity and evenness. The restrictions expressed in the Immigration Act of 1924 were a policy devised to produce an "American culture" rather

quickly. The 1965 version of that law expressed an openness to cultural differences, made the act less restrictive, and opened the way for a great variety
of immigrants from many different cultures. Instead of conformity, current
policy seems destined to produce diversity. This challenges the assimilation-
ist/pluralist dialogue anew, and groups such as those of Hispanic origin are
going to be greatly affected by the outcomes of the dialogue.

THE HISTORIC ROLE OF IMMIGRANT CLERGY

Historically, most groups of people who have immigrated to the United
States have engaged in the development of a religious perspective, usually
derived from that already developed in their countries of origin. One of the
most important differences between Hispanics and the Europeans who preceded them had to do with the relative roles of the clergy. The Europeans'
clergy immigrated along with the people and provided "brokerage" services
between the immigrants and the mainstream society. Priests acted as political, social, and economic leaders as well as educators within the fragile new
communities. They provided answers on how best to gain access to the larger
society and how to reap the rewards of such access. The European immigrants built institutions parallel to those of mainstream society to provide
education and health care, and supported them, generally without subsidies
other than the tax exemptions granted to all such institutions. These efforts
provided a separate institutional base for the immigrants that served them
well during their period of transition. Strong-willed priest-leaders like Father
Vincent Barzynski (Parot, 1981) greatly influenced the ways in which immigrant communities related to mainstream society. The fundamental leadership role of the parish pastor has been described by several social scientists
specializing in the early twentieth-century immigrations (Tomasi, 1976;
Wrobel, 1979).

In contrast, Hispanic groups have few indigenous clergy who migrated
with their people. The clergy are frequently from the elite or privileged
classes in the society of origin and are often perceived as being parties to the
social and economic suppression experienced by the immigrants. These
clergy do not have the role of resource broker so common in the European
immigrant groups. As a result, although there are considerable resources in
the "parallel institutions" of the Catholic church, Hispanics are often unable
to use them, know about them, or sometimes even to be welcomed by them.
Instead, the Hispanics' historic relationship with organized religion, especially the Catholic church, has been somewhat strained.

The Catholic church, recognizing the serious problems it faces serving the
needs of its Hispanic members, has begun developing plans and dedicating
resources to address the issue of lack of clerical leadership. For example, in
the Archdiocese of Los Angeles, it is now virtually required for priests in
training to be bilingual. In recent years, the Archdiocese of Chicago has been

the seedbed for such movements as Movimiento Familiar Cristiano, Encuentro Matrimonila, and Comunidades de Base. The Archdiocese of Chicago has also started the Instituto Arquidiocesano Hispano de Catequesis to train lay catechists to work with people in small groups.

Unfortunately, this is all being done just as the most severe clergy shortages in modern history are besetting the Catholic church; however, the prospects for Protestant clergy are different. According to Father Allen Figueroa Deck of the Academy of Catholic Hispanic Theologians, there are 300 Hispanics training in Catholic seminaries and theological schools and 938 Hispanics in Protestant seminaries and theological schools. The current ratio of Hispanic seminarians to Hispanic Catholics is one seminarian for 35,383 people. The ratio for Protestants is one seminarian for 2,278 Hispanic Protestants. This fact is very likely to affect adversely the ability of U.S. Catholicism to serve small local Hispanic communities, which in turn is likely to increase the movement of Hispanics away from Catholicism toward Protestantism.

CULTURAL BEHAVIOR: RELIGIOUS PARTICIPATION AND BELIEFS

Accurate data regarding the religious practices and beliefs of the Hispanic population are difficult to come by for two reasons. First, most of the data concerning Hispanics is derived from the Census Bureau, which is prohibited by law from asking questions concerning religion; and second, too many researchers have felt that religion was a "given" for the Hispanic population—that it was not something that varied within the population. This stemmed from the stereotype that all Hispanics were Catholic and that all were relatively conservative in their attitudes and devout but noninstitutional in their religious practices. The available data, although thin, offer some insight and corrections regarding these impressions.

Even as far back as 1950, a significant proportion of Puerto Rican marriages in New York City were being performed in Protestant churches; by 1960, although there had been a decline caused in part by efforts by the Catholic archdiocese to evangelize more effectively, the proportion was still high. The figure for 1950 was 50 percent, and by 1960 it had declined to 38 percent, according to data analyzed by Fitzpatrick (1976). By the 1980s, most marriages involving Puerto Ricans in New York City were civil marriages (Dohen, 1982), with approximately 40 percent being performed away from any church and the remaining 60 percent about evenly divided between Catholic and Protestant churches.

Less than 15 percent of the Hispanic responders in the New York City study indicated that they felt marriage was a religious event. Only 14 percent said it was a "sacred thing," and less than 1 percent attached any real importance to being married by a priest (Doyle, 1982). Although a majority of respondents in this study identified themselves as Catholic (83 percent), it is not yet clear what these statistics may mean in terms of the religious identity of the next few generations of Hispanics. These figures concern Puerto Ricans and would be quite different for Mexicans, who are more closely connected to the Catholic church. However, the findings are of value precisely because they differ from the existing model, which contends that the link between Hispanics and the Catholic church is virtually unbreakable.

There has been an underlying theme in much of the writing about Hispanic religion, for both Puerto Ricans and Mexicans, concerning the role of folk religion in their lives. The New York City study contains the interesting finding that while folk religion is important for most Puerto Ricans, it is also strongly associated with institutional religion. Those who ranked high on the folk scale also ranked high on the institutional scale, and on both scales it was the Catholics who tended to be at the high end (Doyle, 1982).

As far as Mexican religious experiences and preferences are known, it appears that there has been a good deal of Protestant proselytizing among Mexicans, with the success of such activity varying from place to place (Grebler, Moore, and Guzmán, 1970). A study in Toledo, Ohio, found that being affiliated with the Catholic church ranked fourth among twenty attributes considered necessary to being a community leader (Soto, 1974). Previous studies have also indicated that Catholicism, unlike Protestantism, has been associated with upward mobility for Mexican-Americans (Peñalosa and McDonaugh, 1966). It is difficult to say whether this is changing; more research of this nature needs to be done. One indicator that affiliation with the Catholic church may still be preferred and may express an association with upward mobility is the fact that, during the early 1980s in Chicago, Hispanic candidates for the high-school and college-level seminary of the archdiocese presented themselves in increasing numbers almost every year (McCready, 1983). It does not appear, however, that this is resulting in more Hispanic ordinations. In addition, recent financial conditions in the Archdiocese of Chicago have been cited by church authorities as reasons to close the high-school seminary (of two) that was most heavily utilized by Hispanic and black students. It is reported that those students are unlikely to travel to the other seminary in the center of the archdiocese.

One of the connotations of *iglesias frias* is that the people cannot sense that their church belongs to them. While this is a problem for non-Hispanics, it is an even greater problem for Hispanic Catholics, who frequently feel that the churches of the European immigrants do not welcome them until hardly any descendants of the original immigrants remain. This obstacle to belonging does not exist in the smaller Pentecostal churches, where the warmth of the base community is immediately felt by new members. However, as we shall see in the section on social action and public policy, there are times when a large, albeit impersonal, institution can accomplish much more than a small base community.

HISPANIC ASSIMILATION AND CULTURAL PLURALISM

Although aged, a still apt description of pluralism can be found in the work of Horace Kallen (1944, p. 124):

> The American way is the way of orchestration. As in an orchestra, the different instruments, each with its own characteristic timbre and theme, contribute distinct and recognizable parts of the composition, so in the life and culture of a nation, the different regional ethnic, occupational, religious and other communities compound their different activities to make up the national spirit. The national spirit is constituted by this union of the different. It is sustained not by mutual exclusions, nor by the rule of one over others, but by the free trade between these different equals in every good thing the community's life and culture produce. This is the relation that the Constitution establishes between the States of the Union; this is the relation that develops between the regions within the States and the communities within the regions. In all directions there obtain . . . a mutual give and take in equal liberty on equal terms. The result is a strength and a richness in the arts and sciences which nations of a more homogeneous strain and an imposed culture . . . do not attain.

The policy implications of the dialogue are quite clear. Assimilation can be seen as a weakening of our social fabric, a denial of a source of strength, while pluralism, which reinforces our multicultural nature, can be defined as increasing our social spirit and deepening our resources.

The increased ethnic consciousness and awareness of recent years attest to the resilience of these identities in our society. It is a matter not simply of nostalgia, but rather of considerable importance, as to how people identify themselves vis-à-vis other citizens and the host culture. The legitimation of different identities, initiated by blacks during the 1960s, has been echoed by almost every other group in society. Just as blacks have become a powerful cultural force in society, other groups have begun to assess their own positions. People of Hispanic origin are particularly prepared to engage in a pluralistic lifestyle because of the strength of their own cultural identity. This is due in part to the intertwining of culture and religion in Hispanic life.

A challenge to the pluralistic model has recently been initiated not so much from the assimilationist perspective as from a neo-Marxian approach to the analysis of group behavior in society. Steinberg (1981) contends that ethnic identity persisting long past the point of immigration results from discrimination and social rejection rather than from an effort to preserve something of value. This approach contends that if it were not for oppression and domination by the larger society, ethnic groups, particularly blacks, would have long ago made it into the mainstream of U.S. society.

This perspective concentrates on the economic and status differences among groups and clearly has utility when one is attempting to analyze the differential opportunities that groups may or may not experience. It is not useful, however, when assessing the importance or relevance of those characteristics that groups maintain over time as part of their valued heritage. It is difficult to weave culture, achievement, and religion into one comprehensive understanding of group life, but unless such an integration is attempted, our policies and strategies will always be lacking one or more important and valuable characteristics. If we focus only on equalizing opportunity, as important as that is, we fail to encourage people to retain, as they advance socially and economically, that which ultimately makes their life valuable and worthwhile; this is true cultural deprivation. If, on the other hand, we stress cultural maintenance to the detriment of economic advancement, this can be a subtle form of discrimination and economic oppression.

The pluralistic perspective considers both types of opportunity as important and deserving of support. People should be able to advance socially and economically without having to give up their values and heritage if they do not wish to do so. For Hispanic groups in the United States, these are critically important issues. For these groups, the link between religion and culture is a potentially important one over which they ought to have the final say. A pluralistic perspective might well hold that how people want to define themselves is none of the host society's affair. If they want to maintain cultural enclaves or build parallel social structures, that is fine. If they want to combine their religion and culture into a unique lifestyle, that is also fine.

The essential policy question regarding the role of nonprofit organizations is how the cultural cost of achieving mainstream status can be kept as low as possible for Hispanic population groups. How can progress be made while heritage is preserved? Hispanics, because of their proximity to the sources of their culture, have more opportunity than most other groups to keep these costs low.

Contemporary society bears witness to the fact that religion, culture, and success are not necessarily incompatible. Hispanic religious practice is considerably different from that of most U.S. Catholics, a fact that causes deep concern on the part of many church officials (Doyle, 1982). However, the U.S. Catholic church has learned a great deal about celebrating from Hispanics. More generally, many urban communities are learning about new styles of community organization from Hispanics who are most comfortable with the personal, the informal, and the motivational, and who have adopted the base community techniques to urban environs. Voter education and registration projects have benefited from uniquely Hispanic characteristics in the Southwest, West, and Midwest.

Much of what has been done is due to the cultural "density" in Hispanic life that is supported by the intense connection between religion and culture. To deny this density or to attempt to exclude it from our consideration of planning and agenda setting would be to deny an aspect of Hispanic culture that is powerful, flexible, and socially useful, and that generates a great deal of motivation and inspiration for change and progress. In the final section of this chapter we discuss how the relationship between religion and culture helps shape the context for social change and policy formulation regarding Hispanics and mainstream society. The role of churches and other nonprofits in such areas as community organization, economic development, and education reform needs to be understood in light of this powerful relationship.

RELIGIOUS CULTURE AND SOCIAL CHANGE: CHURCHES, SECTS, AND COMMUNITIES

Organized religion has competition in relating to Hispanic immigrants and to those of Hispanic origin. Partly because many Hispanics have been in this country for decades without an indigenous clergy, the mainstream churches, based largely on the indigenous clergy model, have been losing ground among Hispanics to the smaller, more active sects. While this trend may provide more support for individuals in terms of spiritual warmth, it may also decrease the ability of the Hispanic community to address important policy needs.

St. Mathias Church in Huntington, California, is an example. It is a predominantly Mexican-American parish with an Irish-born pastor and about 5,000 families. During the immigration amnesty program, it registered 10,000 people. It waged a powerful lobby to increase the minimum wage in the state and to increase the number of housing units available for low-income people. Such collective action in support of social change cannot be done as effectively by the smaller, uncoordinated base communities of the pentecostal tradition. (There have been recent attempts on the part of the Pentecostals to address this by creating *concilios* or groups of base communities. However, there is no indication that these are organized toward specific social or political actions.)

The history of community organization in this country indicates that large religious institutions like mainstream churches can also provide protective umbrellas for small, community-oriented nonprofits. Without such protection, many community organizations that have been very instrumental in social change would never have survived. In effect, there is a partnership between the large and the small, the formal and the informal, that needs to be developed and nurtured. This state of affairs affects two concerns of Hispanics in the United States: education and health care.

Research has shown that Hispanic youngsters do very well in Catholic high schools even when they are from extremely disadvantaged homes (Greeley, 1982). The contemporary concern for educational reform has turned to local school boards and local control of schools as a partial solution to the problems of large public-school systems. The reason local schools worked well in the previous eras of immigration was that they interfaced with what

James S. Coleman and Thomas Hoffer have termed "functional communities" (Coleman and Hoffer, 1987, p. 7):

> The norms that pervaded the school were in part those dictated by the needs of youth themselves, but in part by those established by the adult community and enforced by the intergenerational contact that this closure brought about. This structural consistency between generations creates what can be described as a functional community, a community in which social norms and sanctions, including those that cross generations, arise out of the social structure itself, and both reinforce and perpetuate that structure.

Social services, in this context, are an extension of community identity partly because everyone shares a culture, an ethnicity, and a faith. When there is a dislocation between the culture that constructs the institutions and the one that now inhabits or uses them, the sense of ownership and participation begins to erode. This is particularly important now because Hispanics need the educational resources that large nonprofits, like churches, have to provide.

Health care is also a great need among Hispanics, and the churches already have considerable resources devoted to this area (Glaser, 1988). One of the problems with the available services is that many Hispanics do not know where they are or are uncomfortable in going to them. The church could be a leader in devising ways of presenting and delivering services that would reduce access problems. In the same vein, church schools have access to Hispanic homes that public schools do not. Therefore, it behooves these schools to devise ways of using that access for the benefit of the Hispanic population. While it is true that, in general, Hispanics are not exceptionally devout in an institutional sense—they are not very likely to be frequent mass attenders—they nonetheless value the church greatly and are comfortable in seeking it out for assistance. Because U.S. Catholics have focused on attendance at mass as a primary criterion for devotion and because their officials, usually from a European tradition, have supported them in this, it is likely that many Hispanic Catholics will be considered "less than devout." This would be a great mistake and a waste of valuable resources for both the church and the Hispanic people. One of the benefits of closely examining the connections between culture and religion, for the members of the official church, would be that they could thereby avoid this potential pitfall.

Because of the cultural density mentioned, earlier Hispanics are more likely than many other groups to form *cohesive communities,* and this tendency is badly needed in many urban areas. One of the only resources that poor urban communities have is their population. When ways can be found to use the latent skills within the populations, many areas can be organized and can begin to develop economically. Sometimes the first resource that surfaces is anger or frustration, but even those feelings can provide the fuel to generate effective organizations. Deep within many Hispanic communities is a strong commitment by individuals to each other produced partly by the blend of religion and culture. The commitment to the community can provide the initial spark for successfully developing and building self-sufficient and independently functioning neighborhoods. Part of the resistance to utilizing fully the religious dimension of community life comes from the way we educate our community organizers or from the way we select those to whom the host society will listen. This is not a plea for listening to every Hispanic spokesperson cloaked in religion, but rather an exhortation to take account of religion in the "secular" business of community development. Properly done, this can be a powerful tool in helping to rebuild many of our older cities' neighborhoods.

Finally, there is the issue of the *persistence of Hispanic identity,* which may not be as directly related to policy decisions as services or community development but that ultimately may be much more important. Without a sensitivity on the part of educators, service providers, and policymakers to the desire on the part of many Hispanics to raise their children in a Hispanic context, we will run the risk of wasting our future cultural resources and richness and polarizing our already badly polarized society even further.

Hispanics perhaps more than other groups are resisting the notion that being an American means having to be something other than what you are. Other immigrant groups had to deal with this notion; many paid what they now feel was too high a price for "becoming American." Our diversity is our strength and is as much a part of our society as is our commitment to freedom under law. Some groups have an extraordinary ability to preserve their heritage while entering the mainstream. Hispanics, partly because of the link between religion and culture, tend to be a group that transmits identity effectively. This is a rich cultural resource for our society and should not be abandoned or ignored.

CONCLUSION

Young people need to be able to develop their own identity, and if in the process they should also find themselves immersed in a rich cultural heritage, so much the better. Ultimately this strengthens our society by providing the diversity of experience that can allow us to emphatize with, communicate with, and relate to people from very different cultural backgrounds. In the contemporary world, this seems to be very much worth doing. The integration of religion and culture in the development of the social agenda, while easily overlooked, is fundamental to the implementation of that agenda.

The central role of churches and other nonprofit organizations in immigrant communities has traditionally been to elevate the immigrants' quality of life. Hispanics are unique in that they have had members in the United States for a long period of time and also because of the proximity of the countries of origin, which permits regular contact and the maintenance of ethnic identity. Parishes and other such agencies of formal organized religion may perceive local nonprofits as being competitive, and Hispanics may perceive that they are viewed as "outsiders" who do not really belong to the local community.

Unless nonprofits provide some of the resources and leadership to counter this cultural separation, the historically beneficial relationship between immigrants and nonprofit organizations will not work to the advantage of these particular groups. This would ultimately be a greater loss for the religious and other nonprofit institutions than for the Hispanic populations, because it will reduce the richness and diversity of experiences available to all. Our mainstream institutions need energy and regeneration of purpose, especially in terms of social change and delivery of resources to the poor and vulnerable. The strong religious–cultural resources of Hispanic functional communities are invaluable in this regard. Unless these relationships are nurtured and developed, these powerful resources may well be diluted to the detriment of the entire society.

7

Latino Nonprofit Organizations: Ethnic Diversity, Values, and Leadership

Margarita B. Melville

This chapter addresses three topics. First, it clarifies the need to recognize the ethnic, class, and racial diversity within the Latino population in the United States as it affects the formation and development of nonprofit organizations and their response to the needs of their constituents. Second, it analyzes the common value systems on which Latinos tend to pattern their social behavior. Finally, it discusses the leadership styles prevalent in Latino nonprofit organizations, with special attention to the leadership roles that Latina women fill in these organizations.

The identifying label *Latino* will be used interchangeably with *Hispanic*. The latter term is accepted as a label by many individuals and communities that have nothing in common other than their acceptance of this designation as connoting some special relationship of historical significance to Mother Spain. Their willingness to be so labeled may be a function of psychological factors or social identity—as those who would deny any inheritance of Native American blood—or of political expediency, when such a status conveys certain payoffs not available to non-Hispanic individuals. Or it may be mere passive acceptance of a name that has become generalized without adverting to its origins or significance.

WHAT'S IN A NAME?
Nonprofit organizations founded to serve Latinos use many labels to identify their primary or original clients. Some are designated by the name of a par-

ticular group, such as Mexican American Legal Defense and Educational Fund (MALDEF) and Puerto Rican Legal Defense and Education Fund (PRLDEF), while others use a more generic name such as National Council of La Raza, National Association of Hispanic CPAs, or Spanish Speaking Unity Council. Increasingly, these organizations, especially those that are national in scope, are attempting to address the needs of all Latinos. Nevertheless, in areas where a particular subgroup predominates, the names of organizations serving the community will most often refer to that particular subgroup.

The first point of clarification, and one that can become polemical but must nevertheless be faced, is the significance of the label Hispanic. It succeeds a series of unsatisfactory labels that have been applied to Spanish-speaking people in the United States since 1848. The basic reason for its inadequacy is that it groups people with distinct histories and cultural heritages under one conceptual umbrella that pretends historical and cultural uniformity. Their only commonality is that these peoples are considered ethnic minorities in the United States, suffering some form of discrimination as a result, and that the Spanish language is/was, at some point in time, part of their cultural heritage.

The term Hispanic technically refers to people from the Iberian Peninsula, although in the United States it refers primarily to their descendants of Latin American origin. Official use of the label Hispanic originated in the U.S. Congress with the National Hispanic Caucus, which introduced it in 1968. At the time, there was one Latino senator in office. He was one of only two Latinos who have ever served in the U.S. Senate. Both were from New Mexico, where the term Hispanic prevails. The Hispanic Congressional Caucus became a nonprofit organization in 1978. It currently has fourteen members, ten elected Latino representatives serving in the U.S. Congress, and four additional representatives who feel a close alliance.

Spanish colonists settled in New Mexico in the 1600s. When Mexico gained its independence from Spain in 1821, the inhabitants of this northernmost territory, who were far removed from the independence struggle, hardly had time or the inclination to adjust to their new identity as "Mexicans" before they became U.S. citizens through the Treaty of Guadalupe Hidalgo in 1848. The *manitos* of New Mexico have called themselves Hispanics ever since. Their influence in the Congressional Caucus led naturally to the choice of that particular label as embracing all Latinos (Melville, 1988).

The closest contender for an appropriate generalized label is Latino. Although it may not be used by federal agencies, the term Latino is prevalent in many communities and does not exclude the Indian and black components of Latino origins. In addition, educational institutions are beginning to use Chicano, Puerto Rican, and Latino as three distinct categories in order to identify the specific populations they are serving. When the League of

United Latin American Citizens (LULAC) was formed in 1929 in Texas, it chose "Latin American" as its label in order to mitigate the prevalent pejorative attitude toward people of Mexican descent. Its membership has been entirely Mexican-American until very recently when, in some cities, chapters have been formed with other Latinos.

"Spanish speaking" has been used as a label, and it still has some validity. However, in the effort to Americanize and bring this population into the mainstream, the majority of second, third, and subsequent generations have effectively become monolingual in English. Family ties, new immigrants, and proximity to the Mexican border keep the Spanish language alive in some families and communities, but many speak only "kitchen Spanish."

Yet the symbols, celebrations, and ethnic markers that can be used to promote the solidarity, self-esteem, and pride of a group become markers of differences among separate national groups that make up the so-called Hispanic population. In a survey of seventeen randomly selected San Francisco Bay Area nonprofit organizations, seven preferred to be called Hispanic, four were adamantly Chicano, two claimed to be Mexican-American, two chose Latino, one said it was *Raza,* and one expressed no interest in labels, claiming to be "all of the above." However, when asked if they celebrate cultural events with their membership, six said no, and only three said they celebrated one holiday that might be called universally Latino: El Dia de los Meurtos, a Catholic religious event; El Dia de la Raza, Columbus Day, but with emphasis on the *mestizo* character of Latin society; and Labor Day in Latin America, May 1, which is a commemoration of the death of labor leaders in Chicago and generally considered anti-American. Seven said they celebrate the Cinco de Mayo and six the Dieciseis de Septiembre, the two major Mexican national holidays, which is probably appropriate in an enclave where the largest percentage of the population is Mexican-American. In analyzing these results, it is evident that in this California setting, Mexican heritage predominates as a cultural identifier. A similar survey in New York State would have certainly pointed to Puerto Ricans as the predominant group, much as Florida would show Cubans as the predominant influence.

Differences among Hispanics that make problematic the use of one label include a mixed racial makeup, indicated by use of Jose Vasconcelos' term *the cosmic race.* Included within its purview are Europeans, blacks, Asians, Native Americans, and an ample mixture of all of these, especially the European–Native American component, referred to as *mestizos* and in some places *ladinos.* Miscegenation has been the rule. However, in some Latin American countries, one or another racial group predominates or at least dominates. Even in Mexico, where being a *mestizo* has been celebrated, intergroup conflict and inequality exists because of racial origins. Similar black–white attitudes are found in many countries bordering the Caribbean, such as Nicaragua, Costa Rica, Panama, and Colombia. People have brought these attitudes with them to the United States. The term Hispanic glosses over this racial blend and emphasizes the European component, the one that recalls conquest and domination. The label Latino, on the other hand, emphasizes the independence struggles of the nations of the American continent and the racial heterogeneity of their peoples.

Immigration status and political values also militate against unity when the population in question includes citizens by birth, citizens by naturalization, permanent residents, officially recognized political refugees, as well as undocumented immigrants of precarious status who are in the United States for a variety of political and economic reasons. Demographic studies demonstrate that the differences in population characteristics among these groups often exceed their similarities (Portes and Truelove, 1988, p. 34).

The cultural, racial, and political differences among the so-called Hispanic groups demonstrate the difficulty of establishing voluntary organizations designed to serve all such groups. Nation-specific foods, music, heroes, and history can hardly be used to enhance solidarity, pride, and common identity for a heterogenous population. In groups that are more sensitive to cultural diversity, a variety of music and foods from Mexico and the Caribbean is offered to help make their various members feel "at home."

LATINO CLASS DIFFERENCES AND ETHNICITY

Closely tied to attitudes of racial inequality are perceptions of class differences. Latin American society is rigidly stratified because of the feudal land tenure system imposed by the Spanish conquerors. With the exception of a few countries like Costa Rica and Uruguay, most Latin American countries have a history of the exploitation and enslavement of Indians, with the concomitant relationships of domination–subservience–rebellion. Some have a history of black slavery as well. The social personality types and prevalent values and attitudes generated by this history have their place today in the interclass relations among people of Latin American origin.

Latinos in the United States either come from rigidly class-stratified societies in Latin America or the Caribbean, or are descendants of people who come from such societies. Presumably, the more recent their arrival in the United States or the more intimate their contact with relatives still in native lands, the more conscious they are of their class status, whether this is lower, middle, or upper class. It is important to recognize that there are often profound antagonisms among such classes that labels like Latino and Hispanic cannot gloss over. Historical memory is often neither conscious nor rational. For example, individuals of Puerto Rican or Mexican origin have claimed to be Colombian or Argentinian in order to save themselves from being "put down" by Anglos and by Latinos from countries where the black or Indian component was not as large. These class differences and resulting antagonisms are sometimes severe enough to prevent Latino ethnic solidarity even in the face of Anglo indifference or hostility.

In this way, class differences help illuminate the concept of "ethnicity," including what we mean when we talk about "ethnic identity" and "ethnic pride." Ethnicity comes into play where two or more groups with different cultural histories interact. The interaction may be exploitative, competitive, complementary, conflictive, or a combination of these, producing reactions that intensify or reduce the differences between them (Melville, 1983). In order to maintain some degree of solidarity within a particular group, one or more aspects of the members' cultural or biological inheritance will be emphasized as a distinguishing characteristic. Such a diacritic might be language, religion, a cultural value, a celebration of shared history and origin, or even a biological characteristic preserved by endogamy. The particular element is not the important factor, but rather the similarity it emphasizes and solidarity it maintains. In fact, community celebrations are often rituals of solidarity that emphasize commonality and the sense of belonging.

Many social scientists consider ethnicity a sociopsychological necessity, much like nationalism, springing from the need of an individual or group living in a multicultural world to claim and justify one's historical identity or so-called roots. The classic Marxist position sees ethnicity (and "nationalism") as functions of class differences, exploited by the ruling class. A third position, one to which this author subscribes, sees ethnicity as a complex phenomenon or series of phenomena involving sociological (class and race), psychological (identity), and cultural (historical) variables, as these occur in a larger environment shared with one or more groups with differing cultural histories.

In other words, most social scientists see ethnicity as a function of both social and historical heterogeneity. The latter contributes nothing to ethnicity, and cultural differences do not of themselves result in ethnicity. Ethnicity results from the interaction of two or more distinct cultural groups who, for whatever reason, want to maintain their social distinctiveness. A *Mexicano,* as such, is not an "ethnic" in Mexico unless he or she is in constant contact with Anglos or other foreigners, contrasting his or her historical identity with that of such others. But *Mexicanos* are "ethnics" in the United States, until the time, at least, that they or their offspring want and are able to "pass" indistinguished into the majority society. This does not mean that there are no ethnics or ethnic populations in Mexico. The Mexican Indian relating to *mestizos* and the *mestizo* relating to Indians are both ethnics because of different cultural traits. They recognize and cultivate a concept of difference between them, a we/they ethnic dichotomy.

There are two important considerations to this dynamic interface. First, not all members of a particular group espouse the same type of ethnicity. This means, for example, that within an ethnic population, those who are merchants may see themselves in competition with merchants in the majority society. This we can label "competitive ethnicity." At the same time, low-ranking service workers such as domestics may accept their low social status and relate to members of the majority society with subservience, an example of what we might call "colonial ethnicity."

Second, these different types of interethnic relations are not static. At a given point in history, two ethnic groups may interrelate in one way, while at another time their interaction may be quite distinct. For example, after World War II, returning Mexican-American servicemen expected job treatment equal to that given to Anglo veterans. When members of the majority society continued their prewar patterns of discrimination, Mexican-American veterans reacted, organized, and began to work for improved civil rights. The GI Forum, a national nonprofit organization, is the most prominent of such groups, continuing this struggle even today. Its members shifted from a prewar colonial ethnicity to competitive ethnicity in military life and then to conflictive ethnicity as they sought an improved status in Anglo society. Today, GI Forum's members are again involved in competitive ethnicity, challenging the mainstream for equal participation.

Cuba and Central America illustrate how historical events shape interethnic as well as interclass relations. Cuba until 1959, Nicaragua until 1979, and other Central American countries even until today have had leaders in politics and commerce who have preferred to establish complementary relations with leaders in the United States to serve their personal interests while ignoring the well-being of their societies. This same phenomenon was noted by Kluckhohn and Strodbeck (1961) in their study of *jefes politicos* in New Mexico in the 1940s and 1950s. Such a lack of national and ethnic solidarity is part of the political culture of Latin America, a counterpoint to the strong cultural emphasis on familial solidarity and personal loyalty *(personalismo)*.

The successful revolutions in Cuba and Nicaragua overturned their ruling elites, many members of which, including professionals, left in disagreement with the revolutionary changes and have since become U.S. citizens. Because of their higher educational status, these Cuban and Nicaraguan emigres are sometimes seen to possess positions of leadership in an amorphous Hispanic population when they speak on foreign policy issues. In March 1986, for instance, six members of the Florida State Commission for Hispanic Affairs lobbied Congress in favor of President Reagan's military aid request for those trying to overthrow the Nicaraguan government (Garment, 1987) but said nothing about the fate of other Latino populations, such as Salvadoran and Guatemalan war refugees. Such class solidarity and class identity work against any concept of ethnic solidarity or ethnic identity that may be contained in the label Hispanic.

Ethnicity is a complex concept, and ethnic solidarity is an often fragile social principle. It can be trotted out at times to serve the political and economic purposes of a given segment of the ethnic population, sometimes at the expense of the rights and well-being of large percentages of that same ethnic population.

There are three points of pseudocommonality among the diverse components of the Latino population: the label Hispanic, which has been assigned by the majority society; the use of the Spanish language; and Latino values. The first, the appearance of Hispanic unity, is a perception of the mainstream Anglo society that, for reasons of its own, has labeled such a diverse population Hispanic. Such naming often leads to appropriation, albeit with reluctance. It creates a we/they dichotomy. It is important to note that Anglo negative stereotyping of anything Hispanic dates back to the war between England and Spain that saw Spain first as a threat and then as a defeated enemy, when the Spanish Armada was destroyed (Paredes, 1984). This most important factor promoting commonality is Anglo society's desire to simplify its policies and relationships with regard to the Latino population by utilizing one generalized label, whether it is for seventh-generation Mexican *manitos* from New Mexico, second-generation Cuban Americans, Puerto Ricans born on the island but living on the mainland, or newly arrived exiles from the violence in Central America.

A second point of commonality is a real or superficial acquaintance with the Spanish language. A common language is a very strong bond. It serves as an identifier and a powerful sign of commonality. It can also facilitate communication and enhance the we/they difference. Still, the Spanish language itself in some instances becomes an issue of contention. Sometimes people who speak "standard" Spanish will demean or look down on those whose English-language use and training have made them essentially monolingual with only a handicapped version of Spanish, and vice versa. Very few have had the opportunity to become truly bilingual in both written and oral standard language usage. For example, Southern hemisphere Spanish-language professors have been known to ridicule the undeveloped Spanish-language skills of Chicanos. National accents also serve as ethnic markers that emphasize differences.

The third point of commonality is an elusive one, that is, shared ideals and values that we might call Latino. These are explained later in the chapter.

When all is said and done, however, there may be a positive answer to the question regarding the existence of a single Latino population to be serviced by Latino nonprofits. People tend to group themselves according to their needs, their similarities, a common purpose, the need to establish *confianza* (mutual trust), whether or not Anglos try to simplify their dealings with them by labeling people of diverse national heritages with a single designation. This is precisely how a voluntary organization is formed. People decide who they are and what their needs are, and group themselves in whatever configuration they deem appropriate and necessary. The one concern that many at the bottom of the political and economic ladder have is that the use of a single label should not become the cover for further stratification, so that some suffer the double oppression of subordination by the mainstream as well as subordination by Latino individuals and subgroups that see themselves as superior and behave in a dominant fashion.

Nevertheless, I see danger in assigning the generalized title Hispanic to any national organization, whether it is nonprofit or any other, and taking its efforts and pronouncements as somehow representing the point of view or promoting the civic well-being of a generalized Latino population. The diversity must first be recognized and celebrated, and agreements must be formulated as to who the different Latino populations are and how they will work together. Such a united front could then adopt the label Latino or any other and go out to non-Latino groups or to the government and claim to represent the interests of their diverse populations, much as the negotiating process for formation of the European Economic Community has occurred. As of now, this recognition and process has hardly begun.

HISPANIC VALUES

Despite the diversity of Latino subgroups, there are some general, humanistic values that shape behavior patterns. The Latin American tradition inculcates certain ideals of social behavior based on honor and dignity, on the integral value of a person that puts more worth on one's spiritual makeup than on one's economic status, on personal confidence in certain persons, and on self-help justice. And perhaps one of the most basic of all Latino ideals is that it is one's family, primarily of origin but also the nuclear unit, that one must identify with and rely on for emotional and material support (Carlos, 1988, p. 96).

Let us take a look at what these Latino values are and how broadly they are found among the various Latino subgroups. Most studies of Latino values have been done about people in Latin America itself (e.g., Freyre, 1946; Paz, 1963; Ramos, 1962; Wolf and Hansen, 1972; Whyte and Holmberg, 1956). In the United States, studies of Latino values have been specifically about people of Mexican origin. It might be said that Oscar Lewis also wrote about Puerto Ricans in *La Vida* (1966), although it is not specifically a study of values. Most studies have tended to polarize values into a traditional versus modern dichotomy, claiming that Latinos need to assimilate Anglo customs in order to be capable of living effectively in today's society.

Generally, Latinos are said to be profamily, pro-God, and procountry. More analytically oriented (although not necessarily more valid) observations made by Anglos contrast such values as Latino authoritarianism versus Anglo egalitarianism, Latino present-time orientation versus Anglo future-time orientation, Latino fatalism versus Anglo feelings of control over nature, Latino "being" as opposed to Anglo "doing," Latino religion and recreation as opposed to Anglo technology and business, and Latino personalism versus Anglo group orientation (Kluckhohn and Strodbeck, 1961).

The pejorative lens with which these values is viewed is noticeable when they are compared with a similar list made by a Chicano author: Chicano particularism and friendship versus Anglo universalism and society, Chicano spiritualism versus Anglo materialism, Chicano love of life versus Anglo competitiveness, Chicano experience of life as it is versus Anglo future apprehension (Martinez, 1971).

The argument has been made that the Hispanic values listed above are not properly Hispanic at all but are those of an economically disadvantaged class (Liebow, 1967, p. 213). Fatalism, personalism, and religiosity are all values that have been documented repeatedly as pertaining to economically marginalized people.

Peasants, rural dwellers, and others coming from a traditional, barely industrialized, agricultural society have also been observed to possess a constellation of values similar to those attributed to Latinos that necessarily go hand in hand with living off the land and depending on the vagaries of unpredictable weather patterns for economic survival. Such values include lineality and authoritarianism as well as male dominance (emanating from patrilineality and patriarchy), values that are imbedded in the need for land control and the ability to pass it on with unambiguous rights from one generation to the next. A feeling of subjugation by nature, fatalism, and spirituality are also classic values associated with an agricultural culture. Such values are found among agricultural peoples around the globe and across the centuries, and are not particular to Latinos. As might be expected, the more urbanized any group of Latinos might be, the less likely they are to reflect such values.

In other words, when Strodbeck and Kluckhohn and other Anglo observers of Latino populations attribute the foregoing series of values to Latinos and distinguish them from Anglo values, they are mistakenly contrasting agricultural values with industrial values and confusing class characteristics with ethnic characteristics.

When *familism* is held up as a value of primary importance among Latinos, another type of misconception is often at work. Familism among Anglos refers to an individual's love of and devotion to his or her spouse and children (family of procreation or nuclear family), with love for one's family of origin in a distant second place. Familism among Latinos and others from societies that have not felt the atomizing impact of industrialization and the geographical mobility that such an economy demands is primarily a love of and devotion to one's family of origin, to one's mother and father, sisters and brothers, grandparents, uncles, aunts, and cousins, with secondary loyalty required for one's relations by marriage, including spouse and in-laws. This derives from the need to unambiguously define land rights from one generation to the next, a sine qua non of agricultural cultures.

What is called *personalismo,* or the sanctity attributed to personal relationships and the obligation of loyalty that they demand, is an essential characteristic of Latino society in general, as it is of agricultural and just barely industrialized societies. Two such relationships stand out as fundamental in Latino society: *compadrazgo* and *patronismo*.

The system of co-parenthood, *compadres* and *comadres,* serves to extend family relations and loyalty to a larger pool of individuals who are not kin but who become quasi-kin as a result of participating in the children's baptism or other rituals. The relationship of loyalty and trust is established between parent and godparent rather than between godparent and child. The selection of individuals to serve in this capacity is carefully made. Such service establishes a relation of trust and mutual obligation that cannot be lightly offered or accepted.

Second only to family and *compadrazgo* ties, patron–client relationships are a key to social organization and arose from the starkly stratified society of Latin America. The tie between a client and a patron is essentially a relationship between two people of unequal wealth and power. The informal compact between them is that the one with greater wealth and power helps and protects the poorer; the latter, in turn, offers loyalty and support. The implications of this informal but important relationship is illustrated by the fact that in the early days of farm-worker organization in California, workers had to be organized so that workers from one farm were exchanged with those of another to serve on the picket line. This was so that the pickets at any given ranch were workers from another ranch and therefore did not have to face or offend their own patron, to whom they had a sense of loyalty, regardless of the adverse working conditions to which they were subjected.

Is it not, therefore, a somewhat futile exercise to talk about the role of Latino nonprofit organizations in reflecting and shaping Hispanic values, as if these values were found all across the spectrum of groups labeled Hispanic? There is much talk about "traditional Hispanic values" in the political arena, as both Democrats and Republicans attempt to demonstrate that they are in tune with such values so that they can thereby capture the Hispanic vote. Such values as "God" and "family" are generally considered to be "conservative," so that Republicans believe that Latinos are their natural constituency; Democrats take note of the low economic status of the majority of Latinos and appeal to these economically depressed peoples as natural allies of their party.

ETHNIC MINORITY LEADERSHIP

The quality and style of ethnic minority leadership that emerges reflects a style that borrows from the values of an ethnic heritage as well as responding to the demands of the mainstream society. If we understand leadership as the ability to accomplish a goal through the mobilization of human assistants, it is obvious that leaders are more than spokespersons. The ability to lead others toward a goal and inspire their work and commitment to contribute to the group's welfare constitute a leader's essential characteristics.

Three types of ethnic minority leaders can be identified: brokers, advocates, and token-leaders. Broker-leaders are individuals whose main goal is to prepare and promote the acceptance of minority group members in the majority society. They educate people about their rights, and they provide training and skills development. They often serve as unofficial representatives of the community and form organizations to further the community's goals. LULAC is one such organization. But such leaders and the organizations they sponsor function with a greal deal of internal tension. As Arce (1978) noted in his article on Chicanos in academia, one is a leader in a minority ethnic community by first being faithful to ethnic ideals and ethnic solidarity. When such a leader attempts to promote mainstream participation, he or she does so by teaching mainstream skills and values, thereby weakening minority ethnic ideals and creating a degree of cognitive and psychological tension within him- or herself. The source of such tension may be ignored by broker-leaders and broker-nonprofits serving the ethnic minority community, with the tension often remaining unresolved. Other examples of broker organizations include Adelante in Berkeley, California, the goal of which is to increase the capacity of Latinos to gain initial employment, and the Instituto Laboral de la Raza in San Francisco/Oakland, California, whose goal is effective union participation and leadership training for Latinos.

Advocate-leaders are individuals who recognize the unequal distribution of legal and social services to the minority community and create movements designed to seek redress. They attempt to secure for their community those services that mainstream society has put beyond their reach, without sacrificing emphasis on ethnic identity. The United Farm Workers Union is one such organization. MALDEF, another example, provides legal services and initiates class action suits to demand legal and constitutional rights that are denied the Chicano community by Anglo society. La Clinica de la Raza in Oakland, California, and the Galeria de la Raza in San Francisco are two other examples of advocacy-service organizations. One provides health services in a setting and manner appropriate for the Latino community. The other exhibits the works of upcoming and established Latino artists who promote ethnic identity and serve the esthetic needs of the Latino community.

Token-leaders are not leaders in the strict sense of the word as I described earlier, although they may become such. These are individuals selected as minority representatives, not by their peers but by authorities from the majority society. They can, given their positions in the majority power structure, divert resources toward their minority communities and enhance the understanding and acceptance of their groups by the majority society, thereby becoming broker-leaders. However, they will experience the tension of two loyalties. One loyalty is toward those who selected them to serve as token-leaders to assuage the demands of Latinos for representation or to serve as translators of the behaviors, desires, and needs of the Latino communities. The other loyalty is to their communities of origin, which did not actively select them to be its representatives. Such token-leaders often feel greater loyalty to those who named them to their quasi-representative positions of pseudoleadership than to those from whose ranks they were selected. Some of these individuals have risen in administrative ranks, with or without credentials, and are able to function effectively insofar as the majority society is concerned but have neither represented nor advocated for the Latino community. Some token-leaders go on to praise the system that allows "even Chicana women" or "Hispanic men" to get to the top by working hard and competing.

Nonprofit organizations, like individuals, manifest two of the three foregoing attributes: they are either advocate-service organizations or broker organizations. Few, if any, nonprofits would seem to fill the role of token-leadership, probably because organizations tend to take on lives of their own in ways that individuals do not and, therefore, are difficult to manipulate. Individuals continue to serve as tokens of progress and equality while remaining relatively easy to manipulate.

ORIENTATION AND OBJECTIVES OF SELECTED BAY AREA LATINO NONPROFITS

In order to assess the leadership formation potential of nonprofits, a randomly selected group of seventeen of these organizations in the San Francisco Bay Area were questioned about what they felt their institution did best: promote cultural heritage, provide services, enhance mainstream participation, or form coalitions with other groups. Although the results of the investigation cannot be generalized to the universe of U.S. Latino nonprofits, they do provide an initial reading of the orientation and objectives of those found in northern California.

To the request that they identify the first and second goals of their organization, they answered as follows:

	Ranked first	Ranked second
Provide services	8	5
Facilitate mainstream participation	6	2
Promote cultural heritage	3	2
Form coalitions	0	3

The priority given to the role of service-provider is evident. This reflects the perception of minority groups that their needs are not well served by mainstream agencies. Their inferior status in society is clearly felt and their need for self-help initiatives is primary.

Nine of the seventeen nonprofits have some type of leadership training, although for most it is indirect. Those that have no such training are the health service agencies, the professional groups, and the club for the elderly. But in all of them it is participation itself in the organization and management of the group that promotes training and incentive for leadership in activities involving mainstream society.

As with ethnicity, both types of organizations and their leaders exist in a proactive/reactive relationship with the majority society. One or the other type will predominate at a particular time and in a particular place in response to the needs of a particular segment of the Latino population. These organizations existed before the federal or state governments took notice of them, and they will continue to rise and fall in the future in response to the community's felt needs whether Anglo society supports, ignores, or opposes them.

Internal cohesion in nonprofits that embrace Latinos from different national origins is promoted by what we may refer to as the principle of "segmentary opposition." This principle, generally applied to political units formed on the basis of kinship, may also be expressed by the old Arab adage, "The enemy of my enemy is my friend." It simply means that subgroups of relative social or cultural proximity coalesce in the face of pressures emanating from more distant groups, forming a united front as a mutual defense, so that an external threat overcomes what is until then considered internal division. Latinos whose historical heritage produces distinct national, cultural, racial, and class entities can cooperate within U.S. society even when particular subgroups have experienced strained or hostile interaction among themselves, but only if their need for cohesion in the face of opposition is felt strongly enough to overcome their differences.

LATINA WOMEN, VALUES, AND LEADERSHIP IN NONPROFIT ORGANIZATIONS

The social organization of Latino society has promoted gender-specific tasks and behavior patterns. It has very strong adages regarding what is appropriate in female and male behavior, with very distinct demarcation between them. However, these norms have been changing in Latin America and in the United States, with the consequent gaps between generations.

The concept of *machismo,* as male sexist behavior, has been touted as the cause of the oppression of Latina women. More correctly, it is the paternalism that was based on an authoritarian agricultural system that maintained women as dependent daughters and wives. This system gave men an authoritative position and women a dependent, subordinate one. The traditional, ideal gender-related role distribution, whereby the man was expected to earn a living and the woman was expected to bear the children and manage the household, has been recognizably modified in recent years. Latinas have always worked, but those in the upper-middle and upper classes were traditionally exempted because upper-level incomes from land ownership or entrepreneurial enterprises were such that single individuals (almost exclusively males) were self-sufficient enough to support a family in relative luxury. Today, women's participation in the work force has become accepted in all social classes except, perhaps, among the very wealthy. Upper-middle-, middle-, and working-class women have effectively become men's economic partners in a society where two wage earners are necessary for traditional family lifestyles. This partnership is changing sexist attitudes, but the norm that men are in charge and women are to serve is still prevalent in most group or organizational behaviors. In Latino societies, the ideal of traditional gender-role division and authority lines still exists, although it is gradually being modified.

Women participate in greater numbers than men in health-related and social-service agencies. When they become the service providers, they develop experience and leadership qualities. When women who have had opportunities for higher education participate in nonprofits that require entrepreneurial or professional experience, they readily become leaders.

Higher education, especially graduate education, has also contributed to Latina women's leadership capabilities and opportunities. It has given them visibility, experience, and the self-assurance to speak and organize. Their numbers in undergraduate programs are now more or less on a par with Latino men. But the women are fewer than the men in graduate programs, and the ratio of those who receive degrees is 1:2.

Graduate education is particularly difficult for women. When a family has limited financial resources and choices have to be made, it is still an accepted notion that the men in the family should be given the chance for higher education. The women, after all, "are going to get married and don't need it." If a family has never sent members to college, it is very difficult to break that tradition and risk sending their daughters away to school, to an unknown and probably hostile environment.

Expected familial roles take a toll on women's time and availability for participation in nonprofits other than as clients. In those segments of society where education and work roles have changed the position of Latina women, it is evident that they are actively participating in greater numbers in nonprofits. Active participation is producing leaders to the degree that in several major organizations, specifically MALDEF and LULAC, women are the elected or hired directors and managers in local, regional, or national positions. Several women have gone on to mainstream leadership positions from their positions in voluntary organizations. The opportunity to function as local leaders has given these women the experience and visibility to assume such leadership positions. The number of women leaders in the Latino community seems to have increased in direct proportion to their active participation in nonprofits.

In the seventeen organizations surveyed, women's participation ranged from 40 percent to 60 percent. Exceptions were to be expected: In health services, they were most numerous; in drug-related services, they were less so; in the medical professional association, they were 20 percent; and in the club for the elderly, they were 75 percent. Unexpectedly, the local branch of IMAGE, whose purpose is to promote full employment, reported only a 10-percent female membership. Although no organization surveyed claimed to be doing outreach toward women, all but one were effectively incorporating women in response to women's interests and demands.

CONCLUSION

The major issue in this chapter has been the lack of significant analytic and functional value of treating all so-called Hispanics as a single ethnic group. Mexican-American or Chicano organizations predominate in the United States because of their historical and numerical positions, and they use their own cultural symbols to promote a sense of pride and belonging. However, many Chicano and Puerto Rican nonprofits that function in barrios and communities where other Latinos live have successfully opened their doors to a diverse clientele without friction—though the clientele generally belongs to a single class, whether middle or working class. The interests of such minorities that are discriminated against are not served when they are lumped together on the basis of supposed similarity of cultural traditions with wealthy groups or individuals—who are often the discriminators and exploiters.

8

The Management of Hispanic Nonprofit Organizations

Maria Gonzalez Borrero

INTRODUCTION

The 1990s will pose many challenges for Hispanic nonprofit organizations, the biggest of which is that of meeting the needs of an impoverished community in an era of diminishing resources and pressure to diversify funding bases. During the 1980s, institutional funders targeted only about 2 percent of their annual giving to Hispanic organizations and issues (*Hispanics in Philanthropy*, 1989). It is estimated that by 1999, the Hispanic population will have increased by 50 percent and will still be among the most socioeconomically disadvantaged groups in U.S. society, with inordinately high rates of poverty, unemployment, teen pregnancy, drug abuse, and AIDS.

Hispanic nonprofit organizations, like most nonprofits in this country, grew because government and other institutions were not able to meet the needs of poor, multiproblem families, the disenfranchised, or the newcomer. Hispanic nonprofits have often been the only voice of Hispanics in policy matters.

As part of the effort to "do more with less," this chapter focuses on the management and leadership of Hispanic nonprofits, pointing out some of the challenges that Hispanics face in managing their organizations and the actions that need to be taken if the groups are to survive the next decade. The chapter deals with four separate but related issues: the unique issues and contradictions that surround Hispanic nonprofits and affect all attempts to develop and implement effective and efficient management processes, organizational models and administrative issues in Hispanic nonprofits, governance issues and dilemmas surrounding the functioning of boards of directors of community-based Hispanic nonprofits, and the complexities of leadership and leadership training in these organizations.

Most of the observations and analysis offered in this chapter are derived from personal experience. I have ten years' experience as the founder and executive director of a Hispanic nonprofit organization. I am and have been a board member of local, national, and international organizations, and I am also a trustee of a large community foundation. This kind of personal reflection may be useful at this still "anecdotal data" stage of the study of Hispanic nonprofits. The Hispanic nonprofit movement in the United States is relatively young; little attention has been given to the similarities and differences between Hispanic and non-Hispanic nonprofits, and these reflections could help pave the way for the more systematic research (both basic and applied) that is needed in the future.

There are differences between Hispanic and non-Hispanic nonprofit organizations, but the differences may be more in the areas of funding and community involvement than in historical development. A speaker at the 1989 Council on Foundations meeting noted that 75 percent of nonprofit organizations in this country are less than twenty years old and that, in Minnesota, about half of the nonprofits (excluding higher education and hospitals) have annual budgets of less than $163,000. It was further stated that nonprofits in this country have "weak and immature infrastructures, they don't have policies, rules, systems and technology which ultimately are going to be required if they are to be long-lasting, successful, productive organizations." This particular speaker was encouraging the audience of foundation staff and trustees to support technology and strategic planning in nonprofits, to fund organizations and not just projects. It was further claimed that "there is tremendous cynicism about the work of nonprofit organizations, that money has been dumped for the last 20 years and not only have we not solved the problems but we have more" (Council on Foundations, 1989). Participants agreed that nonprofits must have strong organizational structures, supportive and active policymakers, and visionary leaders to survive and be productive.

HISPANIC NONPROFITS: UNIQUE ISSUES AND CONTRADICTIONS

Hispanic and traditional nonprofit organizations have more in common than is generally acknowledged. The differences may be more in the focuses and approaches of the organizations than in their management ability. Unlike other, more traditional and well-established philanthropic organizations, community-based Hispanic nonprofits have rarely been able to be single focused in their approach to needs and problems. While most nonprofits are multiservice in focus, Hispanic nonprofits exhibit this characteristic to a much higher degree, because of the availability of such organizations for Hispanic neighborhoods, and the limited resources and tremendous poverty in the community.

Although on a national and state level, Hispanic nonprofits tend to be more singular in focus—oriented toward either policy (e.g., immigration, discrimination), problem (e.g., housing, education), or group (e.g., Mexican, Cuban, Puerto Rican)—on the community level, on the level most directly and immediately accessible to the people, these groups (often regardless of their mandate, source of funding, or even, at times, their own desires) almost invariably get drawn into the position of providing direct services as well as advocating for social change.

Put somewhat differently, the levels of need and pain in many communities make it difficult to maintain the kind of detachment and singleness of purpose required to fulfill narrow missions and/or circumscribed agendas. Policy- and research-oriented nonprofits cannot avoid the human consequences of the problems they are investigating; advocacy-oriented nonprofits cannot "turn off" and "turn away" from the needs of community residents, and service-oriented nonprofits cannot continue to treat "victims" without beginning to question, organize, and advocate around issues more directly related to the "sources of victimization."

In all of these instances, the nonprofit agency finds itself in the unique situation of continually having to modify either short- or long-term goals, of often having to face problems in which trade-offs become commonplace, and of rarely having the opportunity to marshal and target all of its available resources on a single objective.

In recent years, there has been an attempt to reduce the "shotgun" orientation of many local nonprofits, to help them deal with the impact of policy decisions on the local level. Many such organizations are conducting research, testing intervention models, developing policy recommendations, and becoming more engaged in advocacy. Nevertheless, the combination of immediate needs and chronic resource limitations makes it virtually impossible for these groups to pursue focused agendas singlemindedly or comfortably.

Working in communities with multiple, ongoing needs and being unable or unwilling to refrain from responding to these needs create enormous management problems for the leaders and staffs of local Hispanic nonprofits. Limited resources must be continually reallocated to respond to direct service, research, and advocacy needs. Staffs must be trained as "creative generalists" rather than "unidimensional specialists." The time frames within which specific tasks are to be accomplished change with each new community crisis. Often tension pervades the organization, and uncertainty replaces calm. At times this tension leads to creative thinking and action, but at other times the stress becomes frightening and almost immobilizing. In both cases, the management problems are unique, and there are precious few guidelines, let alone "solutions," to be found. Clearly, Hispanic nonprofits, particularly human service organizations, must respond to the problems confronting their communities; that is the reason for their existence. It is also clear that their responses must be twofold: easing the pain of those who are hurting; and addressing the institutional, social, economic, and political causes of that pain. What is far less clear is how to manage, on a day-to-day basis, an organization whose existence is defined by the tightrope of continually serving two such demanding masters.

For example, a mental health research and demonstration project that focused on the response of police and hospital emergency rooms to mental health crises of Puerto Rican families both collected data and engaged in advocacy for changes in the police departments and hospitals. However, the project involved Puerto Rican families with real mental health crises, and the project staff became advocates, social workers, and sources of support for the families. Often the staff found it hard to focus on the research agenda; they had to respond to the needs of the families while completing the research. They worked longer hours to meet both priorities. Traditional research- and policy-oriented nonprofits do not get involved in solving the problems of their subjects. Hispanic policy and research nonprofits often have nowhere to refer people in need and thus find themselves having to address the immediate problems.

Hispanic nonprofit organizations, unlike traditional nonprofits, serve a population that is quite diverse. A large percentage of this population is monolingual, Spanish-speaking, and lives within a Hispanic cultural context. Another portion of the community is bilingual. A small percentage is monolingual and English-speaking but lives within households and communities whose cultural environment is Hispanic (Mexican, Puerto Rican, Cuban, etc.). Except for the settlement houses that served the European immigrants, traditional nonprofits have not faced such diversity. Hispanic nonprofits by necessity must have multilingual/multicultural staff prepared to meet the needs of this diverse population.

Perhaps the biggest challenge for Hispanic nonprofits is to balance direct service and institutional change while improving the management and internal operations of the organization.

HISPANIC NONPROFITS: ORGANIZATION AND ADMINISTRATION

Hispanic nonprofits often display clear distrust for firm and fixed administrative structures and organizational strategies. This is not unique to Hispanic nonprofits (Miringoff, 1980). Indeed, like so many other nonprofits in this country, Hispanic nonprofits have no unified concept of human service administration. Miringoff (1980, p. 9) explains, "One reason is that in the United States, the existing concepts of 'organization' or 'administration' have evolved separately from social welfare and human services provision and are drawn mostly from the world and theory of business." Nonprofits, rooted as they are in the dynamics and contradictions of community life, generally require a degree of organizational flexibility and openness seen as alien (or, more likely, disruptive) in business. This may be particularly true of Hispanic nonprofits, which, for both ideological and practical reasons, have resisted developing strong management and organizational systems for fear of becoming too bureaucratic. Bureaucracy is seen as a major constraint that reduces the ability of the service provider to make decisions quickly and allocate resources effectively. Bureaucratic administrative systems are seen as serving the interests of the organization rather than those of the client or community.

The ideological resistance of Hispanic nonprofits to the "temptations of bureaucracy" rests on an arguably firm set of assumptions. The most important of these assumptions is that, in the long run, agencies mandated to improve the human condition must themselves become living models of the kind of environment that maximizes the possibilities of inclusion, justice, and equity. It doesn't have to be a complicated bureaucracy, but the organization needs rules, procedures, and a structure that both staff and board understand. Perhaps nonprofits can learn some lessons from management theories in the business and industry sectors. In 1916, Henri Fayol, a French engineer, published an article outlining the functions of management: to plan, organize, direct, coordinate, and control. Since then, management theories have gone through several stages of development and changes. Since the early 1900s, there have been four major stages of management theory development (Scott, 1978). The four stages are each characterized as being either closed- or open-system (depending on whether the theory focuses on the internal dynamics of the organization or also on the external environment and its impact on the organization), or rational (clear goals and straightforward decisions) versus social (decisions are value chosen and not mechanical). Until 1960 the management theorists focused on the internal organization, and, for the most part, "they did not worry about the environment, competition, the marketplace, or anything external to the organization" (Peters and Waterman, 1982, p. 91). Max Weber and Frederick Taylor in the early 1900s presented the view that bureaucracy—order by rule—is the most efficient form of human organization. Taylor's "scientific management" was the first to call attention to people in the work situation as important factors in the quest for efficiency. Basically, the Taylor–Weber theory was that rules and techniques dealing with the breakdown of the work, coupled with defined spans of control, clear lines of authority, and matching responsibility, would solve the problem of managing groups of people.

The next stage in the development of management theory turned away from the "span of control theory" to focus on the human side of the organization. Major theorists in this stage included Elton Mayo, Douglas McGregor, Chester Barnard, and Philip Selznick. Each of them looked at the "human element" or, as Peters and Waterman called it, the "social actors" in the scheme of management in an organization. In the famous Hawthorne experiments, Mayo carried out a series of studies that found when attention is paid to workers, there is a direct effect on their productivity. McGregor, in his book, *The Human Side of Enterprise* (1960), described his "Theory X" and "Theory Y." The first outlined a series of assumptions that said that the worker was basically lazy, lacked ambition, disliked responsibility, is not very bright, did not have a commitment to the organization, and was resistant to change. In contrast, Theory Y contended that most people enjoy work, that there are other reasons for working besides money, that most people are capable of controlling their own work, that employees will accept and seek responsibility, and that most workers want friendly, supportive relationships.

Stage three began in 1960 and lasted about ten years. It was in this stage that theorists began to look at companies as part of an environment that was competitive and was molded by outside forces. Alfred Chandler, in *Strategy and Structure*, stated that organizational structures are driven by changing pressures in the marketplace. The theoretical work conducted in this stage emphasized that organizations were powerfully affected by what happened outside the company.

The final stage saw the development of a management theory based on the "open system–social actor." This theory looks at both the worker and the organization as crucial players. It emphasizes informality, individual entrepreneurship, and evolution. Karl Weick and James March are two leaders in the development of these theories. This line of thought focuses on the "culture of the organization"—what are the dominant values—and the continual evolution of organizations. These theories also put a greater emphasis on the manager as leader, with the vision necessary to move the organization forward.

How do these theories relate to the management of Hispanic nonprofits? First, many funding sources have members of the corporate community making decisions about grants to nonprofits, and the managerial framework of these corporate members leads them to expect nonprofits to have similar frameworks. Second, the paucity of literature on nonprofit management makes it necessary for nonprofits to turn to these models. Research on management models in Hispanic nonprofits would add to the literature and might assist leadership development in the business sector. Hispanic nonprofits may be more "people oriented," and they have been greatly influenced by visionary leaders.

All Hispanic nonprofits spend considerable time dealing with the fundamentals of organization and administration, including fiscal control, resource development, personnel policies and practices, program management and evaluation, staff development, and community relations. Few Hispanic nonprofits, however, have been able to develop alternatives to traditional bureaucracies. In fact, these organizations have changed their overall views of the role and importance of administration and organization. Executives of Hispanic nonprofits have come to realize that sound administrative procedures and systems can indeed facilitate the provision of effective and efficient services.

Sound organizational practices can support decision making, policy development, and the acquisition of new resources. Also, Hispanic nonprofits need to develop and systematically evaluate their managerial structures. Many nonprofits that begin with small budgets give little thought to managerial structures. An organization begins with a small grant, hires staff, and assumes that everyone on staff will do a little bit of everything. Similar concepts in the business world are "flat structure" and "participatory management." While participatory management refers to input in decision making and flat structure refers to minimizing decision-making levels, they are similar in that decisions are made by group process as opposed to one individual.

For example, as the founding executive director, I generated all the financial reports. The organization could afford only a bookkeeper, and that person did not have the skills to put together these reports. I learned by trial and error how to calculate such things as indirect costs in proposals for federal grants. Even though the organization grew significantly, and we were able to hire qualified fiscal staff, I continued to carry out these functions, not only because I had become good at them but also because we weren't clear on the functions of each member of the administrative staff. What I learned from this experience was that nonprofits need to review periodically the managerial structure and make necessary changes and adjustments.

One model puts the executive director in charge of both "inside" and "outside" activities. A layer of managers/supervisors responsible for various management functions reports to the executive director. For example, one person is responsible for fiscal activities, one for personnel, one for programs and program development, and perhaps one for information systems. An advantage of this model is that the director has a large measure of control. A disadvantage is that the director has less time to do both inside and outside work equally well, with the result that one will get less attention.

Another model that needs to be studied is what I call the "inside–outside" team. In this model, the executive director is the "outside person" responsible for leading the organization by securing resources and funds, working with the board of directors and guiding it in policy formulation, staying in touch with the community to be served and playing a role in the Hispanic community as agendas get developed, working with the broader community (public relations), and becoming informed on new developments in the field.

The "inside person" is responsible for overseeing managerial functions, such as fiscal operations, personnel, ensuring that resources are distributed internally, training supervisory/managerial staff, and program development and evaluation.

The problem with this model is that the roles of the inside and outside persons may get confusing. These two persons must work as a team and have good communication, but the lines of authority are not clearly drawn. Ultimately, the executive director makes all decisions whatever model is adopted. The inside person needs to understand this and be able to function within that framework.

The inside person is the manager, and the executive director is the leader. Current managerial theories—such as those of Peters and Waterman, Warren Bennis, Burt Nanus, Peter Vail, Rosabeth Moss Kanter, and John Gardner—all talk about managers as leaders and challenge the corporate United States to demand leadership from their managers. As Bennis and Nanus (1985, p. 20) put it:

> A business short on capital can borrow money, and one with a poor location can move. But a business short on leadership has little chance for survival. . . . Leadership is what gives an organization its vision and its ability to translate that vision into reality. Without this translation, a transaction between leaders and followers, there is no organizational heartbeat. . . . "To manage" means "to bring about, to accomplish, to have charge of or responsibility for, to conduct." "Leading" is "influencing, guiding in direction, course action, opinion." The distinction is crucial. Managers are people who do things right and leaders are people who do the right thing.

Nonprofits are often founded on visionary leadership. The visions and dreams of some person or persons get a nonprofit organization going. That leadership often determines its survival and success. As we have seen, most nonprofits have very small budgets. It is not strong managerial structures that have kept them alive—it is the commitment of the leadership. Nonprofits should have good, strong managerial structures, but one should not be sacrificed for the other. Managerial theories have been moving in the direction of visionary leadership over the last 60 years.

In nonprofits it is the leadership that secures funding and resources. When the organization that I was director of submitted proposals to a new funding source, the first thing the funder wanted to do was meet the director. Now, as a trustee of a community foundation that makes grants to nonprofits, I understand fully the need to know the director and feel that the director is clearly a leader. A leader in an organizational setting makes things happen, both within the organization and in the community the organization serves.

Hispanic nonprofits, for the most part, have had visionary leaders. These organizations have received the least amount of funding of any group of nonprofits in this country, whether governmental, foundation, or corporate funding. It takes leadership to be able to survive and grow despite very limited resources.

The situation confronting Hispanic nonprofits is reasonably easy to define. We cannot avoid the implications and consequences of poor organizational dynamics and faulty administrative practices. Neither can we simply adopt and implement procedures that have proven successful in settings very different than our own. Instead, we must develop models of functioning that enhance administrative efficiency while preserving the quality of openness that arms our nonprofits with community legitimacy and internal credibility.

HISPANIC NONPROFITS: GOVERNANCE AND BOARDS OF DIRECTORS

As is the case with all nonprofits, the management of Hispanic nonprofit organizations depends on the ability of boards to set/monitor policy and of executives to implement policy. Here, however, a distinction needs to be made between larger, national Hispanic organizations and the smaller, community-based Hispanic nonprofits.

Larger, more stable organizations (particularly national Hispanic nonprofits) are able, both because of their visibility and comparative prestige, to deal with board of director functions and general governance issues in ways similar to those of non-Hispanic nonprofits. National Hispanic nonprofits tend to have diverse membership (e.g., Latinos, non-Latinos, professionals and/or persons with high visibility), are better able to distinguish and separate the roles and responsibilities of board members and executive staff, and tend to recruit more experienced, well-known, and highly educated board members.

Consistent and stable resources enable such boards to focus attention on the development and implementation of organizational policy and direction. Because of their "fishbowl" existence, however, such boards spend a good deal of time on short-term organizational goals and have limited ability to attract, recruit, and train new and younger leadership. Consequently, there is less investment in the longer-range goal of developing the kind of board leadership that can take over and ensure the survival of organizations that are responsive to changing community needs.

Local, smaller, community-based nonprofits have their own strengths and weaknesses when it comes to issues of governance and the role of boards of trustees or directors. The pluses and minuses that accrue to such organizations are a reflection of the volatility that encapsulates all such settings. Clearly, the boards of local nonprofits are in better positions to develop board leadership. Being close to neighborhoods and communities means that boards can more easily identify newcomers, particularly those with leadership potential. Such organizations can take more risks. They are not as "exposed" as national organizations and can better tolerate mistakes because of the personal closeness of board members and the comparative looseness (i.e., openness) of the organization.

On the other hand, local nonprofits often have great difficulty in separating the roles and responsibilities of board members and executive staff. In part, this is due to limited resources, community politics, and varying levels of information, skills, and experience. Limited resources often result in board members assuming staff functions; community politics sometimes leads to board disagreements whose causes lie outside the nonprofit itself; and varying levels of information, skills, and experience often decrease the clarity needed to reach consensus or make decisions.

A common complaint of board members is that they feel underutilized. This is understandable, given the fact that most local nonprofit boards are composed of people who care deeply about an agency's mandate, are serving in voluntary/unpaid positions, and very rarely enhance their own status in the community as a function of board membership. Nevertheless, leadership tends to fall on a small core of people and is seldom shared. It is not uncommon to find Hispanic nonprofits in which the same board president and officers have served for many years. The implications of this situation on the twin issues of governance and management are many and varied. While community support is facilitated, problems involving agency direction and operations are often exacerbated. Board members often lack a clear understanding of what is expected of them. In many cases, they do not know (or will not accept) where their responsibilities end and those of the professional staff begin. At times, board members do not know the right questions to ask. Despite the fact that agencies usually provide board orientation, training, and information, board members do not always have adequate data with which to make decisions. And, finally, the situation often results in the agency executive(s) being uncertain as to how to share responsibilities or determine accountability.

Given the above, I would suggest the following as appropriate board roles in community-based Hispanic nonprofits:

1. Determining, defining, and proselytizing the agency's mission and basic agenda

2. Providing financial guidance and fiscal overview

3. Establishing and maintaining personnel policies

4. Developing close, ongoing ties with the community

5. Ensuring that the agency's charter and laws are followed

United Way of America (UWA) developed a booklet that outlines the responsibilities of voluntary boards. The UWA developed the booklet because:

> Of all volunteers, those elected to boards of directors of voluntary agencies perform the most important service. They lend their expertise and experience to the guidance of their organizations and thus have the greatest impact on the success of these agencies. Serving on a voluntary board, however, places considerable demands on the volunteer's time and a large measure of responsibility. (United Way of America, 1979, n. p.)

HISPANIC NONPROFITS: LEADERSHIP

One of the prevailing fictions in most Hispanic nonprofits, especially those that operate at the local community level, is that leaders (executive directors, principal investigators, project managers, and the like), will be "persons for all seasons." Also, because of limited and decreasing resources, we expect these people to work for comparatively little money. A significant and growing gap exists between the salaries paid to Hispanic nonprofit executives and expectations held of them.

The executive director of any nonprofit organization is its primary leader and manager. As such, he or she has a broad set of administrative responsibilities and is expected to relate to three very different constituencies. These constituencies include the organization's staff, the board of directors, and the external community. The specific responsibilities for which we hold leaders accountable include fiscal operations and management, programmatic integrity, staff development, program planning, policy development, resource development, community relations, and crisis management. Leaders are generally expected to possess two very different sets of skills, those associated with human relations and those related to institutional operations. In addition, however, leadership implies a whole set of personal variables that are much more difficult to define and almost impossible to measure. These include charisma, inspiration, strength, the willingness to risk, sensitivity, and compassion. One of the main problems in locating and recruiting leaders for nonprofits is the difficulty in specifying the particular blend of characteristics required for a particular organization at a particular point in time. The "sought-after blend" varies with both the national political climate and the local situation. Generally speaking, we seek more person-oriented leaders during times of comparative resource availability and during periods of greater national concern for the redressing of historical inequities. During times of conservative political and economic retrenchment, we seek leaders who are more "nuts and bolts oriented." During all times, however, we seek leaders with the ability to inspire, motivate, and harness the energies of coworkers, boards of directors, and communities.

During the relatively short history of Hispanic nonprofits, boards of directors have tended to choose leaders with backgrounds in the areas of social work and/or social activism, not for their managerial abilities or skills.

As noted earlier, there is an interesting movement in the profit-making world where managers are being challenged to be leaders. Clearly, it is leadership that has marked the development of Hispanic nonprofits. Current attempts to improve Hispanic nonprofit management must not sacrifice the leadership that made these organizations possible.

Hispanic nonprofits have been far more concerned with issues of commitment, vision, and values than with administrative experience and expertise. In line with the movement to encourage and support visionary leaders, Hispanic nonprofits should build on their strengths in this area. For the survival of Hispanic nonprofits, it is clear that both leadership and management are crucial.

CONCLUSION/SUMMARY

Hispanic nonprofit organizations are not very different from the more traditional nonprofits in this country. There are certain areas that Hispanic nonprofits need to concentrate on if they are to strengthen their management and leadership and continue as a major force in the development of the community. These are described below.

Funding and Resources

While this chapter does not focus on the issue of funding and resources, it is clear that both are needed to support a strong organizational base. Hispanic nonprofits should seek funding support for administrative structures, technology (e.g., computers), staff development, board development, and long-range planning. Funders increasingly recognize their role in supporting these efforts. Hispanic nonprofits must make the case that support for programs and projects alone will not ensure long-term impact in Hispanic communities.

Single-focused Versus Multifocused Agendas

Hispanic NPOs will continue to be multifocused because of the complex issues in Hispanic communities. It is important, however, that the nonprofits be clear about their missions and have goals/objectives and work plans. Some organizations are collaborating with other organizations (both Hispanic and non-Hispanic) on projects that address a particular issue in the community. Collaboration is certainly a technique that can bring more resources both to the organization and the community. Another approach is to develop agreements with service organizations for referrals and use of their services for Hispanics. This is similar to collaboration, except that the organization sends the individual needing the service to the provider. Finally, Hispanic nonprofits must continue to pressure and demand that non-Hispanic organizations and institutions develop ways to reach out into the Hispanic community, be sensitive to the particular needs of Hispanics, and hire Latinos to better serve the Hispanic populations.

Administrative Structures

Hispanic nonprofits must deliberately choose the administrative structure that best meets their needs and periodically review these structures to assess their effectivenss. These include:

1. the flat structure, where decisions are made by group process; this is particularly appropriate for organizations that are small or just beginning.

2. the more hierarchical structure, where all program supervisors and fiscal staff report directly to the director and program staff report to the supervisors.

3. the "inside–outside" team, where the executive director is responsible for working with the board of directors, bringing in the resources, representing the organization and in some cases the community on broader levels, and marketing and advocating for the organization's agenda. The "inside" person is an organizational manager responsible for the day-to-day fiscal, personnel, and program development operations. This is an emerging model and depends on good communication and clear division of work by the director and manager. In all these models, the executive director has the full responsibility and authority, but the key is what areas he or she is willing to share and delegate.

Board of Directors

The board must be clear about its functions and responsibilities. The board sets policy, develops long-range plans, sets the mission and goals and objectives, hires and fires the director, and brings in resources to the organization. The board must be very careful to observe the fine line between policy and administration.

Staff Development

Hispanic nonprofits in many ways are the schools where Hispanics learn and grow. Boards and executive directors should create staff development strategies that enhance the skills and experiences of their employees. Since it is difficult to compensate nonprofit workers adequately, investing in their development is an important supplement. Some colleges and universities are interested in collaborating with nonprofit organizations in developing degree programs specifically for nonprofits. The areas of development should focus not just on the skills to provide better services but also on fiscal management, supervisory and managerial skills, personnel, and the like.

I have attempted in this chapter to provide an overview of a complex set of variables that affect the management and leadership of Hispanic nonprofit organizations. In describing each variable, I have tried to offer the kind of analysis that could serve as a reasonable basis for further research and theory building. Taken together, this analysis points to the need for us to process, hopefully in a collective manner, the contradictions and experiences that define our lives as leaders of Hispanic nonprofits. Unless and until this collective analysis is undertaken, we may very well squander or use poorly the limited resources we currently possess. If we allow this to happen, we will have violated our most solemn and collective oath—our oath to serve the people.

9

Survival Profiles of Latino Nonprofit Organizations

Leobardo F. Estrada

According to Independent Sector, in 1987 there were approximately 561,000 charitable nonprofit organizations (excluding churches) with approximately $290 billion in expenditures in the United States (Hodgkinson and Weitzman, 1989). This figure represents a 38-percent increase in the number of charitable nonprofit organizations since 1977. Separate information for Latino nonprofit organizations is very limited.

The *Encyclopedia of Associations* (1988) reported 20,076 national nonprofit organizations in the United States and listed 117 organizations with the terms *Hispanic, Latino* (Latin American), *Puerto Rican,* or *Cuban* in the titles. Thus, approximately 0.6 percent of these national nonprofit organizations appear to be specifically directed toward Latino concerns and issues. Data from Independent Sector about Hispanic organizations are also limited, but, applying a similar rate, there would seem to be at least 2,200 Latino nonprofits in the United States.

The most current reporting of the *Encyclopedia of Associations* indicates that national Latino nonprofit organizations are most likely to be (1) public affairs organizations (e.g., civil rights and legal defense organizations, community development corporations, immigration service providers, political affiliates, and public policy institutes), followed by (2) educational organizations (e.g., concerned with scholarships, dropout prevention, and bilingual education), (3) social welfare organizations (e.g., Hispanic elderly services, family counseling services, child abuse prevention), (4) cultural organizations (e.g., arts and letters, historic preservation, museums, music, theatre), and (5) trade and business organizations (e.g., building industries, public relations, communications).

According to the *Encyclopedia of Associations,* the budgets of the Latino organizations ranged from over $200 to over $9 million with an approximate median budget of $36,000. Among the top ten nonprofits listed (and omitting the organization with a budget over $9 million), the median annual budget is approximately $270,000 a year. As these figures indicate, once the salaries of the director and minimal staff are taken into account, the activity level of the organization is severely limited unless it can attract and obtain additional funding.

Neither of these references reveal the funding sources of Hispanic organizations. However, those who have worked for and with Latino nonprofits over the past three decades know that major changes have occurred in funding sources. The shifts in these sources mirror changes in governmental and foundation funding priorities but also reflect changing expectations and changing activities in Latino nonprofit organizations. The following section reviews these changes and attempts to provide a framework for understanding how Latino nonprofits have responded to the need to sustain funding over the years in a constantly changing funding environment.

FROM LOCAL TO NATIONAL EXPECTATIONS

Latino nonprofits have evolved over the past three decades, and funders have increasingly responded as these organizations enlarged their scope and activities from local to national level. In the 1950s and early 1960s, the vast majority of Hispanic nonprofits were small in size and dispersed throughout the United States, with most located in areas of Hispanic concentration and activism, such as San Antonio, Corpus Christi, and El Paso, Texas; Albuquerque, New Mexico; Los Angeles and San Francisco; and New York City. As might be expected, these small Latino nonprofits focused primarily on local issues, particularly in response to inequitable schooling and political representation. These nonprofits were usually directed on a part-time volunteer basis by highly committed individuals. At this stage of development, most Latino nonprofits were funded by membership fees and local donors. The Southwest Council of La Raza was among the first Latino nonprofits to attract national funding, largely because of its expanded, regional approach and role as an umbrella for affiliate organizations.

In the early 1960s, several major foundations identified the lack of Latino national visibility as a critical weakness. Latino issues simply did not arise among decision makers on the East Coast. As long as Latino issues were viewed as regional concerns, congressional legislation and national policymakers could ignore Latinos. Interest in creating a national presence for Latinos resulted in the relocation of several major nonprofits to the Washington, D.C., area with the support of major foundations and the federal government. In a brief period, a dozen Latino nonprofits established offices close to the legislative process in the nation's capital. Major national foundations provided the start-up funds for newly created Latino nonprofits. The types of organizations that obtained support mirrored the recognized national black organizations located in Washington. Thus, the Mexican American Legal Defense and Educational Fund (MALDEF) and the National Council of La Raza were comparable to the National Association for the Advancement of Colored People (NAACP) and the Urban League. Beyond the foundation funding, Latino nonprofit organizations also successfully sought federal funding to support many of their projects and programs. The fact that the 1960s was a period of governmental budget expansion and that poverty, civil rights, and community development were at the forefront of the national agenda allowed these national Latino organizations to grow rapidly.

This period represents a milestone in the evolution of Latino nonprofits, for it was during this time that most of these organizations forged the capacity for grantsmanship, learned to direct project-oriented programs, employed professional staff to carry out their programs, and learned to value the role of public relations. During this period, millions of dollars were invested by foundations in a small number of Latino organizations, and millions more were invested by the federal government in a large number of Hispanic groups and programs. Of particular importance was the fact that foundations awarded funding on three-to-five-year cycles, providing a few Latino nonprofit organizations with a stable financial base, at a time when the groups appeared to be limited only by their imagination and ability to write quality proposals. It was also a period when the leaders of these organizations began to attain wider recognition as Latino leaders.

Many factors converged at this time. Foundation support provided credibility, federal support provided opportunities to initiate programs, and the many successful projects solidified the special niche that Latino nonprofit organizations filled as institutional representatives for Latino concerns. These East Coast-headquartered Latino nonprofits fulfilled the objective of bringing Latino issues to the national public-policy arena. Evidence of the influence of these nonprofits includes the number of presentations before congressional committees; the insertion of language in legislation related to bilingual children, migrant workers, and immigrants; studies conducted by the Civil Rights Commission; and the inclusion of Latino leaders in White House briefings.

CHANGING NATIONAL AND REGIONAL FOCI

As national Latino nonprofit organizations gained in sophistication, federal agencies and foundations became more aware of the Latino community.

Funders began to recognize the heterogeneity and diversity of Latinos as well as the significance of regional concentration of Latino subgroups. In the minds of policymakers, Puerto Ricans' poverty needs in the New York City area became distinct from the refugee issues of Cuban-Americans in Miami and the educational concerns of Mexican-Americans in the Southwest. Latino national organizations were well aware of these differences and attempted to be sensitive to these localized concerns, but, in general, they had been structured to respond to federal agencies and congressional legislation rather than to resolutions for local or regional issues. Only a few national Latino organizations had affiliated organizations, and at that time none had affiliates in *all* the primary regions of Hispanic concentration (i.e., southwestern states, south Florida, New York metropolitan area, and greater Chicago area). National Latino nonprofit organizations lacking an affiliated structure responded by setting up regional offices or developing strong ties to organizations in other parts of the country in order to respond to those regional needs. Despite these efforts, the decision-making power remained in Washington, D.C.

In time, funders saw the need for Latino nonprofits at the regional level that could respond to the urgent, localized, Latino subgroup concerns. The Ford Foundation's Hispanic initiative represents another benchmark because it recognized the need to support national organizations as well as to provide support for regional institutions.

As foundations began to disperse their funds among more Latino nonprofits, the national Latino organizations were pushed to diversify their funding sources further. Some efforts had previously been made along these lines, but suddenly national Latino nonprofits had to shift their funding strategies to include a wider variety of funders, such as major corporations. Despite the advocacy nature of many of these national organizations, new inroads were made in obtaining corporate funding. This success can be attributed in part to the discovery by corporations of the Latino consumer market and their members' increased concern with being good corporate citizens. The decision to seek corporate funding did not come easily. Within advocacy and other organizations, battles were fought regarding the organizational self-image and the acceptance of corporate support, but, in general, the need for new sources of funding won out. Meanwhile, regional Latino nonprofits, which were forced early on to utilize a mix of funding sources, found they could survive with monies from local foundations, funding intermediaries (e.g., United Way), the local private sector, and limited, intermittent funding from national foundations.

This brief review describes some of the general trends that explain shifts in funding sources. At the beginning, Latino nonprofit organizations were dependent upon one or two major sources of funding and then shifted to mixed funding, as they sought to survive declining federal budgets and changing funding priorities by foundations. Finally, as major foundations began to disperse funding to a greater number of national and regional organizations, Latino nonprofits were forced to diversify their funding further into the corporate sector. Within their broad mission, Latino nonprofits made a remarkable leap from tiny institutions with localized concerns to national, multipolicy-oriented institutions that continue to exist but that are complemented today by more regional forms of policy, research, and advocacy activity.

Through the last three decades, Latino nonprofits have learned to define the appropriate scope and scale of their organizations. They have experienced times of expansion as well as lean times, during which they tried to sustain the same level of staffing and program activity. Most Latino nonprofit chief executive officers (CEOs) have learned to accept the fact that there exists an optimum size for such organizations. Arriving at the appropriate scale for a Latino nonprofit organization is not a simple task, but it is essential if the organization is to survive.

Changes in the role and funding mix of Latino nonprofits allow one to appreciate the adaptability of these organizations. New Latino nonprofits continue to emerge, while others are now defunct. Why have some managed to survive while others have not? The following section considers two organizational perspectives that help to provide a framework for understanding the survival of these groups.

SURVIVAL OF THE FITTEST: ORGANIZATIONAL DARWINISM

One view emphasizes the need for organizations to change in response to the funding environment. This viewpoint posits that the priorities of the funding sources determine the environment. In turn, Latino nonprofits that adjust to changes in the funding environment are more likely to survive.

There are several examples of Latino nonprofits dependent on a single source of funding, primarily the federal government, which by necessity experienced the urgency to anticipate federal funding priorities and to shift their focus in line with those changes. For example, Latino nonprofits interested in manpower issues (SER, Jobs for Progress) had to adapt to the shifts in funding priorities from the Department of Labor as its primary legislation, the Comprehensive Employment and Training Act (CETA) with its emphasis upon public service employment, job training, and youth employment was modified by the Job Training Partnership Act (JTPA) with its emphasis upon on-the-job training and public/private initiatives.

Federal funding priorities tend to shift with changes in the administration. While the exact changes are sometimes surprising, most are predictable from congressional testimony, legislative language, and regulations.

Latino nonprofits dependent on foundation funding had a more difficult

situation, since foundation funding priorities are always somewhat myste-
rious. The best indication of past and current priorities is found in previous
grants, but those trends are insufficient to predict future priorities. Foundations differ as to the decision-making autonomy of program officers, and at
times a single, assertive trustee can significantly change a foundation's funding priorities. In most cases, only a close working relationship with foundation staff can throw light on present and future funding priorities. Corporate funding is even less predictable and is influenced as much by corporate
self-interest as by genuine support for a particular Latino organization. Few
corporations announce their funding priorities.

At some point or another, every Latino nonprofit organization has
adapted to changes in funding environments. The last decade, for example,
has been a period of decreased funding for bilingual education that affected
education-oriented nonprofits (e.g., National Association of Bilingual Educators), and of declining funds for community development, which reduced
the activities of organizations such as Chicanos por la Causa, Spanish Speaking Unity Council, and The East Los Angeles Community Union (TELACU).
Furthermore, U.S. Supreme Court decisions regarding class action suits
changed the approach and direction of MALDEF and the Puerto Rican Legal
Defense and Education Fund (PRLDEF). Likewise, during the last decade,
there has been increased funding for elderly persons to the benefit of Latino
nonprofits such as the Asociacion Pro Personas Mayores; increased concerns
with AIDS health education; and, most recently, foundation concerns with
persistent poverty have stimulated responses by Latino nonprofits like the
National Council of la Raza.

In order to anticipate the changing funding environment, Latino nonprofits experimented until they arrived at the best forms of early warning
systems. In many cases, the result was a nonprofit organization with a strong
network of resources that kept the organization informed about anticipated
changes in funding. Among the more successful operations were Latino nonprofits with broad missions and diverse funding that maintained staffing flexibility and used that flexibility to respond quickly to the changing funding
environment. From this perspective, those Latino nonprofits that adapted
were able to thrive and expand. This is particularly clear in the evolution of
Latino community development corporations that took several forms in the
beginning but near the end of the community development corporation
movement became remarkably similar in organization and business venture
strategies.

The concept of niche is very important to this viewpoint. A distinctive
sphere of action that provides a combination of resources and improves an
organization's chances of survival is known as a *niche* within a particular
sector. Niches are not constant; Latino nonprofits may expand or decline
within a niche if unprepared to respond to change. Examples of niches

include legal defense (PRLDEF), educational policy (Hispanic Policy Development Project [HPDP]), community economic development (TELACU), political participation (Latino Institute of Chicago), and professional associations (National Association of Hispanic CPAs).

One such niche was created by Latino nonprofit presence at the national level in Washington, D.C. Major Latino nonprofit organizations thrived in Washington because a void had to be filled for Latino institutional responses to pending legislation, ongoing policy debates, and federal agency concerns for public comment. During the Reagan administration, federal funding was decentralized from the federal government to the state and local levels. As the initiative for many programs shifted to the state and local levels, the Latino national policy niche declined somewhat even as the credibility and recognition of the national Latino organizations increased among policymakers.

The "survival of the fittest" concept is useful in understanding organizational persistence. Those Latino nonprofits with the flexibility of a small core staff, accessibility to a wide range of additional expert staff as required, and sophisticated grantsmanship capacities exhibit the highest rates of survival.

This "natural selection" model, however, downplays "strategic choices" that explain the wide variation in forms that Latino nonprofits take. Otherwise, these organizations might be much more alike. This model also ignores the influence of the leaders who direct these organizations. There is ample reason to believe that these Latino leaders influence the focus of the organizations as much as if not more than the funding environment. The survival model also ignores issues of power and conflict, including the jurisdictional "turf" issues that are resolved through organizational power struggles.

ORGANIZATIONAL DECISION MAKING AND DECISION MAKERS

A second viewpoint gives primary emphasis to decisions that are made within organizations and the political context of the organization. In this model, unlike the first, organizations are not regarded as passive recipients but rather as dealing actively with their environment, including attempts to manipulate it. An excellent example of this is a Latino nonprofit organization that lobbied until it was written into legislation as one of five national organizations providing public service employment, thus assuring its continued role and grant support. Most Latino nonprofits are not as successful in controlling their environment, but all organizations make strategic decisions about adapting to the environment rather than simply reacting to it.

Many variations in Latino organizations result from the values and personal background of their leaders. Leaders such as Vilma Martinez, Raúl Yzaguirre, Ernesto Robles, Carmela Lacayo, the late Willie Velasquez, Guarione Díaz, Juan Rosario, Lupe Anguiano, Harry Pachón, Mario Obledo, Tony and Ruben Bonilla, Pablo Sedillo, and Luis Nuñez, to name a few, exhibit an influence that far exceeds their official leadership role. Case studies of these leaders would demonstrate the unique impact of their decision making.

In their more candid moments, most of these leaders will discuss internal power arrangements, in the form of constituents, boards of directors, and core staff, that influenced many of their decisions. Additionally, there are the demands of external groups such as funders, fundraisers, political officials, and the media. How CEOs of Latino nonprofits balance these demands is not easy to explain, but the longevity of these leaders is an indication that they have successfully responded to these often conflicting demands. This discussion reminds us, once again, of the political context within which Latino CEOs make decisions.

What are some of the ways that Latino CEOs are able to affect the funding environment? First, they create personal linkages with key individuals in funding agencies that are likely to fund Latino nonprofit organizations. These personal contracts are used to influence funding requests, guidelines, and methods (e.g., sole-source funding). Second, they have a strong network with other Latino nonprofits through overlapping board memberships (sitting on the boards of other Latino nonprofits), personal interaction, and collaborative funding efforts, as in the case where one organization serves as the prime contractor and others serve as subcontractors. These cooperative efforts also provide Latino nonprofits with the opportunity to display a united front to outside funders on important policy issues affecting Latinos. SER, Jobs for Progress is an example of two major Latino organizations joining efforts for a major thrust on manpower issues. Other examples are the Interuniversity Consortium and the National Forum of Hispanic Organizations.

While the former model stresses the environment's impact on organizational forms, the latter point of view suggests that those Latino nonprofits that survive are those that have dealt proactively with the changing environment. Survival techniques include bureaucratization, specialization, standardization, and a hierarchical structure.

A separate type of survival technique derives from the socialization process by which the culture of the organization is transmitted to new staff members. Since few Latino nonprofits have formal orientation programs for new staff members, it is usually left to the senior staff members to provide a sense of the culture of the Latino nonprofit to the newcomer. This ensures that organizational forms and grantsmanship strategies that have proven successful in the past will be retained.

Viewing an organization as an active entity appears to be more reflective of the proactive Latino nonprofits that have overcome fluctuations in funding by actively seeking to influence funding and by attaining access to the funder community at the point where funding is being considered or planned, rather than the point at which it is announced. Furthermore, this approach recognizes that difficult decisions have to be made within a highly politicized organizational structure. In sum, Latino nonprofit organizations learn to deal directly with changes in the funding environment by anticipating its impact on their decisions and accounting for them in deliberations with staff and boards.

The major flaw in this viewpoint is that the primary organizational mission is not considered. Most Latino nonprofits, for example, advocate for Latino issues, and these activities represent a large portion of their organizational goals. Latino nonprofits tend to carry out activities that are not funded or inadequately funded, and they devote considerable uncompensated time to extraorganizational activities that are only indirectly related to the organization's primary mission. These actions can only be explained by the overriding commitment of Latino nonprofits to their organizational mission.

CONCLUSION

Most of the notable Latino nonprofits matured when foundation funding was provided for almost two decades in cycles of three to five years. The consistency of foundation funding during those early years is the primary reason major national Latino organizations have been able to achieve longevity. Recently, there have been signs that major foundations are reverting back to single-year funding, reducing support, and opting for tie-off grants to many of the organizations they have funded since the 1960s. Highly visible national Latino nonprofits may soon find themselves with moderate endowments that will not allow them to continue at their present staffing levels, even though they would be assured of continued existence.

Government funding for Latino nonprofits has been steadily declining since the mid-1970s. More importantly, the general trend has been for a decentralization in funding that benefits Latino regional nonprofits over the more centralized (i.e., Washington, D.C.-based) Latino nonprofits. If this trend continues, the number of organizations based in the capital may decline further.

Private-sector funding to Latino nonprofits has been increasing, but corporate support has tended to fluctuate widely from year to year. The inconsistency of this funding makes it unlikely that Latino organizations can ever become dependent on corporate support unless it is transformed along the lines of "adopt-a-school" programs. Corporate funding for the most part prefers to associate its giving with specific projects, and it is rare for Latino nonprofits to obtain basic operating support from corporations. What is encouraging about future corporate support is the business world's growing awareness of the potential of Latino consumers. In addition, corporate donors are more willing than foundations to allow Latino nonprofits to suggest funding opportunities. This prognosis for the future has to be discouraging to Latino nonprofit CEOs, on whom the constant struggle for funding has taken a serious toll. It is a tiring and stressful process that contributes more to burnout than any other factor. However, there are a few promising trends that have begun to emerge, such as community development corporations that have survived the decline in funding because of having an asset base. That is, the profit-making investments that these corporations have in their portfolios generate funds for their continued support and maintenance. No community development corporation is actually self-sufficient, but several provide close to two-thirds of their basic support from management of their assets.

From this observation have emerged several related asset management strategies. One such business venture is for Latino nonprofits to build low-income and affordable housing and then to create a for-profit management company to manage the properties while using the gains to support the agency. Another example is that of Latino nonprofits that own office buildings: They occupy some of the space but lease the remaining office or retail space and use the profits to support themselves. Other nonprofits are looking into floating their own bonds for housing construction, providing technical assistance through consulting contracts, and even becoming real-estate developers. Latino nonprofits must begin by establishing a for-profit arm (within the constraints of the law and the regulations of the Internal Revenue Service) that can purchase, manage, and finance business ventures. Asset management is likely to be the key word for Latino nonprofits in the 1990s.

Most trends point to a transition in Latino nonprofits in the very near future, to a middle ground between the "pure" nonprofits they once were, where their existence was dependent on others, and the self-reliant, "enterprising" nonprofit/for-profit organizations that are profit driven for the sake of continued existence. Somewhere between these two is the ground being sought by nonprofits to secure their futures.

Should there be a concern with the direction that Latino nonprofits are being forced to take in order to survive? Some could argue that when a nonprofit becomes intertwined in the marketplace, it could lose its edge. Most Latino nonprofits are characterized by their willingness to confront the "system/authorities" on behalf of the unempowered. It is obviously easier to be assertive when an organization is outside the system.

A significant counterargument is to remember that a characteristic of Latino nonprofits is their capacity to act "irrationally" as organizations. Examples exist of Latino nonprofits whose concerns with improving the quality of life for Latinos has been accomplished even when it meant taking a stance that might result in the possible loss of funding, when it meant alienating federal agency heads, when it required ignoring the advice of foundation officers, and even when it meant refusing funds when too many strings were attached.

Latino nonprofit organizations have been able to act irrationally and defiantly because they are willing to believe that they have the *right* agenda and that some funders can be persuaded to respond even as others disappear. More importantly, some Latino nonprofits are moving toward self-sufficiency development strategies that will loosen the constraints based on funding dependencies. This trend can only result in stronger and enduring Latino nonprofit organizations.

10

Philanthropy and Latino Nonprofits: A Research Agenda

Michael Cortés

As the nation's Latino population continues its dramatic increase, leaders of Latino nonprofit organizations and their financial supporters ask, How can we do better? Leaders and managers of nonprofits want more money to initiate, strengthen, and expand community service, development, and advocacy projects. Grantmaking executives and trustees wonder what kinds of projects and organizations to fund in Latino communities and how to go about it. Nonprofit leaders and concerned philanthropists wonder how to generate more support for Latino nonprofits among uninvolved donors and grantmakers.

Research can help answer those questions. Applied research findings, conclusions, and program recommendations can help reduce the perceived risks of innovative funding strategies involving Latinos. Sooner or later, prospective funders will learn more about the societal risks of ignoring Latino community needs. Hopefully, funders will also learn more about the unique roles played by Latino nonprofit organizations in meeting those needs through education, job placement and training, community economic development, housing, social services, legal assistance, civic participation, public policy research and advocacy, cultural programs, and the fine arts. As the social risks of ignoring Latinos become more apparent, research can help reduce the institutional risks of taking positive action.

This chapter presents many unanswered questions about philanthropy and Latino nonprofits. Questions are organized into seven general topics, comprising a proposed research agenda. Other researchers interested in philanthropy and Latino nonprofits should consider adopting at least the applied orientation implicit in this agenda.

To be most effective, research on philanthropy and Latino nonprofits should meet three criteria. First, it should serve a strategy that is agreed upon. Second, research should inform practical policy and program decisions flowing from that strategy, as perceived by grantors and Latino grantees. Third, it should be conducted by researchers and institutions trusted and respected by grantmakers and Latino grantees.

Research Should Service Strategy

Exactly what should be researched? That depends upon the strategy. Unfortunately, a general strategy for increasing philanthropic support for Latino nonprofits has only partially emerged and remains fragmentary. Elements of the strategy have been suggested, at least implicitly, by several advocates, including the Council on Foundations (1975, p. VI-2), Díaz (1981), Facundo (1980a, pp. xvii–xviii, 56–57), Forum of National Hispanic Organizations (1982), Gallegos (1975, 1987), Johnson (1981), Moreno (1983), Nason (1977, pp. 41–45), National Puerto Rican Coalition (1987, pp. iv–v), *Neustro* (1982), Ríos (1981), San Juan Cafferty and Rivera-Martínez (1981), Silha (1981), Struckhoff (1981a, 1981b, 1981c), and Wilson (1981a, 1981b). But those elements of strategy remain disconnected. A complete and coherent larger strategy remains to be explicated, agreed upon, and implemented.

There is no general consensus among Latino nonprofits and concerned philanthropists on all the things they should do together to increase resources for Latinos. Without a common sense of direction, we don't know what research questions, if any, are important to Latino nonprofits and their philanthropic advocates. To be useful, research on philanthropy and Latinos should focus on plans for action and practical decisions facing prospective donors and Latino donees. Strong assumptions about future strategy can provide that focus.

A Strategy

In this chapter, I assume that proposals developed and considered during the past three years by Hispanics in Philanthropy, a national association of Latino foundation and corporate contributions staff and trustees, will be adopted as a general strategy by concerned philanthropists and Latino nonprofits. (Rationales are outlined by Cortés [1987, 1988].) The research agenda presented in this chapter assumes the strategy described below.

Let us assume that leading donors and grantmakers will take the following seven steps, or linking strategies, to promote cooperative relations between Latino nonprofits and other, prospective donors.

1. Concerned chief executives and board chairs of grantmaking foundations will initiate a long-term series of local, regional, and national
   meetings to encourage their less committed peers and colleagues to
   begin working with greater numbers of potential Latino grantees.

2. Leading national foundations will expand their matching-grant programs to encourage previously uninvolved regional and local foundations to reach out to Latino community-based nonprofits.

3. Regional and local foundations and corporate contributions programs
   will establish joint pools of consultants experienced in working with
   Latino nonprofits to assist with program planning, outreach, and technical assistance to prospective applicants, and evaluation of proposals
   and project outcomes.

4. Foundations and corporations will begin looking to such pools as
   sources of Latino candidates for grantmaking staff and trustee appoint-
   ments and will encourage other grant makers to do likewise.

5. Grantmakers will allocate more funds for long-term, renewable core
   support grants to effective Latino nonprofits whose survival is endan-
   gered by shifting public and private sector priorities.

6. In areas experiencing rapid Latino population growth, cooperating
   grantmakers will develop and support new community service, development, and advocacy agencies in cooperation with existing Latino
   nonprofits.

7. Cooperating grantmakers will fund new grantmaking agencies
   designed to involve local Latino community leaders and advisors in
   allocational decisions and funding initiatives.

Let us also assume that Latino nonprofits will take the following five steps
to diversify their income. Latino nonprofits will

1. diversify their base of government and private grants and contracts by
   making broader inroads among foundations and corporations that do
   not presently fund Latinos,

2. place greater emphasis on seeking core support grants and long-term
   renewable project support for preexisting organizational priorities,

3. initiate and expand solicitation of individual contributions, both inside
   and outside Latino communities,

4. experiment with generating unrelated business income through rents
   and sales of goods and services,

5. pursue more grants and contracts from state and local governments.

A Research Agenda

What if opinion leaders among Latino nonprofits and philanthropic organizations adopt this joint strategy? How will they persuade their peers and colleagues to join them? Persuasion will be easier if advocates are armed with credible research answering the following practical questions:

1. Why worry about Latinos? Aren't they just another special interest group competing in the world of philanthropy?

2. Why fund Latino nonprofits? Are they the best vehicle for reaching out to the nation's growing Latino population?

3. What works? Why have some philanthropists succeeded at funding Latinos while others have not?

4. Who should do more? What kinds of philanthropic organizations are best positioned to respond to Latino community needs?

5. What kinds of fundraising assistance do Latino nonprofits need?

6. Should Latino nonprofits invest more in soliciting donations from individuals? Should they focus more on potential Latino donors?

7. Should Latino nonprofits support themselves? What else besides philanthropy will keep them afloat?

Those seven questions comprise a research agenda; the rest of the chapter is organized around those questions. If addressed by credible researchers, the agenda should help increase funding for Latino nonprofits.

WHY WORRY ABOUT LATINOS?

Are Latinos just another special interest group competing in the world of philanthropy? Or are philanthropists oblivious to broader national problems posed by current demographic trends involving Latinos? A growing body of literature supports the latter case. But who reads it? Growing Latino populations in the United States pose serious problems and choices for the nation as a whole. Only a limited amount of time remains for organized philanthropy to help determine some of the more important outcomes. What is needed is competent research that summarizes, synthesizes, and evaluates existing knowledge on the subject and disseminates it in forms that are easily accepted and absorbed by relatively uninvolved philanthropists.

Latinos Are Changing Society

More than 19.4 million Latinos reside on the U.S. mainland today, comprising 8.1 percent of the U.S. population. By the end of the century, Latinos will number between 23.1 and 26.9 million—nearly 10 percent of the population. High domestic fertility rates—not immigration—will cause most of the increase. For the remainder of the twentieth century, Latinos will be a relatively poor, uneducated, and ethnically diverse segment of U.S. society (Davis, Haub, and Wilette, 1983; Gann and Duignan, 1986; Levy, Tebbets, and Brousseau, 1982; Mackelprang and Longbrake, 1984; Teller, Estrada, Hernández, and Alvírez, 1977; U.S. Department of Commerce, 1982, 1988).

The future place of Latinos in U.S. society is being shaped by current social conditions. The percentage of Latinos who work or are seeking work is unusually high. But while the percentages of Latinos in the work force are high, their earnings are low. Twenty-five percent overall, 39 percent of Latino children, and 71 percent of Latino children in female-headed households live in poverty. Latino workers are concentrated in low-skilled, low-paying jobs. Fewer than 51 percent of Latino adults have a high-school education (Borjas and Tienda, 1985; Escutia and Prieto, 1986; Santiestevan and Santiestevan, 1985; Santos, 1984; Tienda, 1985; U.S. Congress, 1985).

Latino youth have the nation's largest high-school dropout rates. There are important future consequences of high dropout rates, not just for Latinos, but for society in general. Long-term educational and economic disparities in society represent suboptimal investments in human capital and enhance prospects for costly social conflicts across racial, ethnic, and class lines (Astin, 1982; Hayes-Bautista, Schink, and Chapa, 1988; National Commission on Secondary Schooling for Hispanics, 1984; Olivas, 1986; Orum, 1986; Torres-Gil, 1986; U.S. Department of Education, 1980).

Continued social, educational, and economic isolation of the nation's growing Latino population is a challenge to traditional U.S. ideals of democratic government, equal opportunity, and social justice. Ameliorative strategies are complicated by U.S. Latinos' cultural diversity and changing geographic distribution. Increasing but unknown numbers of undocumented Central American refugees are moving into Chicano and Mexican immigrant population centers in the Southwest. Cuban-Americans have developed a relatively cohesive community in Miami, but the proportion of Cuban-Americans is declining among Miami's Latino population as they migrate to other areas of the state and the nation. Puerto Ricans and other Latino subgroups in northeastern cities are becoming increasingly diffused into surrounding suburbs. The nation's Latino population is dynamic and heterogeneous, with ethnic subgroups remaining differentiated by distinctive traditions, values, institutions, dialects, identities, and community organizations (Cortés, 1980).

Implications for Philanthropy

The social consequences of such trends should be explained by researchers with standing in both philanthropic and Latino nonprofit communities. Ethnic diversity and demographic change affect charitable program outcomes.

Implications for every kind of charitable program activity, including the arts, community development, consumer protection, education, employment, environmental protection, health, housing, human services, public safety, recreation, religion, and social justice, should be explained in forms readily understood by prospective donors and grantmakers.

Approach

The case for increasing philanthropic interest in the nation's growing Latino population can be made by surveying current sociological, demographic, economic, social welfare, and other research literature on Latinos, and summarizing and analyzing it in terms of charitable program consequences and opportunities. Organization, style, format, and dissemination of resulting publications should be designed with a particular set of decision makers in mind: busy, open-minded, but uncommitted donors; foundation trustees; and philanthropic program executives.

One Council on Foundations publication about Latinos (Santiestevan, 1981) provides an excellent example of broad dissemination among that particular audience by a credible institution. Others have suggested dissemination under the auspices of a blue-ribbon ad hoc commission charged with implementing a larger research agenda (Cortés, 1988). Alternative ways of getting research results into the hands of relatively uninvolved philanthropists should also be considered.

WHY FUND LATINO NONPROFITS?

Are Latino nonprofits the best vehicle for reaching out to the nation's growing Latino population? Or are philanthropists better advised to encourage other, more familiar grantees to include more Latinos among their clientele? If donors and grantmakers choose to do both—to fund Latino nonprofits and other agencies reaching out to Latino communities—how might an acceptable balance be struck between the two approaches?

Do Latino Nonprofits Receive a Fair Share?

Most grantmaking foundations ignore Latinos. The total amount of funds granted by U.S. foundations for Latino communities has been estimated by analyzing the *Foundation Grants Index* database (Kovacs, 1988). Gallegos (1975) estimated that 0.75 percent of foundation funds go to Latinos. Facundo's (1980a, p. 9) estimate was 1.0 percent. Time periods covered by the two studies were 1972–1974 and 1977–1978, respectively. Since then, publishers of the index have included Latinos in their special population group statistics. Those statistics show an upward trend in giving to Latinos, although methodological difficulties leave some doubt.

The possibility of an upward trend is supported by National Puerto Rican

**FOUNDATION GRANTS AWARDED
FOR LATINO POPULATIONS**

Year	Dollar value	Percent of total dollars awarded
1980	$7,574,670	0.6
1981	10,182,753	0.8
1982	14,782,000	1.0
1983	17,333,000	1.0
1984	15,663,000	1.0
1985	38,777,000	1.9
1986	28,930,000	1.3
1987	34,148,000	1.3

Sources: Garonzik, 1984, pp. x–xii; Kovacs, 1988, pp. xv–xvi.

Coalition (1987) findings that foundation and corporate giving to Puerto Rican organizations increased between 1979 and 1985. Similarly, Latino organizations' share of grants awarded by Chicago area grantmakers rose from 1.5 percent in 1981 (Claudio, 1983) to 2.7 percent in 1984 (Attinasi, Flores, and Osorio, 1986, p. 5). Valdez (1984, pp. 14–23) found variation by geographic region. He stated, "Foundation awards . . . show an inverse relationship between the size of the region's Hispanic population and the amount of foundation funds awarded to organizations serving Hispanics in the region" (pp. 14, 21). (All conclusions about giving to Latinos, based on the *Foundation Grants Index,* are problematic because of data limitations. Unfortunately, Grants Index data are the best available. See Facundo, 1980b, pp. 24–37.)

It is often argued that the 1 percent of grant dollars going to Latinos is inequitably small, given their growing share of the U.S. population (now above 8 percent) and their disproportionately large share of the nation's social ills. Facundo, Gallegos, and Valdez agree that roughly three-fourths of all foundation funds for Latinos are given by seven large foundations. Over half the funds (or 38 percent, according to Valdez, p. 9) are provided by the Ford Foundation. Less than a quarter of foundations listed in the index give any money at all to Latinos.

Roughly half of grant funds intended for Latinos are granted to Latino nonprofits. Gallegos (1975) found that at least 39 percent of the number of grants for Latinos or Asians went to "organizations actually controlled by minorities." Facundo found that 59 percent of grants for Latinos went to agencies "where at least 50 percent of the board members are of Hispanic origin" (1980a, pp. 12–14).

Unfortunately, the *Foundation Grants Index* database is unrepresentative of philanthropy in general. The *Grants Index* lists grants of $5,000 or more awarded to nonprofit organizations by about 460 major U.S. foundations. A small proportion of other foundations voluntarily contribute to the database. Nevertheless, the database represents a small share of the approximately 26,000 grantmaking foundations in the United States, 5,100 of which award 92 percent of foundation grant funds (Renz, 1987, pp. v, lv). And all 26,000 foundations account for only 5.9 percent of the $87 billion donated annually to nonprofit organizations in the United States (American Association of Fund-Raising Counsel, 1987).

The case for a more equitable share for Latino communities can still be argued, despite the unsatisfactory data. But the argument for funding Latino nonprofits is less convincing, as presented by available research on philanthropy. We lack reports summarizing quantitative research findings about the relative merits of various kinds of agencies serving Latino populations. Compelling anecdotes about the relative effectiveness of today's community-based organizations abound within Latino communities, but they have yet to be recorded, evaluated, and published by scholars. A few qualitative descriptive case histories of Latino nonprofits funded by philanthropic organizations have been published. Santiestevan (1981) provides a modest but well-disseminated collection of success stories.

What Can Latino Nonprofits Accomplish?

Elsewhere in this book, Camarillo and Rodríguez-Fraticelli et al. provide helpful overviews of the distinguished history of Latino nonprofits. Various forms of Latino nonprofits, community organizations, and voluntary associations have enabled the survival and progress of Latino communities in the United States for more than 140 years. The case for funding Latino nonprofits today would be strengthened if additional research addressed the current and future functions of those organizations in relation to their economic, social, philanthropic, and public policy environments.

What roles are Latino organizations playing today, as U.S. society tries to assimilate, integrate, or adjust to its growing Latino population? What is the role of organizations of, by, and for members of Latino communities in improving relations between Latinos and the dominant social, economic, educational, civic, and cultural institutions of U.S. society? In what ways are Latino community leaders and their organizations initiating public- and private-sector efforts on behalf of Latinos? How do the efforts of Latino nonprofits compare with those of other service organizations? How do Latino and other nonprofits interrelate, and what are the consequences for Latino communities? A holistic, independent look at those questions by credible researchers, reported succinctly and disseminated widely among interested but relatively uninvolved philanthropists, would improve the funding environment for Latino nonprofits.

External (i.e., non-Latino) philanthropic and public financial support for secular Latino nonprofits is a relatively recent phenomenon. Most of it began

25 years ago with the Ford Foundation Hispanic initiative and the federal War on Poverty and Great Society programs. (For an example of earlier, catalytic external support, see Santiestevan's [1981, p. 83] brief report on the Rosenberg Foundation.) The end of the first decade of the past 25 years marked a high point in external support for Latino organizations. Many— perhaps most—Latino secular nonprofits in existence today were established with the aid of the Ford Foundation initiative, the federal Equal Opportunity Act and related programs, or Latino veterans of those two initiatives. More recently, as federal support has disappeared and federal grantees have faltered, there remains a reserve of Latino human capital—veteran community organizers and project staff—who, from the point of view of Latino community interests, might now be underutilized.

During the past fifteen years, federal support has been withdrawn in fits and starts. Many federally funded organizations and their spun-off progeny have since disbanded. Others have survived federal policy changes by transforming themselves into smaller-scale projects supported by other public and private grants and contracts. The numbers are unknown. Unknown numbers continue with unknown effectiveness to provide—or advocate provision of—publicly and privately funded services targeted on Latino community needs, in ways compatible with the distinctive characteristics of Latino communities.

What are the current trends in the relationship between organized philanthropy and Latino nonprofits? Will the seven foundations providing the bulk of indexed grant funds for Latinos continue to do so? Of the large majority of foundations that apparently do not fund Latino nonprofits, is there a trend toward increasing interest and involvement? Whatever the other trends, it appears likely that the combined income of all Latino nonprofits from public and private sources has been shrinking for the past fifteen years, at a time when the nation's low-income Latino population is undergoing rapid growth.

Approach

The case for funding Latino nonprofits can be strengthened by research addressing the past, present, and future of external support for Latino nonprofits. Quantitative estimates should consider income from both public and private sources, as well as types of programs funded and related outcomes. Analysis of today's Latino nonprofits, in relation to public and private funding institutions and the nation's changing Latino population, would enable a better appreciation of nonprofits' unrealized potential. Survey research of Latino organizations receiving federal funds or foundation grants during the last 25 years could estimate the survival rate, current financial health, current and propsective funding base, and service capabilities of today's Latino nonprofits.

The case for future funding can also be strengthened by assembling a richer, more comprehensive, and systematic array of case histories modeling effective interventions by Latino nonprofits in Latino community problems, needs, and issues. Cases allowing comparisons between Latino nonprofits, non-Latino nonprofits, and relevant public agencies, as they attempt to serve Latino clientele and community interests, would be particularly helpful. Comparative studies should describe instances of competition and complementarity between Latino nonprofits and other agencies attempting to serve the same communities.

Continued analysis of the *Foundation Grants Index* database would be helpful despite data limitations. If analysis were standardized, trends could be charted on equity issues, such as whether funding of Latinos involves a larger number of foundations and, as Valdez (1984) recommended, a larger and more diverse set of Latino grantees. It would help if the Foundation Center revised its coding procedures to facilitate differentiation between Latino grantees and other grantees addressing Latino beneficiaries (see Facundo, 1980b, pp. 24–37). Representative sampling of the larger population of 26,000 foundations, or at least the 5,100 foundations listed in *The Foundation Directory* (Renz, 1987), would allow more accurate estimates of total grant funds awarded to and for Latinos. Such a survey could also relate foundation size, geographic area, board composition, and other factors to proportion of funding allocated to Latino nonprofits and beneficiaries. Facundo's (1980a, pp. 35–41) findings are a step in that direction.

WHAT WORKS?

Why have some philanthropists succeeded at funding Latinos while others have not? What might private foundations, community foundations, corporate giving programs, and religious philanthropies learn from each other about effective outreach to Latino nonprofits? The brief, informal case histories in Santiestevan (1981) by Aranda, Díaz (p. 72), Johnson, Ríos, San Juan Cafferty and Rivera-Martínez, Oppenheimer-Nicolau, Santiestevan (p. 83), Silha, Stauber, Teltsch, Thiel, and Wagenheim (pp. 54–55) are suggestive. Procedural suggestions are also given by Facundo (1980a, pp. 41–58).

Learning from Experience

As in any new venture, reaching out for the first time to Latino nonprofits requires some risk taking, allowing for trial-and-error learning by grantors and grantees. A systematic collection of case histories reporting the results of innovative foundation initiatives toward Latino nonprofits could help funders develop alternatives to the usual passive and ineffective procedure of issuing grant guidelines and evaluating resultant grant applications.

Case histories could help refine questions for more systematic future research. Are grants that are restricted to time-limited projects more cost-effective than are annually renewable, unrestricted core support grants? Do one-shot project grants enhance Latino grantees' long-term organizational stability and growth? Do seed grants, predicated on the assumption that grantees can hustle up larger support elsewhere without further assistance from the initial funding source, work well with Latino nonprofits? Is cost-effectiveness enhanced by disallowing Latino nonprofits' indirect or overhead costs on project grant application budgets? Is income from individual donations a reliable indicator of Latino nonprofits' legitimacy within local Latino communities? My own experience suggests that each of these questions reflects common misconceptions among grantmakers about Latino nonprofits. Researchers have yet to address those questions.

The Politics of Funding Initiatives

Other underlying causes of small allocations for Latinos remain largely unexplained. Why haven't more funders initiated projects with Latino nonprofits? Many observers suggest that lack of Latino representation within philanthropic organizations is one reason, for example, Cortés (1987), Council on Foundations (1975, pp. vi–2), Facundo (1980a, pp. 52–57), Gallegos (1987), Nason (1977, pp. 41–45), and Wilson (1981a). My own recruitment efforts for Hispanics in Philanthropy led me to guess that, in 1987, there were fewer than 140 Latino foundation and corporate contributions staff and trustees in the United States. The preexisting personal interests, preferences, and experiences of most non-Latino foundation staff and trustees seem to limit relations between funders and Latino nonprofits.

It seems unlikely that corporate contributions programs have done any better than foundations at allocating funds for Latino nonprofits. As yet, there are no systematic studies measuring or estimating corporate contributions to Latinos, and there does not appear to be any research examining corporate policies, practices, and staffing patterns as possible causal factors. Data collected annually by the Conference Board (Troy, 1982) might be augmented to that end. Also unexplored are the extent and outcomes of corporate attempts to work with Latino nonprofits as "partners" instead of "grantees," as was done with the Hispanic Association for Corporate Responsibility (HACER), led by the National Council of la Raza in Washington, D.C. Consequences of such quid pro quo relationships for the internal policy and program decisions of Latino nonprofits have been the subject of casual speculation by critics, but they have not been addressed by research.

Approach

Case histories could be assembled illustrating different sorts of Latino funding strategies attempted by various funders. The Ford Foundation Hispanic initiative (described in part by Nicolau and Santiestevan in Chap. 4) provides a starting point. A review of staff working papers and grant documents, sup-

plemented by exploratory staff interviews, focusing on successful and unsuc-
cessful efforts at working with Latino grantees, might be conducted with
funders with extensive experience at funding Latino nonprofits, like the
Akbar Fund, the Anheuser-Busch Companies, the ARCO Foundation, the
Carnegie Corporation of New York, the Ford Foundation, the Robert Wood
Johnson Foundation, the Joyce Foundation, the W. K. Kellogg Foundation,
the Rockefeller Brothers Fund, the Rockefeller Foundation, and the Victoria
Foundation. Internal events and leadership leading to foundation initiatives
toward Latino communities could be identified. The role of Latino staff and
trustees could be explored. Particular attention might also be paid to local
and regional foundations, like the Irvine Foundation, the William Penn
Foundation, the Puerto Rico Community Foundation, the Rosenberg Foundation, and the San Francisco Foundation, all with experience in innovative
working relationships with Latino community-based nonprofits.

WHO SHOULD DO MORE?

What kinds of philanthropic organizations are best positioned to respond to
Latino community needs? Analysis of *The Foundation Grants Index* led Valdez (1984, pp. 30–36) to observe that most funds for Latino nonprofits are
awarded to national organizations by foundations with national giving programs. Facundo's findings and conclusions (1980a, pp. 22–25) were similar
but less emphatic. Valdez does not argue that national nonprofits are adequately funded. Nevertheless, he urges funders to give more attention to
local, community-based Latino nonprofits (Stanford University News Service, 1984).

National giving programs are not as well positioned as local, regional, and
corporate donors to initiate grants to community-based nonprofits. But analyses of the *Grants Index* cited thus far suggest that more proximate funders
rarely fund Latino nonprofits at all. As mentioned earlier, *Grants Index* data
are least useful when one is trying to estimate giving by smaller regional,
local, and family foundations, which comprise the vast majority of grantmaking foundations in the United States. There is even less information from
which to estimate corporate and individual donations to Latino nonprofits,
whether local or national. Do local and regional funders generally ignore
Latino nonprofits in their own backyards? It looks that way, but we really
don't know.

The *Grants Index* covers grantmaking by 460 of the nation's largest foundations. The seven foundations providing three-quarters of all funds granted
to or for Latinos include some of the nation's largest grantmakers. Given
their very large share of grantmaking in general, it is not clear just how
disproportionately large their share of funding for Latinos might be. Further
analysis could explore more carefully the relationship of foundation size and
other characteristics to the proportion of grant funds awarded to or for Lati-

nos. A "fair-share" percentage criterion might be developed for comparing the performance of individual foundations and categories of foundations.

FUNDRAISING ASSISTANCE

What kinds of fundraising assistance do Latino nonprofits need in order to make broader inroads among funders with little or no experience with Latino communities? If grantmakers should take more initiative in reaching out to Latinos, shouldn't Latino nonprofits improve their fundraising skills and knowledge?

Limited Training and Experience

In the early days of Hispanics in Philanthropy, several of its members volunteered to spend time helping nearby Latino community organizations improve their grantsmanship. Volunteers found the need overwhelming. The Latinos they worked with typically had no training and very little experience at fundraising. There was little or no prior contact with fundraising training programs, such as those listed by the Independent Sector (Gray, 1987).

A national survey commissioned by Hispanics in Philanthropy found that, among the 25 fundraising training organizations surveyed, "a lack of Latino trainers, board members and staff in the field was reported as the major factor contributing to the respondents' limited success in attracting Latinos to training workshops" (De Necochea, 1989). Just one of the organizations surveyed, the National Council of la Raza, specializes in training Latino nonprofits (Espinoza, 1988). Five others have programs addressing minorities in general. The survey did not contact or get responses from all available training organizations. At least one other organization, the National Puerto Rican Coalition, helps Latino nonprofits gain funding for themselves (Figueroa, 1988). Nevertheless, if my own experience at the National Council of la Raza is typical, the unmet need for training far exceeds what large Latino nonprofits like the council can supply, given their own funding constraints. Even national and other relatively sophisticated Latino nonprofit organizations could benefit from additional fundraising training and assistance, particularly when they are soliciting individual contributions.

Fundraising and Internal Management

The relationship of staffing patterns and other management practices to effective fundraising by Latino nonprofits has not been researched. Which Latino organizations are most efficient at integrating internal policymaking, strategic planning, programmatic expertise, and fundraising knowledge, in the course of seeking support? What factors underlie successful and unsuccessful integration? For example, how important are specialized training, job titles and qualifications, internal communication practices, executive leadership, allocation of unrestricted funds, use of external fundraising consultants, and involvement of board members?

At least one foundation has tried funding development officers within national Latino nonprofits. The outcomes have not been studied. What became of the officers originally hired? Were their positions retained after they left? How well did they train their successors? Was their expertise integrated into internal planning and decision making?

Investment by Latino organizations in their own fundraising capabilities have not been studied. How many organizations purchase staff training services from the Fund Raising School, the Grantsmanship Center, the National Council of la Raza fundraising workshops, American Association of Fund-Raising Council (AAFRC) conferences, and the like? How many Latino organizations are aware of such resources or consider them to be good investments? How well-trained and skilled at fundraising are their staffs? How have external training outcomes compared with other approaches, such as on-the-job training by other staff, use of on-site consultants for training in conjunction with fundraising, and hiring new staff on the basis of their fundraising credentials and experience?

Some students of nonprofit management recommend that a large proportion of each board of directors be selected on the basis of candidates' ability and willingness to tap personal networks to raise funds for the organization. The appropriateness of this criterion for boards of Latino organizations needs to be explored. What conflicts does that criterion pose for organizations whose mission is to detect and respond to Latino community problems and aspirations? How sensitive can organizational policymakers be to community hopes for economic, educational, social, and cultural achievement in the context of U.S. society, if their networks run instead among resource networks outside Latino communities? Are there good models for balancing representation of community and external resource networks on Latino boards of directors? Can funders and donors be engaged without detracting from the primary mission of Latino organizations? Or should boards remain sensitive primarily to Latino communities, at the expense of their potential fundraising roles?

Approach

Case studies of Latino nonprofits with a history of successful fundraising could search for explanations. What accounts for their successes? What aspects of staff and board training, personnel practices, and other internal management practices are critical to success? Why haven't Latino nonprofits invested more in specialized fundraising and training services offered by other organizations? Should training by Latinos for Latinos, like that offered by the National Council of la Raza and the National Puerto Rican Coalition, be expanded? Have unrestricted core support grants to Latino nonprofits allowed more optimal levels of fundraising? Case histories should focus on a variety of Latino nonprofits, national and local, large and small, old and young. Conclusions could focus on kinds of fundraising, capacity-building grants that work best with Latino organizations. Particular attention should be paid to development of bases of individual contributors, both inside and outside the Latino community.

SOLICITING INDIVIDUAL DONATIONS

Should Latino nonprofits invest more in solicitation of individual donations? Can individual donor pools become a major source of income for Latino nonprofits? Should they focus their fundraising efforts on the people they serve, and other, more affluent Latinos? Or should Latino nonprofits target non-Latino donors instead?

Assessing the Market

Of the $87.22 billion in contributions made to U.S. nonprofits in 1986, 82.2 percent were from individuals, 6.7 percent were from bequests, 5.9 percent were from foundations, and 5.2 percent were from corporations (American Association of Fund-Raising Counsel, 1987). Seventy-one percent of all households in the United States contribute to charity. Contributors give an average of 1.5 percent of their household income (Hodgkinson and Weitzman, 1988, p. 13). Only 56 percent of Latinos contribute to charity. Latino contributors give an average of 1.0 percent of their household income (p. 14). Those estimates are from a survey of charitable giving and volunteering conducted by the Gallup Organization for Independent Sector. The survey found the following (Hodgkinson and Weitzman, 1988, p. 21):

> The Hispanic group . . . showed unusual patterns. The 21 percent of Hispanic respondents who reported both contributions [and] volunteering had the lowest average household income ($21,145) of all Hispanics. . . . In contrast, the 38 percent of Hispanic respondents who reported that their households did not contribute and they did not volunteer had the highest average household income ($31,773) of all Hispanics. This large group affected the overall statistics for Hispanics, which show all [contributing and non-contributing] Hispanics giving [an average of] 0.5 percent of household income to charity even though their average household income is higher than that of blacks, who gave an average of 0.9 percent of their household income to charity. These findings for the Hispanic group deserve more study.

Why don't individual Latinos contribute more? Does the nation's growing Latino population represent an underdeveloped market for charitable causes? Has the direct-mail solicitation industry failed to interpret demographic characteristics correctly when compiling mailing lists of Latino prospects? Have direct-mail consultants failed to develop materials with mass appeal among our nation's diverse Latino cultures? Are Latinos traditionally suspicious of, or isolated from, the philanthropic and charitable traditions of a mainstream U.S. culture that has historically excluded them? Would Latino nonprofits have an easier time than other charities at increasing Latino charitable giving, assuming Latino nonprofits had enough fundraising resources?

Building Upon Tradition

In contrast to the Independent Sector survey findings, there is a long history of cooperative self-help and organized mutual aid among Latinos in the United States, as Camarillo (Chap. 2) and Rodríguez-Fraticelli, Sanabria, and Tirado (Chap. 3) discuss elsewhere in this book. Camarillo, for example, describes *mutualistas* organized during the last century to, among other things, insure members against the financial costs of sickness and death. Do Latino cultural traditions facilitate or hinder more individual support for Latino nonprofits by the nation's growing Latino population? Questions about Latino philanthropy left unanswered by the Independent Sector survey might best be explored by historians, sociologists, and cultural anthropologists concerned about the applied research needs of Latino nonprofits (see Cortés, 1989).

Externally supported Latino nonprofits are a recent phenomenon. Some of the older Latino nonprofit corporations, community organizations, and voluntary associations adapted their programs and structure when external support became available 25 years ago. For example, two voluntary associations—the American GI Forum and the League of United Latin American Citizens—created SER, Jobs for Progress to provide employment training and placement services under contract to federal agencies with War on Poverty funds. But the two parent organizations have retained their traditional, self-supporting base of members. The potential roles of traditional organizations in fundraising for Latino nonprofits remain to be explored.

Which Latino Nonprofits?

What types of Latino nonprofits are best positioned to develop individual funding bases? Do geographic location, types of services offered, organizational experience, or other factors account for varying records among Latino nonprofits at individual fundraising?

The amount and kind of income received by the nation's Latino nonprofits as a whole are unknown. My impression is that an overwhelming majority of externally supported secular Latino nonprofits founded within the past 25 years are almost entirely financially dependent upon grants from foundations and corporations, and grants and contracts from governmental agencies.

Externally supported Latino nonprofits appear to be well outside the charitable mainstream. They have made very few inroads into the $82 billion market among individual donors for charitable causes. Perhaps the externally funded Latino nonprofits receiving the most foundation grants and corporate contributions are also the ones with the most experience at soliciting individual contributions. That list would roughly correspond to rankings by Facundo (1980a, p. 23) and Valdez (1984, p. 17).

Successful fundraising among foundations might predispose nonprofits to additional, more innovative fundraising methods. For example, among Latino nonprofits, the Mexican American Legal Defense and Educational Fund (MALDEF) receives the largest amount of foundation and corporate contributions. While presenting a draft of her contribution to this book, Martinez related how MALDEF gradually adapted and developed fundraising dinners as part of its overall fundraising strategy. MALDEF also has a relatively long history (as externally supported Latino nonprofits go) with development of an individual donor base. More recently, MALDEF has begun raising funds from Latinos who might benefit from class action civil rights suits being brought by the organization. Of the 95 contributors of funds for MALDEF's suit charging Los Angeles County with discrimination against Latino voters, the large majority are affluent Latino individuals, businessmen, or public officials residing within the voting districts in question (*MALDEF Newsletter,* January 1989, p. 3). Similarly, MALDEF is raising funds from Latino employees of the U.S. Customs Service. MALDEF has sued that agency, charging it with discrimination against Latino employees (*MALDEF Newsletter,* May 1989, p. 1). Although more successful at individual fundraising than other Latino nonprofits, MALDEF continues to depend on foundation grants and corporate contributions for the bulk of its income (MALDEF, 1988, p. 18).

Case studies of MALDEF and other successful fundraisers should be instructive. The National Council of la Raza has adapted very effectively to federal cutbacks by increasing its corporate support. The council also charges its affiliated community-based organizations modest dues and has some experience with individual fundraising. The National Hispanic Scholarship Fund began by trying to develop an individual donor base but eventually proved more successful at gaining corporate and foundation support. The National Concilio of America and other nonprofit coalitions have had some limited success at increasing the number of Latino agencies receiving funds from local United Way campaigns. Latinos have not organized their own federated fundraising campaigns. However, Latinos apparently contribute to some black united funds, especially in Los Angeles (Castillo, 1988). In the early 1980s, the Puerto Rican Legal Defense and Education Fund and five other non-Latino public-interest law organizations successfully sued to participate in the Combined Federal Campaign, through which federal employees make charitable contributions by payroll deduction. Since then, a few other national Latino nonprofits have also begun participating. The National Farm Workers Union (AFL–CIO)—not really a Latino nonprofit in the sense meant here, but generally perceived to be a Latino organization—has mounted several successful direct mail solicitations throughout much of its history.

Priorities

Which potential individual donors should be targeted first by Latino non-profits—the wealthy or the middle class? the public in general or Latino donors in particular? Cost–benefit analysis, based on test mailings and other solicitation experiments, could help define the options. Which donors yield the greatest return on each fundraising dollar expended for Latino nonprof-its? During the past 25 years, the best yield has been from grants from the public sector and organized philanthropy. Latino nonprofits' first fundraising priority continues to be foundation grants and corporate contributions.

For Latino nonprofits, the yield on solicitations for individual donations has been relatively low. With careful planning, training, and technical assis-tance, perhaps Latino nonprofits could dramatically increase that yield, espe-cially among Latino contributors. But are Latino nonprofits prepared to invest adequately, to develop an individual donor base? Research on past successes and failures will probably show a positive correlation between external institutional support and investment by Latino nonprofits in culti-vating individual donors. Even so, such investment is probably suboptimal in all cases.

Such research might conclude that development of individual donor bases will remain a low priority for Latino nonprofits because of financial and technical constraints. Individual fundraising might remain a low priority unless and until sufficient unrestricted core support or fundraising project grants are awarded by foundations and corporations. It might also remain a low priority until the direct-mail solicitation industry and providers of fund-raising training and technical assistance begin addressing themselves more effectively to the nation's growing Latino market.

Philosophy

What philosophical, ideological, equity, and political issues will Latino non-profits face when they are considering new solicitations for funds from mem-bers of the communities they serve? The movement to empower Latinos pre-dates the advent of external funding for Latino nonprofits 25 years ago. Latino researchers, advocates, and community organizers played essential roles in development of the Ford Foundation Hispanic initiative and in implementation of federal War on Poverty and Great Society programs in the mid-1960s.

The development of external support for Latinos was widely viewed as partial compensation to entire communities long victimized by discrimina-tory public policies and private prejudices. Latino nonprofits today are largely dedicated to continued struggle against vestiges of discrimination and prejudice against Latinos in the United States. Among veterans of the Latino nonprofit movement, there remains a degree of anger and a sense of injustice over traditional disenfranchisement and relegation of Latinos to economic and social roles considered inferior in U.S. society. Many Chicano veterans of the movement, for example, consider the advent of external support 25 years ago in a context of 140 years of social injustice (Estrada, García, Macías, Flores, and Maldonado, 1981; Moquin and Van Doren, 1972; Morales, 1972; Santiestevan, 1973; Sierra, 1983, pp. 51–101; Steiner, 1970; Tyler, 1975; see U.S. Commission on Civil Rights, 1968, 1970).

Perhaps the financial and technical resources for development of a Latino individual donor base are already available for Latino nonprofits. Perhaps the resources are not yet available but soon will be, thanks to concerned foundations and corporations. There remains the philosophical question of the appropriateness of shifting the burden of support for Latino nonprofits to the communities they are trying to help. The case for doing so should be made with care.

Approach

To determine promising future directions in development of individual donor bases for Latino nonprofits, we must begin by understanding the status quo. A survey of Latino nonprofits could determine the current extent of fundraising from individuals and the sorts of approaches that work for particular organizations.

An inventory of outside technical assistance and fundraising contractors could also be conducted to discover what, if any, experience exists among direct-mail solicitors and other consultants with fundraising for Latino nonprofits. If such experience proves practically nonexistent, a small symposium might be organized among selected fundraising consultants and Latino direct-mail political and commercial advertising specialists, to explore and develop options. Exploration might done in cooperation with the Council on Foundations' Pluralism in Philanthropy Project, which attempts to promote individual philanthropy among wealthy and affluent members of disadvantaged minority groups.

New directions in fundraising from individuals could be refined through experimentation. Promising approaches revealed by the survey could be adapted to other Latino nonprofits and tested in their respective communities. Ideas developed at the symposium could be test-marketed and evaluated.

Another symposium could explore the philosophical and ethical issues posed by diversion of Latino nonprofits' scarce fundraising resources to development of individual donor bases. Opinion leaders within the Latino empowerment movement and its constituent ethnic subgroups should be included. The objective would be to reach a consensus that could then be written and disseminated.

SHOULD LATINO NONPROFITS SUPPORT THEMSELVES?

What else besides philanthropy might keep Latino nonprofits afloat? Is it reasonable to expect Latino nonprofits to become more self-sufficient? Funding by nonphilanthropic sources is beyond the scope of this chapter, except to the extent that organized philanthropy might facilitate it. The relationship between philanthropy and Latino nonprofits might be expanded to include promotion of increased self-sufficiency. The desirability of doing so poses both philosophical and feasibility issues. Research addressing the following questions could help frame, explore, and resolve those issues.

Returning to the Public Sector

Should Latino nonprofits founded within the past 25 years as government grantees and contractors return to that role, where the bulk of their fundraising experience lies? Can lost federal funding be replaced by contracts with state and local government agencies? The political feasibility of increased public support for Latino nonprofits might be explored. The sorts of technical assistance needed to help Latino nonprofits make the transition to different public-sector funding agencies, programs, and levels of government might also be identified.

Unrelated Business Income

What models of income-generating enterprises (to produce "unrelated business income," in the parlance of Internal Revenue Service regulations governing nonprofit tax-exempt organizations) have worked for Latino nonprofits? What models used by other types of nonprofits might be adapted for Latinos? What sorts of goods and services might Latino nonprofit-controlled enterprises develop and market without distorting the parent nonprofit's social goals and values? What do the experiences of the Latino community development corporations funded by the Ford Foundation through the Southwest Council of la Raza in the late 1960s suggest for income-generating enterprises? Will increasing political backlash by tax-paying, for-profit competitors foreclose that option?

Should organized philanthropy help endow Latino nonprofits with investment portfolios and real estate instead of making project grants? How can optimal balances be struck between conventional and community-based investments? How have some Latino nonprofits managed to acquire their own buildings? Does leasing space out to other Latino nonprofits help or hinder Latino nonprofit landlords?

Approach

Exploratory descriptive research and a survey of Latino nonprofits could help identify useful models. Replication and demonstration could follow.

Such projects are inherently risky and should be treated in an experimental spirit by Latino nonprofits and their funders. Well-established, stable non-profits with diversified programs and funding bases would best withstand the inevitable stresses of new ventures.

CONCLUSION

The seven topics reviewed in this chapter comprise a research agenda. That agenda addresses the information needs of a general strategy for concerned philanthropists and Latinos working together to increase funding for Latino nonprofits. But that strategy has little standing at present. It is loosely based on conclusions reached in 1986 at a membership conference of one voluntary association, Hispanics in Philanthropy. It remains to be seen whether other philanthropists and Latino organizations will adopt it.

A broad consensus on general strategy for increasing funds for Latino non-profits might never emerge, at least not in permanent form. But opinion lead-ers among Latino nonprofits and concerned philanthropists can continue working together to refine and gain general acceptance of elements of that strategy. Those same opinion leaders might never agree upon a final agenda for applied research in the field of philanthropy and Latinos. But they might still agree on the strategic utility of addressing specific research questions, including some of the agenda items proposed here. Strategy and its attendant information needs can be debated forever, but a succession of more limited agreements may be reached along the way.

There is already a broad consensus on the goal of increasing funds for Latino nonprofits. But do researchers care? There is a paucity of research on philanthropy and Latinos emanating from respected universities, centers for the study of nonprofit organizations and philanthropy, and other influential institutions. Some of the works cited in this chapter might not pass academic muster, but they are all we have on the subject.

Sympathetic research professionals needn't wait for a clear mandate from Latinos and philanthropists. Researchers certainly don't have to agree with all my assumptions or adopt my problem formulations. But I would urge researchers to address the field of philanthropy and Latinos. A committed audience of advocates awaits credible research findings and conclusions. Concerned research professionals can make their own strong assumptions about strategy, formulate their own consequent research projects, and join the fray.

11

The Future of Hispanic Nonprofits

Paul N. Ylvisaker

INTRODUCTION

The absorbing and insightful account by Siobhan Oppenheimer Nicolau and Henry Santiestevan (Chap. 4) of the Ford Foundation's role in encouraging Hispanic nonprofits draws me into some retrospectives of my own. I left the Ford Foundation about the time their story begins; let me briefly review what went before.

At Ford, we had spent a decade evolving an interest in urban affairs. We had begun in the usual mode, researching the economic, governmental, and physical planning issues of U.S. sprawling metropolitan areas—with an occasional leap into the problems of Europe and the Far East, particularly Calcutta. The more we looked, the more we were taken by the human dimension of cities, especially the plight of migrants struggling to adapt from rural to urban cultures, too many of them trapped in the poverty of the near downtown. Eventually that interest evolved into Ford's "Gray Areas" program: experimental grants to five major cities and the state of North Carolina—and then suddenly, with President Johnson's burst of national energy, into the War on Poverty's Community Action Program.

But something preceded those Gray Areas grants. Fascinated by the trail of poor migrants struggling to find a better lot in the cities, we assembled a group of thoughtful observers of each of the major streams: Puerto Rican, Appalachian, Mexican, and Southern black. Principal consultants were Clarence Senior, Perley Ayer, Julian Samora-Ernesto Galarza-Herman Gallegos, and Robert Weaver. Weaver, shortly to become President Kennedy's principal urban administrator, spent a year working on the assignment; the two of us collaborated on a proposal to make migration the global theme of the foundation for the next quarter century. It went nowhere; the officers of the foundation had a hard time visualizing what in retrospect has turned out to be one of the dominant forces at work both here and abroad.

So we stayed at home, concentrating on the rural–urban movement within the United States, with the perhaps quixotic hope that we could ease the process and accelerate from three generations to one the transition from rural life to urban acceptance. But we kept two emphases alive: one, the inclusion of all immigrants involved, including Hispanics (on which subsequent programs were built); and two, the conceptual frame of migration. It is within that frame that I would like to begin dealing with the subject assigned me.

CONCEPTUAL FRAME: MIGRATION AND THE LOGICS FLOWING FROM IT

We are in a historical period where "God's eggbeater" is creating massive swirls of human movement on a global scale. I will not belabor the causes or the process; they are well known. Nor will I dwell on the scale, except to wonder whether we yet appreciate the potential. I shall never forget Ted Hesburgh's quiet wondering, after his experience as chair of a commission on immigration, what the world's reaction would be if suddenly 100 million of the subcontinent's poor picked up their meager belongings and headed for Europe, or if an equivalent mass marched from Latin America to the United States.

The magnitude Hesburgh mused about may not yet have materialized, but the flows are mounting, both globally and to the United States. Immigration to this country has reached a historic high, and sources of origin have spread from a concentrated sector (Europe) to all corners of the earth.

Wherever the source, whatever the magnitude, migration has characteristically ignited a psychological syndrome: fear/defensiveness leading to hostility/denigration/repression leading to self-protection/mutual assistance and then to assertiveness. My Norwegian forbearers experienced a faint taste of this in the last century when they were demeaned as "roundheads" and "squareheads" and scorned for their smelly mud houses, but they were too few to touch off much of a hostile reaction. They neither evoked the specter of an oncoming horde nor experienced a correspondingly savage antipathy. Still, one can find evidence of self-protection in their creation of mutual aid and cultural awareness associations.

In Chapter 7, Margarita Melville refers to that rhythm of response to migration, creating sooner or later a sense—if not pervasively a reality—of Hispanic "solidarity": people in a besieged situation needing and tending to feel alike, despite their many other diversities, then organizing spontaneously around a number of defensive and assertive strategies; in this context, note also Albert Camarillo's seven categories of nonprofit action in Chapter 2.

Not all social juxtapositions brought on by migration are peacefully resolved with the passing of time and the evolving of strategies to overcome tensions. Violence and civil strife are too conspicuous a part of history to draw that comforting conclusion. But even when time, rationality, and social mobility work their slow miracles, problems lie ahead. "Self-confidence," Puerto Rican poet Martin Espada said, "is the best defense against hostility." But as self-confidence grows, the divisive process of individualization begins. Ethnic cohesiveness slips away, and class differences emerge between those who have "made it" and those who prosper through what they perceive as self-help.

Ours is a society that begets individualism. And in a singular way, it spawns a culture that gnaws at its own vitals: the sense of community, of common identity and common purpose. De Tocqueville long ago discerned that dualism and marked it as one of the eventual threats to this nation of migrants. Robert Bellah and his associates returned to this theme recently in *Habits of the Heart.* And Chinese anthropologist Fei Xiao Deng faced me with it in a friendly argument I will never forget. "You," he charged, "are the White Devil. Your society defines human potential by what the individual can attain on his own. We do not believe that an individual can realize human potential apart from, or at the risk of, the community to which he belongs."

Without cohesiveness, can there be progress? And with progress, can cohesiveness be sustained? The dilemma is one that sooner or later faces every participant in the migrant process. It is part of the implicit logic of migrations—a seemingly inevitable stage or progression in social displacement and relocation.

A NOTE ON THE ROLE OF NONPROFITS

One driving force in the resolution of that dilemma is the room and the role the United States has given to voluntary associations, what we know as the world of nonprofits. Any collection of people can form such an affinity group anywhere, at any time, with freedom to adopt the goals and strategies that best define their own interests. These organizations may be local or national, single- or multipurpose, conventional or radical, inclusive or exclusive, combative or conciliatory, providers of advocacy or service. What they allow for is a way of acting publicly without waiting for political consensus, a way of expressing unity as well as diversity.

It is no accident or wonder that the host of different groups we now label as *Hispanics* would take recourse to voluntary action as a means to achieve their common and more often divergent purposes. They found themselves in a society where they were too outnumbered to count on the support of government or the majority that by definition controls the government. One reads the chapters in this book and their chronicling of Hispanic reliance on nonprofits with that appreciation in mind, and also with an awareness of two persistent problems: one, the difficulty of finding common ground and presenting a united front; and two, the arduous, even improbable, task of accumulating the resources needed for effective action by a mostly impoverished minority in a chronically hostile and increasingly diffused environment.

FORCES AT WORK

Demographic

The volume of migration, both globally and toward the United States, is likely to hold steady and just as likely to increase. Poverty and war will be pushing millions of the world's population toward safer havens and more affluent and promising economies. Class differences within these migrant groups will be inherent and endemic: Some members will be more educated, more skilled, and more affluent, and a greater number will be of a circumstance two economic stages behind—agricultural, not yet industrial, and far from the service/informational world that is breaking upon us. Age differences will also be evident, with the migrating cohort a good deal younger than the receiving country's population (including earlier migrants—as in the case of southwestern Mexicans native to the area and longer part of the dominant culture). Geographical distribution will also vary, although generally concentrating along U.S. boundaries. We do not have to recount here the distribution of Hispanics, although the consequences of their concentration and dispersion deserve analyzing and projecting, as do the rates—common and differential—of their social mobility and individualization. Also, given the increasing flow and scattering of other ethnic migrants, one can predict the further juxtaposition (melding, confrontation?) of socially diverse populations.

Economic

Ours will be a world of tightening resources and continuing, if not increasing, disparities both within and among nations. Ecological disasters such as ozone depletion and global warming are no longer speculative but imminent. Any combination of the two, plus the social strife that would accompany it, would dramatically increase social displacement and migration. Whatever may transpire will not be in the direction of reduced population flows.

Social and Political

The global response to increased migration has ranged along an entire continuum from almost total prohibition of immigration (Japan) to encouragement (Canada). The U.S. response has been schizophrenic, historically open, then closed, and now warring with itself over welcoming, tolerating, screening, or excluding. On the one hand, charitable instinct, a long tradition of civil rights, and chronic need for an ample work force (now accentuated by a depleting and insufficiently educated cadre of entries) have been on the side of encouragement. On the other hand, xenophobia, racial and ethnic prejudice, fear of linguistic diversity, and political differences have voted discouragement.

Generally, the U.S. response can be expected to remain schizophrenic. The balance can at any time be tipped by sudden bursts of immigration, especially in localities that are heavily impacted, or by particular considerations, as when foreign policy concerns, critical needs for specialized labor, or conspicuously humane considerations enter and become politically attractive. Whatever the immediate balance, continuous screening and endemic social resistance will be constants in U.S. politics. Eternal vigilance will be the price that affected minorities and their allies throughout society will have to pay.

LIMITATIONS OF MIGRATION AS A CONCEPTUAL FRAME

While it is an embracing and provocative concept, migration also has its explanatory shortcomings, not least in the case of Hispanics. Mexicans—now Mexican-Americans—were, after all, the host culture for the oncoming Anglo hordes; they suffered through conquest, not migration. And only as a residue of the original confrontation brought on by migration can the persistent and ever-changing forms of resistance and prejudice be explained. Neither the brutally enforced migration of African blacks into U.S. slavery nor the migration to northern cities of southern blacks (forced even when free) find adequate places within the migration scheme. Even as the volume of immigration grows, there will be more migrants already residing in the United States than will be newly coming to it—except flows from countries minimally or not at all represented yet. Their experience as residents of longer standing inevitably distances them from the newly arrived. That perspective needs to be added to the migratory scheme and logic sketched out in the preceding pages.

FUTURE TRENDS AND NEEDS—HISPANICS AND THEIR NONPROFITS

Hispanic Need for and Use of Nonprofits Are Almost Certain to Increase. To the degree that tension and discrimination ease, a shift from advocacy to service may well take place. In the opinion of some knowledgeable people, this is already occurring. But advocacy will always remain an essential part of the nonprofit scene. Brian O'Connell of Independent Sector has often stated his belief that advocacy is the most precious facet of voluntary activity. In the world of Hispanics and other minorities, advocacy is essential as long as any trace of hostility and discrimination remains. But numerically, as Professor Melville found in her admittedly limited sampling in California, Hispanic nonprofits seem to be predominantly engaged in the provision of services. The reasons are many: the difficulty of securing funding for advocacy, both from public and private sources; the preference of recipients for working with sympathetic and language-friendly service providers; the critical nature of health, education, and other social services in a complicating society; and the often hostile reception given to immigrants and minorities by public and private agencies, themselves experiencing a steady diminution of funds.

Increased Demand Does Not Automatically Ensure Increased Supply. As Lester Salamon has documented, government assistance to nonprofits has been cut by more than a score of billions during the Reagan administration, and the difference has not been made up by private funders. It is likely that public funding will continue to fall off, while private giving, although steadily increasing, has not shown much responsiveness to Hispanic organizations (although the argument is made, sometimes persuasively, that grants, even when minimal to Hispanic nonprofits as such, often directly benefit Hispanic groups and individuals). Also, one is struck by Michael Cortés' observation that Latino response to invitations for funding have been disappointing. If so, that too will most likely change.

Hispanics Will Become More Aggressive and Effective in the Growing Competition for Resources. As I reread the chapters of this book, I am impressed with the steepness of the learning curve of Hispanics and their nonprofit organizations. Necessity is the mother of invention, and the necessity is there. Leadership and sophistication continue to emerge in the Hispanic community. I am particularly struck by the emergence of assertive leadership and participation by Hispanic women.

Much of philanthropy's slowness to respond is due to donors' unfamiliarity with Hispanic circumstances and needs. This knowledge gap arises less from hostility than from social distance separating donors and Hispanics. Closing the gap will require movement on both sides—more from the donor community because of its advantaged position. That includes Hispanic donors as well: the growing number of those who have "made it" in the United States. These rising professionals and entrepreneurs—the Bill Cosbys, if you will—within the Hispanic community can make powerfully symbolic statements. But the burden of that mission must fall on donors of the larger community: first, to increase the representation of Hispanics on their boards and staff; and second, to take the initiative in learning about Hispanic needs and then to respond with some measure of proportion and fairness. With the steady emergence of qualified Hispanic community leaders and professionals, philanthropic response can and should be expected increasingly from regional and local sources, particularly community foundations. Until now, national foundations have been the major suppliers: As Michael Cortés points out, seven funders accounted for 75 percent of all grants to Hispanic nonprofits over the past fifteen years, the Ford Foundation alone contributing half of the total. There are signs that national foundations are not continuing that effort; in the squeeze that may follow, it will probably be the start-up rate of new national Hispanic organizations that will be at risk. Sharply felt, too, will be the switch from institutional support to project funding, a pattern so characteristic of organized philanthropy.

The Growing Size and Presence of the Hispanic Population Will Be Another Favorable Influence on Both Private and Public Funding. I have not yet seen an analysis of the Hispanic vote in the last presidential election, Undoubtedly, it was not as concentrated as the Democratic vote among blacks and was more influential in local than in national balloting. Whether concentrated or not, with the nation moving from one-fifth to one-third minority in the next decade or two, the minority and Hispanic vote will increasingly be courted; funders, as it was once said of the Supreme Court, do follow the election returns. But again, the increasingly competitive potential of Hispanics and their nonprofits may assure a larger share of what could well be a shrinking pie.

Full Realization of That Potential Depends on a Number of Contingencies. Will increasing numbers reignite hostility and attempts at repression and exclusion? Will numbers translate into votes? This is certainly a challenge not only in registering but even more in getting out the vote, converting the undocumented into citizens, and showing adroitness in political leadership. Evidence of hostility lurks behind the English only movement that has been discouragingly successful in several state elections. Encouragingly, one sees the effectiveness of the late Willie Velasquez and his successor, Andy Hernandez, as well as the emergence of extraordinarily competent political action and leadership in places like San Antonio, Texas.

Most of All, Hispanic Effectiveness and Progress Depend on the Degree to Which the Waste of Hispanic Human Talent Through Educational Deficiencies Is Radically Reduced and the Level of Academic Achievement Raised. This deserves the highest priority for both advocacy and service nonprofits, as well as for agencies and leaders throughout the general society. The task is a formidable one, ranging from curbing prejudice to strengthening the family and improving job prospects. The Hispanic dropout rate is as tragic as it is inexcusable. The new president's leadershp task certainly includes efforts to reduce the current waste of the nation's Hispanic and other human resources. Education has always been the stepping stone if not the cornerstone of progress for newcoming populations: Irish, German, Jewish, Scandinavian, and others of European origin; and blacks through the creation of an entire system of higher education. Hispanics have not had the advantage of concerted efforts to ensure greater access and to stimulate enhanced performance, certainly not the establishment of educational institutions in which they could feel a sense of ownership and full participation, as blacks and certain ethnic–religious groups have had. Interestingly, however, there are now twenty institutions of higher education in which Hispanics constitute 50 percent or more of total enrollment and another twenty with 40 percent or more.

One Special Field in Which Hispanic Talent Needs to Be Mobilized and Trained Is Nonprofit Leadership and Management. Hispanic talent is painfully scarce in the independent sector, both in Anglo and Hispanic institutions. In this era of rising needs and limited resources, such talent will be sorely needed, as will the recruitment and stimulation of volunteers. The rapidly multiplying academic and training centers in the nonprofit field must aggressively recruit Hispanics, provide the necessary financial aid, concentrate on leadership development, give appropriate curricular attention to the Hispanic circumstance, and make sure that persons indigenous to or more than casually familiar with that circumstance be represented on their faculties. The level of support of Hispanic nonprofits and the attention paid to them will undoubtedly reflect the increased confidence and competence such new expertise would generate.

Of Equal Importance Is the Strengthening of the Research Capacity of Hispanic Nonprofits. As Henry Santiestevan is fond of saying, the game ahead is going to be one of "hardball based on hard facts." There is no Brookings Institution or other established research facility dedicated more than marginally to the progress and problems of Latinos in this country—or, for that matter, in their countries of origin. All varieties of nonprofits, not to mention public legislatures and executives, are badly in need of such research. This is an intellectual infrastructure that is missing and needs to be put in place. It could be provided by expanding the resources and capacity of existing and emerging centers (such as the Tomás Rivera Center in Claremont, California) as well as by special institutes and incentive grants.

Effectiveness of Pro-Hispanic Efforts Will More and More Depend on the Capacity to Coalesce, Link, and Bridge. Isolation, heterogeneity, and further erosion of solidarity by stratification and individualization have made it exceptionally difficult to build a Hispanic self-consciousness and a proportionally significant impact on the U.S. scene, given the power, persistence, and pervasiveness of those forces. The answer, and the art of maximizing Hispanic influence, will probably lie more in linking and bridging than in forcing or otherwise artificially obscuring and obliterating those internal differences. Consciousness raising among both Hispanics and non-Hispanics is always a worthy and needed endeavor, but never in such a way that it presents a false picture or restrictive standard of unity.

This does not rule out a continuous search for common themes and aspirations that unify rather than divide. On the contrary, it puts a premium on such efforts. It would therefore seem beneficial, at least to this outsider, to encourage a Pan-Hispanic coalition to define and advance a common agenda and joint efforts among all the constituent parts of the Hispanic population, including the more and less advantaged. (I note with some surprise—certainly with fascination—William McCready's description (Chap. 6) of the gap between the Catholic church and Hispanic social movements and his urging that there be more of an alliance most people would assume to have long existed.)

Even with such coalescence, the "Hispanic agenda" still will not have enough votes and influence to carry. Linking and bridging with other elements of the U.S. population are essential. The gulf between Hispanics and blacks—and, if the eternal tendency of minorities to fight over crumbs persists, between Hispanics and other beleaguered groups as well—is wide and ever in danger of widening. Efforts to link those disparate elements deserve encouragement and an explicit place among nonprofit priorities.

My own experience with such linking demonstrates, at least to me, the advantage and promise they hold. The Hispanic Policy Development Project, designed deliberately as an Anglo–Hispanic partnership, has been a remarkably effective instrument, despite the almost inevitable controversy and tensions. Shortly, our "Anglo" contingent will include black representation—another bridging step that is long in coming.

A Critical Determinant in Advancing Hispanic and Other Minority Causes Will Be the Future Role That Outnumbered and Less Advantaged Populations Will Choose to Play in the Political Process. The options are essentially two. The first is to work within one of the two major parties, presumably the Democratic Party, which has traditionally been far more open to minority concerns. That option has its own attractions, not least being the imminent restructuring of the Democratic Party and the emergence of minority leaders such as Jesse Jackson with proven vote-getting records. But if, as is likely, the Democratic Party will be realigning its orientation toward mainstream and majority interests, the tendency will be, as in the Republican Party, to play down and submerge minority issues. The other option is to play independent and hard to get, contributing a swing vote for which both parties must compete. Both strategies will require a discipline among Hispanics that is not congruent with their history but not beyond all likelihood.

A third option is to concentrate locally and differentially, as has been mostly characteristic of Hispanic politics so far. That tactic has produced results in areas where Hispanics are concentrated, but it leaves national elections relatively untouched by an Hispanic presence.

Still, who knows? Our new president has said he wants a "kinder and gentler America." Is this political rhetoric or a genuine promise of greater empathy with the plight of newcomers and minorities? The evidence for the latter is at best mixed.

Appendix A: Conference Participants

Note: * = conference planning committee.

Raydean Acevedo
Program Manager
National Computer Systems
Washington, D.C.

Audrey Alvarado
Executive Director
Latin American Research and Service Agency
Denver, Colorado

Luis Alvarez
President
National Urban Fellows Program
New York City, New York

Miguel Barragan
President
National Concilio of America
San Francisco, California

Camen Bolden
Executive Director
Congreso de Latinos Unidos
Philadelphia, Pennsylvania

Carmen Bolt
District Manager for Hillsborough County
Social Security Administration
Tampa, Florida

Maria Gonzalez Borrero
Assistant City Manager
Hartford, Connecticut

Albert Camarillo
Professor
History Department
Stanford University
Stanford, California

Dennis A. Collins
President
The James Irvine Foundation
San Francisco, California

Michael Cortés*
Department of Architecture and Urban Planning
University of California at Los Angeles
Los Angeles, California

Christina Cuevas*
Program Executive
San Francisco Foundation
San Francisco, California

Grace Montañez Davis
Deputy Mayor
Los Angeles, California

Gloria De Necochea
Senior Program Officer
California Community Foundation
Los Angeles, California

Guarione M. Diaz
President and Executive Director
Cuban American National Council
Miami, Florida

William A. Diaz
Program Officer
Ford Foundation
New York City, New York

Thomas Donahoe
President
Pacific Telesis Foundation
San Francisco, California

Wilma Espinoza*
Consultant
Kahlo Group
San Francisco, California

Leobardo F. Estrada
Associate Professor
Department of Architecture and Urban Planning
University of California at Los Angeles
Los Angeles, California

Angelo Falcón
President
Institute for Puerto Rican Policy
New York City, New York

Ruben Franco
President and General Counsel
Puerto Rican Legal Defense and Education Fund
New York City, New York

Herman Gallegos*
Chair of the Board
Gallegos Institutional Investors Corporation
San Francisco, California

Margarita Garcia
Director of Special Programs
International Rescue Committee
West New York, New Jersey

Miguel Garcia, Jr.
Program Officer
Primerica Corporation
Greenwich, Connecticut

Andrew Hernandez
Executive Director
Southwest Voter Registration Education Project
San Antonio, Texas

Antonia Hernandez
President and General Counsel
Mexican American Legal Defense and Educational Fund
Los Angeles, California

Carmela Lacayo
President and Executive Director
National Association for Hispanic Elderly
Los Angeles, California

Douglas Lawson
Allocations Specialist
Campaign for Human Development
National Conference of Catholic Bishops
Washington, D.C.

Mary E. Leslie
Executive Director
Pacific Telesis Foundation
San Francisco, California

Arturo Madrid
President
Tomás Rivera Center
Claremont, California

Arabella Martinez*
President
Center for Policy Development
Berkeley, California

Vilma S. Martinez
Attorney at Law
Los Angeles, California

José Matos-Real
Consultant
Chicago, Illinois

William C. McCready
Associate Director
Public Opinion Research Laboratory
Northern Illinois University
DeKalb, Illinois

Margarita B. Melville
Associate Professor and Coordinator of Chicano Studies
Department of Ethnic Studies
University of California at Berkeley
Berkeley, California

Alex Mercure
Mercure Realty
Albuquerque, New Mexico

Henry Mestre*
Consultant
San Leandro, California

Hugo Morales
President
Radio Bilingue Foundation
Fresno, California

Siobhan Oppenheimer Nicolau
President
Hispanic Policy Development Project
New York City, New York

Abdin Noboa
Vice President for Research and Evaluation
Quest International
Granville, Ohio

Louis Nuñez
President
National Puerto Rican Coalition
Washington, D.C.

Michael O'Neill*
Professor and Director
Institute for Nonprofit Organization Management
University of San Francisco
San Francisco, California

Joel Orosz
Associate Program Officer
W. K. Kellogg Foundation
Battle Creek, Michigan

Douglas X. Patiño
President and Chief Executive Officer
Marin Community Foundation
Larkspur, California

James R. Perez*
Branch Chief
Office of Civil Rights
U.S. Department of Health and Human Services,
    Region IX

Cruz Reynoso
Attorney at Law
Old Sacramento, California

J. W. Rhodes, Jr.
Manager, Corporate Contributions
Chevron USA
San Francisco, California

Aida Rodriguez
Research Associate/Policy Analyst
Equal Opportunity Division
Rockefeller Foundation
New York City, New York

Carlos Rodriguez-Fraticelli
Assistant Professor
University of Puerto Rico
San Juan, Puerto Rico

Harriett Romo
Project Coordinator, IUP/SSRC
Center for Mexican American Studies
University of Texas at Austin
Austin, Texas

Julian Samora
Professor Emeritus
University of Notre Dame
South Bend, Indiana

Henry Santiestevan
Executive Vice President
Hispanic Policy Development Project
Washington, D.C.

Marta Sotomayor
President
National Hispanic Council on Aging
Washington, D.C.

B. Stotzer
Consultant
Los Angeles, California

Diana Torres
Director, Project Blueprint
United Way of America
Arlington, Virginia

Rev. Rosendo Urrabazo, CMF
President
Mexican American Cultural Center
San Antonio, Texas

Luz A. Vega*
Senior Program Officer
James Irvine Foundation
San Francisco, California

Kirke Wilson*
Executive Director

Rosenberg Foundation
San Francisco, California

Paul N. Ylvisaker
Charles W. Eliot Professor of Education
Harvard University
Cambridge, Massachusetts

Alex Zermeno*
Human Resources Development Specialist
Bay Area Rapid Transit
Oakland, California

Appendix B: Authors

Maria Gonzalez Borrero is assistant city manager in Hartford, Connecticut. She is a director and the founder of Hispanic Health Council, a community-based research and training institute. She has served on the boards of several local and national nonprofit organizations, including the National Puerto Rican Coalition. Her publications include articles and monographs on health issues in the Hispanic community.

Albert M. Camarillo is professor of history at Stanford University, former executive director of the Interuniversity Program for Latino Research, and former director of Stanford's Center for Chicano Research. His publications include *Chicanos in a Changing Society: From Mexican Pueblos to American Barrios in Santa Barbara and Southern California, 1848–1930* (Harvard University Press, 1979), *Chicanos in California: A History of Mexican Americans* (Boyd and Fraser, 1984), and *Mexicans in American Cities: Mexican Americans in American Ethnic and Immigrant Group History* (Oxford University Press, forthcoming).

Michael Eduardo Cortés is completing his doctoral dissertation at the Graduate School of Public Policy at the University of California at Berkeley. He has taught at U.C. Berkeley and UCLA, and was the director of Planning, Finance, and Administration at the Levi Strauss Foundation, and the vice president for Research, Advocacy, and Legislation at the National Council of La Raza. He served for several years as a consultant to Hispanics in Philanthropy.

Leobardo F. Estrada is associate professor in the Graduate School of Architecture and Urban Planning at the University of California at Los Angeles. He is a former staff assistant to the deputy director, U.S. Bureau of the Census, and chairs the Hispanic Advisory Committee on the 1990 Census. His principal research interests are racial and ethnic statistics, particularly with reference to the Hispanic population of the United States.

Herman E. Gallegos is Chair of the Board, Gallegos Institutional Investors Corporation, San Francisco. He was the founding executive director of the Southwest (later National) Council of La Raza. From 1979 to 1989, he was a trustee of the Rockefeller Foundation. He is a former trustee of the Rosenberg Foundation and the Dole Foundation and is currently a director of Pacific Telesis Group, Union Bank, Independent Sector, and the San Francisco Foundation.

Vilma S. Martinez is a partner in the Los Angeles law firm of Munger, Tolles, and Olson. From 1973 to 1982, she was president and general counsel of the Mexican American Legal Defense and Educational Fund (MALDEF). She served for three years as a staff attorney for the NAACP Legal Defense Fund. She is a former regent of the University of California (1976–1990) and is a director of the Anheuser Busch Companies, the Southwest Voter Registration Education Project, and the Edward W. Hazen Foundation.

William C. McCready is associate director of the Public Opinion Laboratory and associate professor of sociology at Northern Illinois University. He has been a faculty member at the University of Chicago, Loyola University of Chicago, and St. Xavier College in Chicago, and was program director in the Center for the Study of American Pluralism at the National Opinion Research Center. His publications include *Hispanics in the United States* (Transaction Press, 1985; with Pastora Cafferty) and several books and articles on ethnicity in the United States.

Margarita B. Melville is associate professor in the Chicano Studies Department at the University of California at Berkeley. She has written widely on culture, class, gender, and ethnicity in the United States, Mexico, and Central America. Her publications include *Guatemala: The Politics of Land Ownership* (Free Press, 1971) and *Twice a Minority: Mexican American Women* (Mosby, 1980).

Michael O'Neill is professor and director, Institute for Nonprofit Organization Management, University of San Francisco. His publications include *Educating Managers of Nonprofit Organizations* (Praeger, 1988; with Dennis R. Young) and *The Third America: The Emergence of the Nonprofit Sector in the United States* (Jossey-Bass, 1989).

Siobhan Oppenheimer Nicolau is president and founder of the Hispanic Policy Development Project. From 1968 to 1981, she was a program officer at the Ford Foundation, where she was responsible for Ford's Hispanic project funding. Prior to her years at Ford, she worked for Stamford, Connecticut, and New York City in social service and community action programs. She has authored or co-authored numerous reports on Hispanic youth, and serves as consultant on Hispanic affairs to several foundations and corporations.

Carlos Rodriguez-Fraticelli is assistant professor at the University of Puerto Rico and former director of the Higher Education Task Force at the Centro de Estudios Puertorriqueños, Hunter College, City University of New York. He has also taught at Haverford College and Yale University. He has published several articles on the Puerto Rican experience in the United States.

Carlos Sanabria is a research associate at the Centro de Estudios Puertorriqueños, Hunter College, City University of New York. His work has focused on the history of Puerto Rican migration to the United States.

Henry Santiestevan is the president of Santiestevan Associates, a Hispanic-oriented public relations firm. He is senior fellow and former executive vice president at the Hispanic Policy Development Project. He worked for the United Auto Workers, the CIO, the AFL–CIO, and was the second executive director of the Southwest (later National) Council of La Raza. His publications include several articles on Mexican-American organizations, labor issues, and immigration.

Amílcar Tirado is librarian and researcher at the Centro de Estudios Puertorriqueños, Hunter College, City University of New York, and a member of the editorial committee of the *Centro Bulletin*.

Paul N. Ylvisaker is Charles William Eliot Professor of Education at Harvard University and former dean of the Harvard Graduate School of Education. He was director of the Public Affairs Program at the Ford Foundation from 1959 to 1967, where he established Ford's "Gray Areas" program, widely considered to have had a major formative influence on the Johnson administration's War on Poverty. He has written extensively on issues relating to philanthropy, urban problems, education, and government. He is a director of the Mary Reynolds Babcock Foundation and the Hispanic Policy Development Project, and a consulting director of the Dayton Hudson Corporation.

References

Acuña, Rodolfo. *Occupied America: A History of Chicanos,* 2d ed. New York: Harper and Row, 1981.

Alba, Richard, and Kessler, R. "Patterns of Interethnic Marriage among American Catholics." *Social Forces* 57(1980):1124–1140.

Alinsky, Saul. *Reveille for Radicals.* Chicago: University of Chicago Press, 1946.

Allsup, Carl. *The American G.I. Forum: Origins and Evolution.* Mexican American Monograph No. 6. Austin: University of Texas Press, 1982.

American Association of Fund-Raising Counsel. *Giving U.S.A.: A Compilation of Facts and Trends on American Philanthropy for the Year 1986.* New York: AAFRC, 1987.

Arce, Carlos. "Chicano Participation in Academe: A Case of Academic Colonialism." *Grito del Sol* 3(1978):75–104.

Aspira. "Building Career and Leadership Opportunities for Puerto Rican Youth in New York City: A Proposal." Mimeographed, 1959.

Astin, Alexander W. *Final Report of the Commission on the Higher Education of Minorities.* Los Angeles: Higher Education Research Institute, 1982.

Attinasi, John J., Flores, Raymundo, and Osorio, Rufino. *Strangers in the Philanthropic World: The Limited Latino Share of Chicago Grants.* Chicago: Latino Institute, 1986.

Barrera, Mario. "The Historical Evolution of Chicano Political Goals." *Sage Race Relations Abstracts* 10(1)(1985):1–15.

Bennis, Warren, and Nanus, Burt. *Leaders: The Strategies for Taking Charge.* New York: Harper & Row, 1985.

Blawis, Patricia B. *Tijerina and the Land Grants: Mexican Americans in Struggle for Their Heritage.* New York: International Publishers Company, 1971.

Bonilla, Frank. "Rationale for a Culturally Based Program of Action Against Poverty Among New York Puerto Ricans." New York: Puerto Rican Forum, 1965.

Borjas, George J., and Tienda, Marta (eds.). *Hispanics in the U.S. Economy.* New York: Academic Press, 1985.

Briegel, Kaye L. "Alianza Hispano-Americana, 1894–1965: A Mexican American Fraternal Insurance Society." Ph.D. diss., University of Southern California, 1974.

Camarillo, Albert. *Chicanos in a Changing Society: From Mexican Pueblos to American Barrios in Santa Barbara and Southern California, 1848–1930.* Cambridge, Mass.: Harvard University Press, 1979.

Camarillo, Albert. *Chicanos in California: A History of Mexican Americans.* San Francisco: Boyd and Fraser, 1984.

Carlos, Manuel Luis. "Identidad y raices culturales de los enclaves hispanos de los EE.UU." In *Hispanos en los Estados Unidos,* R. J. Cortina and Alberto Moncada (eds.). Madrid: Ediciones de Cultura Hispanica, 1988.

Castillo, Lilia Frankel. "An Exploratory-Descriptive Study of the Historical Development of Independent Fundraising in the Los Angeles Chicano Community." MSW thesis, University of California, Los Angeles, 1988.

Centro de Estudios Puertorriqueños. *Labor Migration Under Capitalism.* New York: Monthly Review Press, 1979.

Centro de Estudios Puertorriqueños. *Sources for the Study of Puerto Rican Migration, 1879–1930.* New York: Centro de Estudios Puertorriqueños, City University of New York, 1982.

Chenault, Lawrence R. *The Puerto Rican Migrant in New York City.* New York: Russell and Russell, 1970.

Claudio, Edwin. "Hispanic Organizations and Philanthropy in Chicago." Unpublished report. Chicago: Latino Institute, 1983.

Coleman, James S., and Hoffer, Thomas. *Public and Private High Schools: The Impact of Communities.* New York: Basic Books, 1987.

Cortés, Carlos E. (ed.). *Latinos in the United States: An Original Anthology.* New York: Arno Press, 1980.

Cortés, Michael. "Hispanics and Grantmakers: New Approaches to Growing Hispanic Communities." Working Paper No. 1987-1. San Francisco: Hispanics in Philanthropy, 1987.

Cortés, Michael. "Hispanics and Philanthropy: A Research Agenda." Unpublished draft of Working Paper No. 1988-1. San Francisco: Hispanics in Philanthropy, 1988.

Cortés, Michael. "Latino Philanthropy: Some Unanswered Questions." Paper presented to the Council on Foundations, Pluralism in Philanthropy Project, Washington, D.C., June 1, 1989.

Council on Foundations. "Revised Report and Recommendations to the Commission on Private Philanthropy and Public Needs on Private Philanthropic Foundations." New York: The Council, August, 1975.

Council of Foundations. Annual Conference, Toronto, 1989.

Davis, Gary, Haub, Carl, and Wilette, Joanne. "U.S. Hispanics: Changing the Face of America." *Population Bulletin* 38(3)(1983).

Del Castillo, Richard G. *The Los Angeles Barrio, 1859–1890: A Social History.* Los Angeles: University of California Press, 1979.

De León, Arnoldo. *The Tejano Community, 1836–1900.* Albuquerque: University of New Mexico Press, 1982.

De Necochea, Gloria. "HIP Conducts Survey of Latino Grantseeker Training Needs." *Hispanics in Philanthropy News* 3(1)(Winter/Spring 1989):1.

Díaz, Guarione M. "Meeting Cubans' Needs: How Can Grantmakers Help?" In *Hispanics and Grantmakers: A Special Report of Foundation News,* Henry Santiestevan (ed.). Washington, D.C.: Council on Foundations, 1981.

Dohen, Dorothy. "Marriage, Family, and Fertility Patterns Among Puerto Ricans." In *Hispanics in New York: Religious, Cultural, and Social Experiences,* Vol. 1. New York: The Office of Pastoral Research, Archdiocese of New York, 1982.

Doyle, Ruth. *Hispanics in New York: Religious, Cultural, and Social Experiences,* Vol. 1. New York: The Office of Pastoral Research, Archdiocese of New York, 1982.

Encyclopedia of Associations, 22nd ed. Detroit: Gale Research Co., 1988.

Escutia, Marta M., and Prieto, Margarita. *Hispanics in the Work Force.* Washington, D.C.: National Council of la Raza, 1986.

Espinoza, Wilma. Memorandum and Report to Hispanics in Philanthropy on the "Grantseekers Training Project Survey." San Francisco, 1988.

Estrada, Leobardo F., García, F. Chris, Macías, Reynaldo Flores, and Maldonado, Lionel. "Chicanos in the United States: A History of Exploitation and Resistance." *Daedalus* 110 (Spring 1981):103–132.

Facundo, Blanca. *Responsiveness of U.S. Foundations to Hispanic Needs and Concerns: Results of a Survey on Institutional Policies and Procedures Relevant to Hispanics and an Analysis of Grant Information in the 1977 and 1978 Foundation Grants Index.* Reston, Va.: Latino Institute, Research Division, 1980a.

Facundo, Blanca. "Responsiveness of U.S. Foundations to Hispanic Needs and Concerns: Results of a Survey on Institutional Policies and Procedures Relevant to Hispanics in Educational R&D and Other Related Areas, and an Analysis of Grants Information in the 1977 and 1978 Foundation Grants Index." Unpublished technical report submitted by the Latino Institute Research Division, Reston, Va., to the U.S. National Institute of Education, Minorities and Women Program, Grant No. NIE-G-79-0069, June, 1980b.

Figueroa, Darryl. "Lois Athey Becomes NPRC Training and Technical Assistance Coordinator." *NPRC Reports* 8(10)(December 1988):4.

Fitzpatrick, Joseph P. "The Puerto Rican Family." In *Ethnic Families in America,* Charles H. Mindel and Robert W. Haberstein (eds.). New York: Elsevier, 1976.

Fitzpatrick, Joseph P. *Puerto Rican Americans: The Meaning of Migration to the Mainland,* 2d ed. Englewood Cliffs, N.J.: Prentice-Hall, 1987.

Foley, Douglas E. *From Peones to Politicos: Ethnic Relations in a South Texas Town, 1900–1977.* Mexican American Monograph No. 3. Austin: University of Texas Press, 1977.

Forum of National Hispanic Organizations. "Issue Review: Corporate and Foundation Philanthropy." Briefing packet for "First Corporate/Hispanic Partnership Summit," conference of the Forum of National Hispanic Organizations, San Francisco, October 23, 1982.

Freyre, G. *The Masters and the Slaves.* New York: Knopf, 1946.

Gallegos, Herman. *U.S. Foundations and Minority Group Interests.* Report prepared by the U.S. Human Resources Corporation. San Antonio: Mexican American Cultural Center, 1975.

Gallegos, Herman. "Hispanics in America: Opportunities for Responsive Philanthropy." Paper presented to the Ford Foundation, Conference on Hispanic Public Policy and Research Issues, New York City, February 9, 1987.

Gann, Lewis H., and Duignan, Peter J. *The Hispanics in the United States: A History.* Boulder, Colo.: Westview Press, 1986.

Garment, Suzanne. "Nicaragua Debate Will Make Waves Among Hispanics." *Wall Street Journal,* March 21, 1987.

Garonzik, Elan (ed.). *The Foundation Grants Index, 13th ed.: A Cumulative Listing of Foundation Grants.* New York: Foundation Center, 1984.

Geertz, Clifford. "Religion as a Cultural System." In *The Religious Situation,* Donald Cutler (ed.). Boston: Beacon, 1968.

Glaser, Pamela. A. *Immigrants at Risk*. Chicago: Traveler's & Immigrants Aid of Chicago, May, 1988.

Glazer, Nathan, and Moynihan, Daniel Patrick. *Beyond the Melting Pot: The Negroes, Puerto Ricans, Jewish, Italian and Irish in New York City*. Cambridge, Mass.: Harvard University Press, 1963.

Gonzales, Sylvia A. *Hispanic American Voluntary Organizations*. Westport, Conn.: Greenwood Press, 1985.

Gotsch, John Warren. "Puerto Rican Leadership in New York." Master's thesis, New York University, 1966.

Gray, Sandra T. (ed.). *An Independent Sector Resource Directory of Education and Training Opportunities and Other Services*, 2d ed. Washington, D.C.: Independent Sector, 1987.

Grebler, L., Moore, W., and Guzmán, R. *The Mexican American People*. New York: Free Press, 1970.

Greeley, Andrew. *Catholic High Schools and Minority Students*. New Brunswick, N.J.: Transaction, 1982.

Gutierrez, Armando G., and Hirsh, Herbert. "Political Maturation and Political Awareness: The Case of the Crystal City Chicano," *Aztlan* 5(1, 2)(Spring/Fall, 1974):295–312.

Gutierrez, Davis. "CASA and the Chicano Movement: A Study of Organizational Politics and Ideology in the Chicano Community, 1968–1978." Working Paper No. 5, Stanford Center for Chicano Research, Stanford University, August 1984.

Hayes-Bautista, David E., Schink, Werner O., and Chapa, Jorge. *The Burden of Support: Young Latinos in an Aging Society*. Stanford, Calif.: Stanford University Press, 1988.

Herbstein, Judith. "Rituals and Politics of the Puerto Rican 'Community' in New York City." Doctoral dissertation, City University of New York, 1978.

Hernandez, José A. *Mutual Aid for Survival: The Case of the Mexican American*. Malabar, Fla.: Krieger, 1983.

Hispanics In Philanthropy: An Overview. San Francisco: Hispanics In Philanthropy, 1989.

Hodgkinson, Virginia A., and Weitzman, Murray S. *Giving and Volunteering in the United States: Findings from a National Survey*. Washington, D.C.: Independent Sector, 1988.

Hodgkinson, Virginia A., and Weitzman, Murray S. *Dimensions of the IndependentSector: A StatisticalProfile,* 3ded. Washington, D.C.: IndependentSector, 1989.

Hodgkinson, Virginia A., Weitzman, Murray S., and Kirsch, Arthur D. *From Belief to Commitment: The Activities and Finances of Religious Congregations in the United States.* Washington, D.C.: Independent Sector, 1988.

International Commission for Central American Recovery and Development. "Poverty, Conflict, and Hope: A Turning Point in Central America." Duke University Center for International Development, February 1989.

Johnson, Robert M. "Investing in Your Own Community." In *Hispanics and Grantmakers: A Special Report of Foundation News,* Henry Santiestevan (ed.). Washington, D.C.: Council on Foundations, 1981.

Kallen, Horace M. *Americanism and Its Makers.* New York: Bureau of Jewish Education, 1944.

Keane, John G. "Changing Population Patterns." In *The World Almanac.* New York: Pharos Books, 1989.

Kluckhohn, Florence, and Strodbeck, Fred. *Variations in Value Orientations.* New York: Row, Peterson and Co., 1961.

Kovacs, Ruth (ed.). *The Foundation Grants Index, 17th ed.: A Cumulative Listing of Foundation Grants Reported in 1987.* New York: Foundation Center, 1988.

Levy, Stephen, Tebbets, Ruth, and Brousseau, Fred. *Projections of Hispanic Population for California: 1985–2000: With Projections of Non-Hispanic White, Black and Asian and Other Population Groups.* Palo Alto, Calif.: Center for Continuing Study of the California Economy, 1982.

Lewis, Oscar. *La Vida: A Puerto Rican Family in the Culture of Poverty— San Juan and New York.* New York: Random House, 1966.

Liebow, Elliot. *Tally's Corner.* Boston: Little, Brown and Co., 1967.

Limón, José E. "El Primer Congreso Mexicanista de 1911: A Precursor to Contemporary Chicanismo." *Aztlan* 5(1, 2)(Spring/Fall 1974):85–106.

Mackelprang, A. J., and Longbrake, David B. "Hispanic Population Growth and Economic Development: Setting the Policy Agenda for the Next Century." *Management Science and Policy Analysis* 4(4)(Fall/Winter 1984):19–29.

Marin, Christine. *A Spokesman of the Mexican American Movement: Rodolfo "Corky" Gonzales and the Fight for Chicano Liberation.* San Francisco: R and E Research Associates, 1977.

Martinez, Tomas M. "Chicanismo." *Epoca I* 2(1971):35–39.

McCready, William C. "The Persistence of Ethnic Variation in American Families." In *Ethnicity in the United States: A Preliminary Reconnaissance,* Andrew M. Greeley and William McCready (eds.). New York: Wiley-Interscience, 1976.

McCready, William C. "Analysis of Seminary Enrollment for the Archdiocese of Chicago." Unpublished paper, 1983.

McGregor, Douglas. *The Human Side of Enterprise.* New York: McGraw Hill, 1960.

Meier, Matt S. *Mexican American Biographies: A Historical Dictionary, 1836–1987.* Westport, Conn.: Greenwood Press, 1988.

Meier, Matt S., and Rivera, Feliciano. *Dictionary of Mexican American History.* Westport, Conn.: Greenwood Press, 1981.

Melville, Margarita. "Ethnicity: An Analysis of Its Dynamism and Variability Focusing on the Mexican/Anglo/Mexican American Interface." *American Ethnologist* 10(2)(1983):272–289.

Melville, Margarita. "Hispanics: Race, Class, or Ethnicity?" *The Journal of Ethnic Studies* 16(1)(1988):67–83.

Mexican American Legal Defense and Educational Fund (MALDEF). *Annual Report: May, 1987, through April, 1988.* Los Angeles, 1988.

Mills, C. Wright, Senior, Clarence, and Goldsen, Rose Kohn. *The Puerto Rican Journey: New York's Newest Migrants.* New York: Harper and Brothers, 1950.

Miringoff, Marc L. *Management in Human Service Organizations.* New York: Macmillan, 1980.

Montejano, David. *Anglos and Mexicans in the Making of Texas, 1836–1986.* Austin: University of Texas Press, 1987.

Moquin, Wayne, and Van Doren, Charles (eds.). *A Documentary History of the Mexican Americans.* New York: Bantam Books, 1972.

Morales, Armando. *Ando Sagrando: A Study of Mexican American—Police Conflict.* La Puente, Calif.: Perspectiva Publications, 1972.

Moreno, Juan. "Foundation Giving to Puerto Rican and Latino Community Organizations, 1972–1981." New York: Institute for Puerto Rican Policy, 1983.

Nabokov, Peter. *Tijerina and the Courthouse Raid.* Albuquerque: University of New Mexico Press, 1969.

Nason, John W. *Trustees and the Future of Foundations*. New York: Council on Foundations, 1977.

National Commission on Secondary Schooling for Hispanics. *Make Something Happen*. Washington, D.C.: Hispanic Policy Development Project, 1984.

National Puerto Rican Coalition. *Major U.S. Foundations' and Corporations' Responsiveness to Puerto Rican Needs and Concerns*. Report NPRC 87-1. New York: NPRC, 1987.

Navarro, Armando. "The Evolution of Chicano Politics." *Aztlan* 5(1, 2)(Spring/Fall 1974):57–84.

New York City. "Interim Report of the Mayor's Committee for Puerto Rican Affairs in New York City." Mimeographed, 1953.

New York State Chamber of Commerce. *Reaction of Puerto Rican Children in New York City to Psychological Tests*. New York: New York State Chamber of Commerce, 1935.

Nuestro. "Corporate Money for Organizations: Who Gives It? Where Does It Go?" *Neustro* (March 1982):27–31.

Olivas, Michael (ed.). *Latino College Students*. New York: Teachers College Press, 1986.

O'Neill, Michael. *The Third America: The Emergence of the Nonprofit Sector in the United States*. San Francisco: Jossey-Bass, 1989.

Orum, Lori S. *The Education of Hispanics: Status and Implications*. Washington, D.C.: National Council of la Raza, 1986.

Paredes, Raymund. "The Origins of Anti-Mexican Sentiment in the United States." In *New Directions in Chicano Scholarship*, R. Romo and R. Paredes (eds.). Santa Barbara, Calif.: Center for Chicano Studies, University of California at Santa Barbara, 1984.

Parot, Joseph J. *Polish Catholics in Chicago, 1850–1920: A Religious History*. De Kalb, Ill.: Northern Illinois University Press, 1981.

Paz, Octavio. *The Labyrinth of Solitude*. New York: Grove Press, 1963.

Peñalosa, Fernando, and McDonaugh, Edward C. "Social Mobility in a Mexican-American Community." *Social Forces* 44(1966):498–505.

Peters, Thomas J., and Waterman, Robert H., Jr. *In Search of Excellence*. New York: Harper & Row, 1982.

Portes, Alejandro, and Truelove, Cynthia. "El sentido de la diversidad: recientes investigaciones sobre las minorias hispanas en los EE.UU." In *His-*

panos en los Estados Unidos, R. Cortina and A. Moncada (eds.). Madrid: Ediciones de Cultura Hispanica, 1988.

Puerto Rican Forum. *The Puerto Rican Community Development Project: A Proposal for a Self-Help Project to Develop the Community by Strengthening the Family, Opening Opportunities for Youth and Making Full Use of Education.* New York: Arno Press, 1975.

Ramos, Samuel. *Profile of Man and Culture in Mexico.* Austin: University of Texas Press, 1962.

Reisler, Mark. *By the Sweat of Their Brow: Mexican Immigrant Labor in the United States, 1900–1940.* Westport, Conn.: Greenwood Press, 1976.

Renz, Loren (ed.). *The Foundation Directory,* 11th ed. New York: Foundation Center, 1987.

Ríos, George J. "A Corporate Perspective." In *Hispanics and Grantmakers: A Special Report of Foundation News,* Henry Santiestevan (ed.). Washington, D.C.: Council on Foundations, 1981.

Rockefeller Foundation. "Proposal for a Latin American Population Sciences Network." Trustee docket item PS6, December 13, 1988.

Romo, Ricardo. *East Los Angeles: History of a Barrio.* Austin: University of Texas Press, 1983.

Rosenbaum, Robert J. *Mexicano Resistance in the Southwest.* Austin: University of Texas Press, 1981.

Ruiz, Vicki. *Cannery Women, Cannery Lives: Unionization and the California Food Processing Industry, 1930–1950.* Albuquerque: University of New Mexico Press, 1987.

San Miguel, Guadalupe. *"Let Them All Take Heed": Mexican Americans and the Campaign for Educational Equality in Texas, 1910–1981.* Austin: University of Texas Press, 1987.

San Juan Cafferty, Pastora, and Rivera-Martínez, Carmen Belén. "The Chicago Example: Foundation Giving for Hispanics." In *Hispanics and Grantmakers: A Special Report of Foundation News,* Henry Santiestevan (ed.). Washington, D.C.: Council on Foundations, 1981.

Sánchez-Korrol, Virginia E. *From Colonia to Community: The History of Puerto Ricans in New York City, 1917–1948.* Westport, Conn.: Greenwood, 1983.

Santiago, Isaura Santiago. "A Community's Struggle for Equal Educational Opportunity: Aspira v. Board of Education." Doctoral dissertation, Fordham University, 1978.

Santiestevan, Henry. "A Movement is Born: National Emergence of la Raza." *Agenda* Summer 1973:4–5.

Santiestevan, Henry (ed.). *Hispanics and Grantmakers: A Special Report of Foundation News.* Washington, D.C.: Council on Foundations, 1981.

Santiestevan, Henry, and Santiestevan, Stina (eds.). *The Hispanic Almanac: A Fact Book of Social and Economic Data.* Washington, D.C.: Hispanic Policy Development Project, 1985.

Santos, Richard. *Hispanic Youth: Emerging Workers.* New York: Praeger, 1984.

Scott, W. Richard. "Theoretical Perspectives." In *Environments and Organizations,* Marshall W. Meyer and Associates (eds.). San Francisco: Jossey-Bass, 1978.

Senior, Clarence. *The Puerto Ricans: Strangers—Then Neighbors.* New York: Quadrangle Books, 1965.

Sheridan, Thomas E. *Los Tucsonenses: The Mexican Community in Tucson, 1854–1941.* Tucson, Ariz.: University of Arizona Press, 1986.

Shockley, John S. *Chicano Revolt in a Texas Town.* Notre Dame, Ind.: University of Notre Dame Press, 1974.

Southwest Voter Research Institute. "Commentary: What 'Kinder, Gentler Nation' Means to Latinos." *Southwest Voter Research Notes* 2(6)(September–December 1988).

Sierra, Christine M. "The Political Transformation of a Minority Organization: The Council of la Raza 1965–1980." Ph.D. diss., Stanford University, 1983.

Silha, Stephen. "The Seattle Situation: Is it Yours?" In *Hispanics and Grantmakers: A Special Report of Foundation News,* Henry Santiestevan (ed.). Washington, D.C.: Council on Foundations, 1981.

Soto, John A. "Mexican-American Community Leadership for Education." Ph.D. diss., University of Michigan, 1974.

Stanford University News Service. "Foundation Grants to Hispanic Groups Highly Concentrated, Stanford Study Shows." Nov. 27, 1984.

Steinberg, Stephen. *The Ethnic Myth.* New York: Atheneum, 1981.

Steiner, Stan. *La Raza: The Mexican Americans.* New York: Harper and Row, Colophon, 1970.

Struckhoff, Eugene C. "About This Special Report." In *Hispanics and Grantmakers: A Special Report of Foundation News,* Henry Santiestevan (ed.). Washington, D.C.: Council on Foundations, 1981a.

Struckhoff, Eugene C. "' . . . But They Said It Couldn't Be Done': Dispelling Some Myths, Misconceptions and Misapprehensions about the IRS." In *Hispanics and Grantmakers: A Special Report of Foundation News,* Henry Santiestevan (ed.). Washington, D.C.: Council on Foundations, 1981b.

Struckhoff, Eugene C. "Coalition: A Lesson for Grantmakers?" In *Hispanics and Grantmakers: A Special Report of Foundation News,* Henry Santiestevan (ed.). Washington, D.C.: Council on Foundations, 1981c.

Teller, Charles H., Estrada, Leo F. Hernández, José, and Alvírez, David (eds.). *Cuantos Somos: A Demographic Study of the Mexican-American Population.* Mexican American Monograph Series, No. 2. Austin: University of Texas Press, 1977.

Tienda, Marta. "The Puerto Rican Worker: Current Labor Market Status and Future Prospects." *Journal of Hispanic Politics* 1(1)(1985):27–51.

Tirado, Miguel. "Mexican American Community Political Organizations: The Key to Chicano Political Power." *Aztlan* 1(1)(Spring, 1970):53–78.

Tomasi, Silvano M. "The Ethnic Church and the Integration of Italian Immigrants in the United States." In *The Italian Experience in the United States,* S. Tomasi and M. Engel (eds.). New York: Center for Migration Studies, 1976.

Torres-Gil, Fernando (ed.). *Hispanics in an Aging Society.* New York: Carnegie Corporation of New York, 1986.

Troy, Katheryn. *Annual Survey of Corporate Contributions, 1982 Edition (An Analysis of Survey Data for the Calendar Year 1980).* New York: The Conference Board, 1982.

Tyler, Gus (ed.). *Mexican-Americans Tomorrow: Educational and Economic Perspectives.* Albuquerque: University of New Mexico Press, 1975.

U.S. Commission on Civil Rights. *The Mexican American.* Washington, D.C.: U.S. Government Printing Office, 1968.

U.S. Commission on Civil Rights. *Mexican Americans and the Administration of Justice in the Southwest.* Washington, D.C.: U.S. Government Printing Office, 1970.

U.S. Congress, Congressional Research Service. "Hispanic Children in Poverty." No. 85-170-EPW. Washington, D.C., 1985.

U.S. Department of Commerce, Bureau of the Census. *Persons of Spanish Origin by State*. 1980 Census, Supplementary Report, PC80-S1-7. Washington, D.C.: U.S. Government Printing Office, 1982.

U.S. Department of Commerce, Bureau of the Census. *Persons of Spanish Origin in the United States: March, 1988* (Advance Report). Current Population Reports, Population Characteristics, Series P-20. Washington, D.C.: U.S. Government Printing Office, 1988.

U.S. Department of Education, National Center for Education Statistics. *The Condition of Education for Hispanic Americans*. Washington, D.C., 1980.

United Way of America. *The Citizen Board in Voluntary Agencies*. Arlington, Va.: United Way of America, 1979.

Urrutia, Liliana. "An Offspring of Discontent: The Asociacion Nacional Mexico-Americana, 1949–1954." *Aztlan* 15(1)(Spring 1984):177–184.

Valdez, Armando. *A Study of Foundation Awards to Hispanic-Oriented Organizations in the U.S.: 1981–1982*. Stanford, Calif.: Stanford University, Center for Chicano Research, 1984.

Vega, Bernardo. *Memoirs of Bernardo Vega*. New York: Monthly Review Press, 1984.

Wagenheim, Kal. *A Survey of Puerto Ricans on the U.S. Mainland in the 1970s*. New York: Praeger, 1975.

Wakefield, Daniel. *Island in the City*. New York: Corinth Books, 1959.

Whyte, William F., and Holmberg, Allan R. "Human Problems of U.S. Enterprise in Latin America." *Human Organization* (3)(Fall 1956).

Wilson, Kirke. "Hispanic Trustees and Staff." In *Hispanics and Grantmakers: A Special Report of Foundation News*, Henry Santiestevan (ed.). Washington, D.C.: Council on Foundations, 1981a.

Wilson, Kirke. "How Grantseekers Can Best Approach Foundations." In *Hispanics and Grantmakers: A Special Report of Foundation News*, Henry Santiestevan (ed.). Washington, D.C.: Council on Foundations, 1981b.

Wolf, Eric R., and Hansen, Edward C. *The Human Condition in Latin America*. New York: Oxford University Press, 1972.

Wrobel, Paul. *Our Way: Family, Parish, and Neighborhood in a Polish-American Community*. South Bend, Ind.: University of Notre Dame Press, 1979.

Wuthnow, Robert, Hodgkinson, Virginia A. and Associates. *Faith and Philanthropy in America: Exploring the Role of Religion in America's Voluntary Sector.* San Francisco: Jossey-Bass, 1990.

Young Lords Party, and Abramson, Michael. *Palante: The Young Lords Party.* New York: McGraw–Hill, 1971.

INDEX